Educating for Human Dignity

University of Pennsylvania Press
Pennsylvania Studies in Human Rights
Edited by Bert B. Lockwood

A complete listing of the books in this series
appears at the back of this volume

Educating for Human Dignity

Learning About Rights and Responsibilities

Betty A. Reardon

PENN

University of Pennsylvania Press

Philadelphia

Library of Congress Cataloging-in-Publication Data

Reardon, Betty.
  Educating for human dignity : learning about rights and
responsibilities / Betty A. Reardon.
      p.   cm. — (Pennsylvania studies in human rights)
    Includes bibliographical references and index.
    ISBN 0-8122-3306-9 (cloth : alk. paper). — ISBN 0-8122-1524-9
(pbk. : alk. paper)
    1. Human rights.   I. Title.   II. Series.
JC571.R4364   1995
323′.07—dc20   95-21590
                                                        CIP

10 9 8 7 6 5 4 3 2

This book is dedicated to Harry B. and Elizabeth J. Hollins, whose lives were a testament to the human right to peace

Contents

Preface and Acknowledgments

This resource is one product of a project on the development of human rights education as a major component of education for peace. The project was carried out by the Peace Education Program at Teachers College Columbia University, supported by two generous grants from the United States Institute of Peace. Beginning with the first course offerings and teacher workshops funded by the grants, attention to the problems and potentials that human rights (as a field of study and as an area of human experience) offers to the achievement of world peace has been central to peace education as it is presented at Teachers College.

A survey also funded by these grants was carried out to ascertain what classroom teachers were doing in human rights education. It revealed very little elementary and secondary curricular material that focused on concepts of human rights as they are articulated in the Universal Declaration of Human Rights, so efforts were also made to reach educators through programs and workshops in a number of areas beyond the Columbia campus. Through these efforts educators were encouraged to develop materials that would address human rights in terms of existing international standards and principles, in a manner suited to their own classrooms. Some of their efforts are included in this volume.

The human rights education framework in which the sample curricula are presented—a values base, multiple approaches, and a developmental sequence—was also developed in the courses offered at Teachers College, and presented in the various workshops to introduce human rights education to practicing teachers.

Materials adapted from previously published curricula are included in this volume to provide wider coverage of human rights themes. All materials included were designed for and used in specific situations. Particular educators, especially workshop participants and educators pursuing graduate degrees at Teachers College, developed the units for use in their own classes. Some of the materials have been widely used, some only by the teachers who designed them. All have been reviewed by human rights educators and found to be appropriate to their purposes. They are offered here as suggestions to be adapted and changed according to the needs and goals of teachers, and to serve as sample materials for use in teacher education at the graduate and undergraduate levels. Their main purpose is to demonstrate how human rights education can be approached throughout elementary and secondary schooling. The materials are instruments to fulfill the purposes and carry out the approaches advocated here. The entire volume is intended as an introduction to human rights education for use by both teacher educators and classroom teachers.

Educating for Human Dignity is organized into three basic components. Chapters 1 and 2 present the theoretical rationale and pedagogical approach developed through the explorations described above. Chapters 3 through 6 comprise curriculum samples presented by grade level. Chapter 7 provides further resources to assist teachers in educating themselves and preparing and developing their own teaching materials.

While the approach is comprehensive, the content certainly is not. The actual development of the field of human rights education to a status adequate to the needs and purposes it has identified is a major goal of the People's Decade for Human Rights Education. The Decade (1991–2000), an enabling agent for the United Nations Decade for Human Rights Education (1995–2004), is a non-governmental initiative combining the efforts of formal and non-formal educators, university professors, researchers, and human rights advocates from various parts of the world. Its purpose, based on the assertion that human rights education is a human right, is to develop informed concern for human rights throughout the world. We hope the users of this resource will join in this endeavor, and that they will inform the Decade Organizing Committee of their efforts and the materials they develop. (See Chapter 7 for the address.) To facilitate this process, the University of Pennsylvania Press grants users permission to copy the "handout" material in this volume (but only that material) for classroom use.

The Teachers College Peace Education Program is grateful to the United States Institute of Peace, whose support of our work has made the theme of human rights more prominent in the field of peace education, and to the Longview Foundation, whose assistance has helped to bring the program's human rights work to a wider audience of teachers through the completion of this book. We are equally grateful to the funders who have sustained and supported the program over the years, among them the Miriam and Ira Wallach Foundation, the Samuel Rubin Foundation, and the Abe and Ethel Lapidus Foundation.

The final draft of the volume was completed with the help of a grant from the Longview Foundation and with the assistance of student interns whose work was made possible by the grants from the United States Institute of Peace and Longview. Teachers and students at Teachers College have been major contributors, among them Deborah Johnston, Joan Klingsberg, Xuchun Jia, and Susan Lechter.

It is our hope that this resource will be one small but constructive step in the larger global effort of the People's Decade for Human Rights Education, a people's movement to bring knowledge of and commitment to human rights to all those who share this beautiful planet, and to demonstrate that the achievement of human rights, like the restoration of the environment and the abolition of war, is essential to human survival. All three goals require massive educational efforts. The Decade is the beginning of one such effort. This book is dedicated to all who share in that struggle.

Chapter 1
Introduction: Purposes and Approaches

The Purposes of This Book

The field of education, like all sectors of society, is presently being profoundly challenged by the rapidly changing global social system. The curricula of schools and teacher education institutions had hardly begun to develop a response to the often repeated litany of global problems when the system in which they evolved began to restructure itself drastically. This situation revealed the limits of the problem centered approach to understanding and teaching global social issues.

The new challenge calls for an approach more readily adaptable to a world experiencing drastic changes, one grounded in a set of fundamental principles by which human affairs can be assessed in a variety of situations. This book proposes one such approach. It is values based and conceptual rather than issue- or problem-centered. It assumes that our social problems at all levels, local through global, are as much a matter of ethics as they are of structures; as personal and social as they are political and economic. It further contends that the subject of human rights most readily lends itself to the curricular requirements of the challenge. Indeed, it can be argued that most of the problems faced by the global system both in the Cold War period and now in its aftermath can be viewed as issues of human rights. This argument is central to the positions and programs of the People's Decade for Human Rights Education and to this curriculum sampler and resource guide designed to implement its purposes.

The underlying intention is that this book will lead to more extensive and detailed human rights curricula. It has been published in the hope that its users will contribute to the further development of human rights education by adaptations of these materials and inventive use of the other resources listed here, and especially by developing their own materials. The Decade for Human Rights Education would be most interested in receiving samples, syllabi, and other resources developed by the users of *Educating for Human Dignity*.

This volume offers a curriculum framework and rationale, resource listings, and sample lesson materials to facilitate human rights education in elementary and secondary schools and teacher education institutions. It is intended to be suggestive rather than definitive. It demonstrates some possibilities for an holistic approach to human rights education that is comprehensive, conceptual, and developmental, that directly confronts the values issues raised by human rights problems within a context of global interrelationships.

Understanding the framework, its values base, approaches, and sequence as set forth here is essential to the effective use of the samples and the resources. All educators using this volume, whether in elementary or secondary school classrooms or in university teacher education courses, will find it helpful to read the introductory chapters even if they intend to use only one or two of the samples. The developmental approach is best applied in a specific situation when the educator has an overview of the general process. The normative conceptual basis is most useful when the educator works in the context of the general value system presented. Some elements may be repetitive for those who do read the opening chapters and introductions to the developmental levels. Certain aspects of the framework have been especially emphasized for users who may have neither time nor inclination to review all the introductory material.

An holistic approach is consistent with the principles of ecological or whole systems thinking that are emerging as the paradigm most appropriate to the formation of planetary citizens. As applied to human rights education, holism interprets all rights and entitlements as interrelated and interdependent components of one central, generative principle: *human dignity*.

Indeed, recent feminist scholarship argues for an holistic approach to human rights that maintains that all human rights are integral one to the other, and cannot be separated or prioritized, as had been the practice in the industrialized nations of East and West. This argument was validated by the conclusions of the United Nations Human Rights Conference of 1993 which declared human rights to be universal and indivisible. Economic rights do not have priority over political rights nor political over economic rights as had been argued by East and West respectively throughout the Cold War. Feminist scholars such as Riane Eisler and Charlotte Bunch (see the list of references at the end of this chapter) argue that the standards of the public and private spheres should be informed by a fundamental respect for the dignity of all human beings. The feminist argument asserts that the separations between private and public morality, as well as between the ethics applied to one's own group and those used in dealings with others, are a major cause of the violation of rights of ethnic minorities, women, and adversaries. Such an argument provides further rationale for a comprehensive conceptual approach devised to illuminate principles of human dignity.

The comprehensiveness of the approach lies in its attempt to touch on all areas of rights and in the assertion that human rights can find some appropriate place in the curricula of all grade levels and subject areas. The sample lessons are presented by grade level not subject area; most can be adapted to several subjects. The range of materials becoming available makes it possible for teachers of all grades and subjects to include human rights topics in their curricula. These resources are presented in the belief that comprehensive human rights education is not only possible, but, more important, is essential to the welfare and survival of human society.

The preference for a conceptual rather than a topical approach derives from the values, both explicit and implied, that infuse the ideas and the evolution of human rights. As a social movement and a field of study, human rights concerns the norms and standards appropriate to a good society. Within a human rights framework, society is not an abstraction divorced from notions of ethics and qualities, but is the forum for human moral development, applied to public and social as well as to private and personal relationships and behavior. Human rights should form the very core of social education.

Education for Civic Responsibility and Political Efficacy

The human rights education framework is intended as social education based on principles and standards. Although both problems and cases are included in the units presented in the sampler, they are intended to illuminate principles and provide opportunities to apply standards. A central purpose of both the holistic framework and the developmental approach is to cultivate the capacities to make moral choices, take principled positions on issues, and devise democratic courses of citizen action—in other words, to develop moral and intellectual integrity. We hold that the vitality of democracy rests on the ability of citizens to exercise the responsibilities of citizenship in the light of principled reflection.

The key concepts that inform the framework are a set of values that help us identify problems such as racism, sexism, and other readily obvious denials of the values that comprise and sustain human dignity. Social problems are frequently recognized as the violation of the fundamental values of the society, such as equality and fairness. Since human rights education is also values education, we seek to educate toward the belief in and commitment to a set of core values and sub-values that derive from the fundamental central value of human dignity. This system comprises a range of values of varying degrees of complexity and abstraction, but the most fundamental of them can be expressed in both simple and sophisticated terms, appropriate in one form or another to all learning and developmental levels, and are woven throughout the developmental sequence suggested in the sampler. The subvalues and problems are more specific and are appropriate to the curriculum of specific grade levels. Thus we present a conceptual-developmental sequence that advocates presenting concepts, problems, and the relevant international human rights standards according to grade levels in a sequence that flows from simpler to more complex issues and topics to illustrate how the concepts can infuse the entire K–12 curriculum.

The ultimate goal of this kind of education is the formation of responsible, committed, and caring planetary citizens with sufficiently informed problem awareness and adequate value commitments to be contributors to a global society that honors human rights. For this purpose some action oriented curricula are included.

Few of the students in our elementary and secondary schools will become human rights experts or human rights workers. Yet it is our hope that some of them will become human rights activists and many, if not most, will become advocates. And, surely, all should be aware of human rights.

Certainly, teacher training should strive at least to develop an awareness of human rights issues and standards among all teachers. The goal we seek in advocating the inclusion of human rights curricula in schools and teacher education is citizenship education that develops both awareness and advocacy. Every citizen of the twenty first century should have knowledge of the fundamental human rights upheld by the international legal standards that provide the norms for a just and peaceful world community. Knowledge of these norms and the obstacles to their fulfillment is as essential to the development of human rights activists and advocates as it is to the universal observation of human rights, and to the achievement of a just world peace. Thus, human rights is an essential subject for courses in educational foundations and other teacher education areas.

Human Rights and Peace Education

Human rights education is as fundamental and constitutive to peace education as human rights are to peace:

Stated most succinctly the general purpose of peace education, as I understand it, is to promote the development of an authentic planetary consciousness that will enable us to function as global citizens and to transform the present human condition by changing the social structures and the patterns of thought that have created it. This transformational imperative must, in my view, be at the center of peace education. (Reardon, *Comprehensive Peace Education*, x)

Human rights education is essential to the fulfillment of the transformational purposes of peace education, for it seeks a set of goals that is, in the aforementioned terms, fundamental to peace. The People's Decade for Human Rights Education has defined two general objectives or purposes of the field. The first objective is that all human beings should be made aware of the rights accorded to them by the Universal Declaration of Human Rights and the international instruments for its implementation, that all may know that procedures exist for the redress of violation of these rights, and that political authorities and citizens know they can be held accountable for rights violations. Second, it seeks to facilitate society's becoming aware of the problems that impede the realization of human rights, and of the ways to resolve those problems.

The Decade's purposes are also a set of tools for the achievement of "the conditions of peace," those structures, processes, and behaviors most likely to limit and ultimately to eliminate social, structural, and political violence. The achievement of the minimum conditions of human rights would provide the foundation of a non-violent social order which could be defined as peace. These conditions, defined by peace research as "positive peace," would also greatly reduce the causes of war. The elimination of armed conflict, (and, I would add, political repression imposed by force) is referred to in the field as "negative peace." It is the assumption of the approach advocated here that human rights education is essential to the achievement of both positive and negative peace, and that these two forms of peace are as inseparable as the various categories of human rights. Human rights education assumes a comprehensive concept of peace which requires an all-inclusive approach based upon the principles of the universality and indivisability of human rights, including all categories and "generations" of rights, a concept to be discussed later in the context of an historic approach.

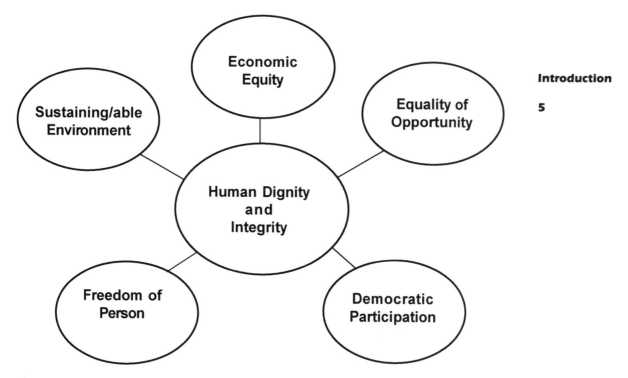

Figure 1. Interrelated values.

An Holistic Values Approach

Human rights is a normative field of study seeking to define and apply standards of justice to human affairs. Both as the subject of research and education and as an arena for political debate and social action, it is thus determined by values. By values we mean concepts of what is good and worth striving for. The fundamental values that inform human rights, we claim, are universal. They are concepts of good that can be found in one form or another in most ethical and religious traditions. They are, as well, an integrated holistic system of ethical standards for all human relations, interrelated normative concepts that inform most notions of a good society, and an inspiration for much of the best reconstructionist education. Figure 1 illustrates this system of interrelated normative concepts.

Human dignity and integrity are the symbiotic concepts at the center of the ethical system comprising the social values that are the essence of human rights. Within this approach *dignity* is defined as the fundamental innate worth of the human person. A good society honors the dignity of all persons and expects all its members to respect the dignity of others. *Integrity* refers to the wholeness of the physical, mental, aesthetic, and spiritual facets of the person. The good society provides for the expression and development of the multiple facets of the person and holds them to be inviolable. Good societies are built on the active recognition of individual and group rights and the fulfillment of individual and social responsibility.

All the other values that give rise to specific concepts of human rights emerge from this core. In the holistic values approach we are using, there are five such values, but other values frameworks for the interpretation and application of human rights can also be of use to human rights educators. The world order values defined by the World Order Models Project for a "just world peace" and the human values–human needs approach put forth by MacDougal, Laswell, and Chen in *Human Rights and World Public Order* (see References and Chapter 7) are two that are especially adaptable to human rights education. The five here, however, stem from the core values of human dignity and integrity and from the proposition of the inseparability of the various categories of human rights. We identify these values as economic equity, equality of opportunity, democratic participation, freedom of person, and a sustaining and sustainable environment.

Economic equity asserts the right to the fulfillment of basic survival needs. It embodies the belief that the material benefits and social values of a society should be distributed so that no one suffers unnecessary deprivation, and that the poverty imposed by the inequitable distribution of the world's wealth is a violation of human rights. It implies the responsibility to work for *distributive justice*.

Equal opportunity calls for all members of the society to have access to the possibilities to develop all the human capacities with which they are endowed. This value defines problems of intolerance and discrimination such as racism, sexism, and colonialism as human rights violations, and entails the responsibility of the society to assure *social justice*.

Democratic participation is the basis for claims to civil and political rights. The value arises from the belief that people are entitled to exercise power and make decisions with regard to public and social issues. They have the right to *participate in formulating the policies* that will affect their lives and in decisions about the use of public resources. Democratic participation requires *acceptance of the responsibilities of citizenship* on the part of all citizens.

Freedom of person is primary in the Western tradition of human rights. It connotes the rights of all to control their own bodies, minds, and spirits, to choose their own personal and cultural identity and way of life, and to move freely where they will, if it does not adversely affect others, neglect important responsibilities, or cause harm to the community. It is the value that rejects slavery, unjust imprisonment, torture, enforced prostitution or pregnancy, restriction of movement within or between countries, limits in access to information, interference with personal choices. It demands the exercise of *individual responsibility* to refrain from and prevent infringement on the freedom of others by individuals, organizations, social groups, and governments.

The right to a *sustaining and sustainable environment* is presently in the process of definition. It may be claimed not only by individuals but human groups and by the entire human species, and perhaps represents a whole new "generation" or category of rights (see discussion below). A sustaining environment implies the right to natural conditions and social circumstances that enable people and groups to make a living, such as the right to development (both economic and social development as pertains to the group and personal development as pertains to the individual), the right to peace, and the right to a *healthful environment*. It also entails individual and group responsibility for preserving the health and integrity of the environment itself, what has been referred to as *ecological responsibility*, caring for the environment and assuring its sustainability.

Most of the conceptual and moral terrain of human rights can be located within these five values. They all not only derive from the same central concept of human dignity, but are so interrelated that none can be fully separated from the others. Many human rights issues fall within the domain of several of the core values, and none can be resolved without some consideration of all. Conflicts between human rights sometimes arise precisely because the interrelationships are overlooked. It is for such reasons that this book uses an holistic, ecological approach emphasizing interrelationships.

Defining positive peace, "the good society," as a set of social, political, and economic conditions dependent on the realization of rights and authentic democracy is to say that positive peace derives from social responsibility and active citizenship. In a planetary age, this definition translates to global responsibility, participating as global citizens in the world political order:

. . . three fundamental value concepts found throughout peace education efforts of all kinds . . . are . . . positive human relationships based on the dignity of all persons; stewardship of the planet based on a reverence for the Earth; and global citizenship based on responsibility to a world community. These values sum up the most general notions of what comprises global responsibility in the eyes of most peace educators. (Reardon, *Educating for Global Responsibility*, xv)

These same values suffuse human rights education and thus endow it with a dynamic quality of education for change. They emphasize participation in the struggle for universal human dignity, which can be realized fully only under conditions of a positive peace based on respect for individual persons, social groups, human cultures, and the natural environment. As preparation for this struggle, human rights education becomes a major component in the movement for global transformation articulated as the goal of the peace and environmental movements as well as many human rights movements. Thus human rights education is intended to prepare the learner to become a maker of history, bringing values and concepts into lived human experience and changing the human condition toward the achievement of the "good society." Thus we advocate this values-based conceptual framework and present it in a developmental sequence.

An Historical Approach

The values framework and the developmental sequence for human rights education can be approached through various themes and from various perspectives. The most widely used is the historical approach. Knowledge of the historical origins of human rights as the organizing principles of the good society is important to understanding the human rights movement as a dynamic, living human endeavor. The teaching of history can be enlivened by the story of the conceptualization of and struggle for human rights.

The evolution of the concepts of human rights can be traced to the very roots of Western society. The idea of articulating the social contract in the form of behavioral standards and laws binding on all the members of the society can be seen in such ancient social landmarks as the Code of Hammurabi and the Ten Commandments. The essentially modern idea that such standards should be equally binding on citizens and leaders alike one has given rise to present notions of human rights and democratic government. The political philosophy of representative democracy developed from the argument that the function of the state was to protect the rights and well-being of its citizens. As stated in the United States Declaration of Independence, governments were established "to secure these rights." The obligation of citizens is to ensure that governments fulfill this purpose and "to alter or abolish" governments that flout or fail in this purpose. Resistance to unjust or illegitimate authority is thus a fundamental principle of democracy and an essential responsibility of citizens for the assurance of human rights.

Such concepts reflect a standard interpretation of Western history, but history is seldom taught as the evolution and development of the concepts and assurances of human rights. Yet such an approach offers teachers the opportunity to present historical experience not only as the unfolding of events, but as the intentional evolution of the social and political thought that influenced and was influenced by these events. Further, a human rights context for history emphasizes the human social experience of ordinary people, not just the achievments of outstanding leaders. Perhaps most important for educators who perceive human rights as the fundamental substance of "positive peace," such an approach to history provides a balance to the heavy emphasis on wars and military developments of most standard instruction in history, and shows history to be made of possibilities and choices.

At the very least, all relevant human rights concepts and developments should be included in history courses that deal with events and periods significant to the evolution of human rights standards. History courses could be taught from a human rights perspective, meeting the need to give all students an acquaintance with the history of the fundamental human rights standards of their own nation and of the world community. For students in the United States this means familiarity with the Universal Declaration of Human Rights and the major international covenants and conventions along with the Declaration of Independence and the Constitution. And it should mean that the knowledge of all these standards is required content of the curricula of all our schools.

Human rights have been derived from and defined out of the lived history of human beings. This reality is reflected in the terminology of human rights, which defines categories of rights as "generations." The word connotes the chronology, or the time and age, in which a category of rights is identified and defined. It also means that rights are produced, or "generated," by a set of political, economic, social, or cultural conditions at work in society. These generations offer a fruitful framework for teaching European and American history as human rights evolution, placing the emergence of existing human rights concepts and events in the context of what has been called "modern history," and framing the evolving and yet to be defined human rights concepts as "post-modern." These newly emerging concepts can be viewed as "the future of human rights," or the "rights of the ecological age."

The first generation of rights comprises the political and civil rights articulated as the rationales for the American and French revolutions that closed the eighteenth century. The second generation is the economic and social rights generated by the socialist and workers' movements of the nineteenth century. These two generations were conceptualized as individual rights: the first being restraints on the power of the state over citizens to assure freedom; the second being obligations of the state to the citizens to assure economic and social well-being. The mid-twentieth century with influences from areas beyond the West produced the third generation of collective or "solidarity" rights sought by groups with common identity or experience in the struggles to end colonialism, racism, sexism and the abuse of children. This generation articulates the rights to self-determination of peoples and self-identification of ethnic groups. It also includes the right to development to overcome poverty as the first generation included the right to revolution to overcome political oppression.

As the twentieth century closes, a fourth generation claimed on behalf of all humanity may be emerging. The seeds of this generation lie in the notion of "crimes against humanity" invoked in the international standards condemning genocide and apartheid, and in the notion of the unity of humankind. As they come to understand and internalize the oneness of humanity, students of today will define this new generation, that might apply not only to individual persons, national, ethnic, racial, age or gender groups but to humanity as a whole.

Enlisting students in such a definitional process is to invite them to be actors in history, to be creators of standards that identify and challenge the problems of their times. It enables them to see that human rights standards emerge from notions of "social wrong," conditions society comes to see as contradictory to the fundamental values that uphold the social contract. Thus the political excesses and repression of monarchy produced the first generation of rights; industrialism's unchecked exploitation of the laboring classes produced the second; and the contradictions and injustices of colonialism produced the third, and helped to make human rights a truly global movement. It is up to this generation of citizens to identify and challenge contemporary social wrongs, to formulate and apply the human rights standards that will reduce and prevent such wrongs throughout the world, and perhaps to establish the fourth generation of rights as truly global standards. In so doing they participate in making for themselves and subsequent generations a more humane planetary future, and thus contribute to the achievement of peace.

An International Standards and Institutions Approach

One of the most effective conceptual approaches to human rights education is through the international standards themselves, the principles, declarations, covenants, and conventions that are the foundations of international human rights law promulgated by the United Nations. Here, too, it is possible to apply the approach in a comprehensive and holistic manner, starting with the meaning of universality and the Universal Declaration of Human Rights (see Chapter 7 for an extracted version of the Declaration). While the world has changed considerably, the Declaration is still the most comprehensive conceptual statement of rights. It is recognized to apply to all people the world over, and it is the source for all subsequent standards and treaties. It should be the centerpiece of any human rights curriculum.

The Universal Declaration does not make specific reference to every particular right that has been claimed since it was put forth by the United Nations General Assembly in 1948. However, it has been interpreted to validate most recognized rights, even those of the so-called third generation, which pertain to groups rather than individuals, and those some call the fourth generation. In the latter case, it is claimed that some rights pertain to humankind as a whole; as noted, the claim is based partially on the designation of some of the worst violations of human rights, such as genocide and apartheid, as "crimes against humanity." If crimes are committed against humanity, then humanity can be said to have rights such as the right to peace, or to a healthy, ecologically balanced planet, or to a world of human genetic, cultural, and political diversity. Some also claim that these rights derive from Article 28 of the Universal Declaration, which proclaims the right to an international order conducive to the realization of human rights.

An international standards approach provides two other significant curriculum content possibilities. The standards serve to demonstrate some of the major world problems not only as rights violations but as issues of importance to the order and viability of world society. Even if there were no human rights standards, the conditions that gave rise to them would still be problems for the world. However, human rights standards provide criteria by which to define, assess, and determine the severity of these problems. The approach also makes it possible to consider and assess trends toward and away from world community and global social integration. Human rights standards reflect the growth of an emerging sense of universality and provide norms that strengthen the potential for a system of shared global values, an essential requisite to an authentic world community.

Finally, the promulgation of these standards attests to the phenomenon that rights are defined in the face of "social wrongs"—those acts and conditions which contradict generally accepted assumptions about right human relationships and violate minimal standards of human decency. In short, human rights are a secular code of ethics and morality for the world community, and as such, form the fundamental basis for peace, as is the claim of the Universal Declaration:

. . . recognition of the inherent dignity and of the equal and inalienable rights of all members of the human family is the foundation of freedom, justice, and peace in the world. (Preamble, Universal Declaration of Human Rights)

While not all international instruments (by which we mean intergovernmental agreements with the status of international law) for the protection and realization of human rights are essential to the study of the field, some documents should be familiar to all citizens. Among these are, of course, the Universal Declaration of Human Rights and the Covenants on Civil and Political Rights and on Economic, Social and Cultural Rights. The three together are often referred to as the "International Bill of Rights." Equally important to the actual protection of rights are the regional instruments, such as the African Charter and the American and European Conventions, which should be known generally to all and specifically to the peoples of the respective regions. An international standards approach can be applied in a global perspective as indicated above, but it can also be adapted to regional studies through the regional instruments and charters adopted by the nations of regional organizations such as the Organization of African Unity, the Organization of American States and the Council of Europe. Regional institutions and procedures including the Inter-American and European commissions and courts of human rights might also be studied as phenomena of regional integration and examples of international institutions arising from changes in the international system. These regional commissions and courts together with the world institutions, especially the United Nations machinery, can be studied as consequences of both political change and social movements. They are evidence of an evolving global social order, the institutional core of the society of all humanity.

A Reconstructionist Approach

All current standards stemming from the Universal Declaration of Human Rights are indivisably interrelated and universally applicable, taken together, form a system of norms, values, and aspirations that can serve to guide the development of a healthy and just world social order, and provide the core of a reconstructive approach.

Teachers who undertake human rights education usually do so with the general purpose of developing the capacity to engage in social change. For such a purpose, a reconstructionist approach demonstrates how human rights movements emerge, gain social support, and produce both attitudinal and legal-structural changes in society. When such an approach is presented in a conceptual, values-based framework, it can be used to complement the historical or international standards approaches. It can also stand on its own as an avenue for demonstrating to learners the possibilities for using knowledge of human rights to directly affect the world in which they live.

A reconstructionist approach is basically process oriented, demonstrating how societies learn to identify social wrongs, acknowledge how they violate human dignity and define and apply human rights standards to overcome them. The stages through which rights are recognized by a people, are enacted into law, and become the standards by which a society judges itself can be observed in our own social environments, and in other areas both past and present, on a local as well as a global scale. The process usually starts with persons of conscience becoming aware of a condition they perceive to be against their society's ethical principles or fundamental human values. Such persons are often the initiators of a movement or organization that attempts to bring the conditions or specific situation, for example, slavery or torture, to the attention of their community, their nation, or the international system. Here is an opportunity to show how most human rights organizations have been founded in the face of actual historic circumstances people believed could and should be changed.

It can be observed that in some cases these organizations or ad hoc groups mount campaigns that become major social movements such as the abolitionist, labor, child advocacy, and civil rights movements. When successful, such movements lead to serious public discussion of the problems and proposals for remediation. When political leaders recognize the public concern and support action toward change, specific policies or laws are proposed and debated. If the society acknowledges both the need for remediation and the probability that the proposed policy, national law (such as voting rights), or international convention (such as the Convention on the Rights of the Child) can provide it, a law or convention is likely to be adopted, but only after a further campaign of political action.

Then the task becomes one of implementation and monitoring, very important roles for citizens and non-governmental organizations. The implementation process is the stage at which actual social change takes place. It is that part of the process in which first-stage social action can be taken by learners, be they professors of education and student teachers or classroom teachers and middle and secondary school students. These actions, in fact, may lead to new campaigns and movements because other offenses to human dignity are often uncovered in such an implementation process (e.g., the relation of discrimination against women to the adequate implementation of children's rights). Such continuing processes of uncovering and overcoming obstacles to human dignity can be shown to be a fundamental dynamic of truly democratic societies.

Reconstructionist education is first and foremost education for authentic democracy. The responsibility to provide such education falls upon all teachers, and their professional education should prepare them to carry it out. One of the most effective tools for such teacher education can be found in human rights. Because the struggle is an on-going one likely to be with us through a long period of global change, an approach based on principles and standards arising from clearly articulated values—one that shows social change to be a process affected by individual and group intervention—offers possibilities for hope in the human future.

Selected References

Bunch, Charlotte and Roxanne Carillo. 1990. *Gender Violence: A Development and Human Rights Issue.* New Brunswick, NJ: Center for Women's Global Leadership.

Claude, Richard Pierre and Burns H. Weston, eds. 1992. *Human Rights in the World Community: Issues and Action.* Second edition. Philadelphia: University of Pennsylvania Press.

Eisler, Riane. 1987. *The Chalice and the Blade: Our History, Our Future.* San Francisco: HarperCollins.

McDougal, Myres Smith, Harold D. Laswell, and Lung-chu Chen. 1980. *Human Rights and World Public Order: The Basic Policies of an International Law of Human Dignity.* New Haven, CT: Yale University Press.

Reardon, Betty. 1988a. *Comprehensive Peace Education.* New York: Teachers College Press.

Reardon, Betty. 1988b. *Educating for Global Responsibility: A Guide to Teacher Designed Curricula for Peace Education, K–12.* New York: Teachers College Press.

Chapter 2
A Developmental Sequence for Presentation of the Core Concepts

A developmental sequence to content comprises the final component of the framework for human rights education that is most conducive to the goals of the Decade for Human Rights Education. Table 1 summarizes the sequence.

Using holism (defined as an integrated approach to interrelated issues and concepts) as the context for learning, the last component of the general framework is a developmental approach to a K–12 learning sequence concerning human rights which integrates well into the conceptual core of the framework. The fundamental values and concepts identified in Chapter 1 form the basis for planning curricula suited to the developmental stages of the learners, categorized here as age level or grade groupings. The fundamental values and concepts, organized into subconcepts, are designated in the table as *core concepts and values.*

Most of the concepts and values essential to this framework have been set forth in the international human rights *standards* and *instruments*: declarations, covenants, and conventions, that make up a body of standards through which the achievement of the values of human dignity and social justice can be assessed. They serve as indicators of the development of peaceful and just societies and can serve as well as guides to the development of social responsibility among the learners to whom human rights education is addressed.

Table 1 also illustrates *developmental levels* at which these standards might be introduced into the curriculum, and age and grade levels appropriate to the presentation of the core concepts and various major human rights problems. While the fundamental value concepts seek to articulate values that are universal and comprehensive, the curricular sub-concepts are expressions of these values as defined within particular cultural and historical contexts. The universality of human rights lies in general normative principles of human dignity that are manifested in the many and varied ways cultures have devised for the conduct of human affairs. The intent of these principles is to ensure human dignity, not to impose a conformity that would limit human potential.

The developmental sequence outlined here also recognizes human diversity. It does not presume a universal, unvaried pattern of learning development. It seeks only to provide some general guidelines to assure learner-centered teaching processes, and to offer content as relevant as possible to particular groups of learners, organized by grade level. The core concepts and values appear throughout the sequence, but are presented in more complexity as the development levels move up.

TABLE 1. Developmental Sequence for Core Concepts and Content

Developmental Level	Core Concepts and Values	Human Rights Standards and Instruments	Issues and Problems
Childhood Early grades Ages 5–8 K–grade 3	Rules Order Respect Fairness Diversity Cooperation Personal responsibility	Classroom rules Declaration of the Rights of the Child	Inequality Unfairness Harm
Later childhood Middle grades Ages 9–11 Grades 4–6	Law Citizenship Community rights Charter Constitution Freedom Declaration Social responsibility	Community standards Declaration of Independence African Freedom Charter U.S. Bill of Rights Universal Declaration of Human Rights Convention on the Rights of the Child	Prejudice Discrimination Poverty Injustice
Adolescence Junior high school Ages 12–14 Grades 7–9	Justice Equality Equity Conventions Covenants Global responsibility International law	Regional human rights conventions UN covenants & conventions: Elimination of Racism; Discrimination Against Women; Civil & Political Rights; Economic, Social & Cultural Rights	Ethnocentrism Racism Sexism Authoritarianism Colonialism Hunger
Youth Senior High School Ages 15–17 Grades 10–12	Moral exclusion Moral responsibility Moral inclusion Global citizenship Ecological responsibility	Nuremberg Principles UN conventions: Prevention & Punishment of Genocide; Prevention and Elimination of Torture Defining and developing new standards	Ethnocide Genocide Torture Political repression Environmental abuse

As values serve to identify and illuminate human problems, and human rights standards serve to diagnose and overcome "social wrongs," so particular wrongs can be used as vehicles for learning that will lead students to explore and develop human values and to confront and resolve social problems. Human rights education seeks to develop social responsibility relevant to particular societies yet grounded in the fundamental, universal values that have inspired human rights movements and informed human rights standards. The standards are best understood in light of the *issues and problems* they are intended to address. Such learning objectives are most likely to be achieved in a learner-centered educational process which is sensitive to the concerns and capacities of the students.

Since the concerns and capacities are far too varied to be described or summarized in any one resource, we have selected the limited dimensions of age level development to illustrate one significant factor in learning capacity. Table 1 is intended to illustrate, in a simple fashion, how this factor can be used to plan a curricular sequence for a comprehensive approach to human rights education. Learning activities can be planned and curriculum materials can be selected or developed on the basis of the core concepts. Each concept and instrument was selected as fulfilling two essential aspects of comprehensive human rights education. First the concept is an idea or value that can be addressed in some form at all levels, but is most likely to be first understood at the level at which it is introduced. Second, the subject matter or topics of the human rights problems and standards have particular relevance to the curriculum of the grades and experience of the learners of the levels at which they appear on the chart. It should be noted that teachers are likely to find ways in which all the values and concepts can be introduced at any grade level. And while there is some adaptability of issues and problems to various levels, it is much more limited than the value content.

At the heart of human rights education is the assumption that a society conducive to the fulfillment of human dignity derives from the honoring of a social contract by observing fundamental rules of behavior respectful of the dignity and humanity of all members of the society. Thus *respect for persons* is the first and fundamental concept of this developmental sequence, as *human dignity* is the central concept of a values base for human rights. The social contract of a just society is one in which citizens and state mutually agree to conduct the affairs of the society on the basis of that contract, which comprises reciprocal rights and responsibilities. Citizens support the state so long as it respects the rights of persons and the state assures that citizens respect the rights of others. The social responsibility to respect and defend human rights is significant to the vitality of democratic systems. It derives from the recognition that cooperative relationships are the most advantageous to all members of society. Recognizing this situation reminds us that education must prepare citizens for cooperation. There is thus a preference for cooperative and group learning methods in human rights education that is reflected in this resource.

Childhood and the Early Grades

The foundation of attitudes toward others on which respect for human dignity depends is laid in children's first experiences. How they are received at birth, treated by their care givers, and regarded by their peers and siblings will be reflected in how they regard and treat others. Family-life education and the preparation of care givers are important areas for human rights education, and certainly should figure into the human relations, family life, and sex education courses sometimes offered to early adolescents. In some respects then, what we have designated as the first stage of this developmental sequence, the early grades, is really the *closing* phase of the early social development process. However, it is an extremely significant one in the overall process of social maturation, and for many children represents their first experience with "organized society." This, then, is the time to introduce the concepts of *social order* and *fairness* that are sources of law and social regulation, the major tools for the implementation and protection of human rights, and the concepts of *community* and *responsibility*, the bases of a just social order.

As teachers explain to children the classroom procedures and the *rules* that serve as guidelines to carry them out, they have a responsibility to avoid the actuality or the appearance that rules and discipline are arbitrary, for such is the essence of authoritarianism, in the kindergartens as in the houses of state. The learners should be able to comprehend from explicit instruction and the behavior of the teacher that the purpose of the classroom rules is to assure that the learning tasks can be achieved and that all will be able to learn as much as possible. They should experience the social order of the classroom not as an end in itself but as the means to assure fairness, so that all have equal opportunity to hear, see, speak, act, and engage in all the activities of learning available in the class. It should be stressed that the children themselves are responsible for the order and fairness of the class and that the quality of the classroom experience depends in great part on them.

Respect for others should be presented as a primary rule, demonstrated by the teacher in respect for the children and required by the teacher of the children in their treatment of each other. Toward this end, a learning objective of the early grades is respectful listening. Every member of the class should be able to expect the others to listen when she or he speaks. It is everyone's right as a member of the community to be heard. In these and similar ways the concept of rights as that which we expect to achieve in or receive from our communities can be introduced, stressing the parallel concepts of equality of rights and diversity of persons and circumstances.

Human diversity in the context of *human equality* is a significant factor in the development of human rights. These are notions that should be woven throughout the developmental sequence to be made explicit at the next level. At this first level, the notions can be infused as shared expectations and recognition of differences.

Since human differences have been the basis for so many human rights violations, it is essential that the earliest instruction acknowledge differences among individuals and among the social, cultural, and geographical circumstances in which people live. It can be observed that, while all human beings have the same rights, sometimes *fairness* requires that different rules have to be made for some people because of their circumstances. So it is that the rules in first grade differ in some ways from those in the seventh, but both sets of rules are supposed to serve the same purpose, to assure that all have an equal opportunity to learn and be respected.

By second grade these concepts should be grasped and particular differences observed, such as cultural and ethnic variations. For example, one of our teaching units, Sample 7, addresses these differences as a positive factor: the wonderful diversity that makes up the human family, how different we are as one person from another, one group from another, and yet all human. Most important to young children is the difference between children and grown-ups. With this notion, the rights of the child can be introduced as another example of how fairness sometimes requires different rules for different groups.

Before the end of the third grade children should know that the world society has recognized, though not fulfilled, the special needs of children, so that the human rights of the child have been noted and listed in particular sets of goals and rules about what children should be able to expect from the adults who run their countries. The Declaration of the Rights of the Child, available in a variety of forms (see Chapter 7), should be included in the curricula of the early elementary grades as a description of the goals caring adults have set forth to provide the expectation of human dignity to the world's children. Sample Eight introduces the Declaration. It should be pointed out that grown-ups and children are entitled to the same fundamental rights, and that because children have special needs, there is a particular set of guidelines to make the world aware of the importance of fulfilling these needs. Special needs and circumstances will be noted again when standards regarding racism and sexism are studied.

Finally, though it is undoubtedly painful for teachers as well as the students who are affected by it, the concept of child abuse cannot be ignored even at this early stage. Children, especially those subject to abuse, must know that such treatment is a violation of their fundamental rights, of their human dignity and physical integrity. They should be told that there are rules against this treatment, and that adults are expected to honor these rules. While the Declaration of the Rights of the Child is only a list of *goals* hoped for, there is also a list of *rules*, called the Convention on the Rights of the Child (included in the Appendix to this volume), which should be applied throughout the world. One of its rules is against abuse. The idea behind this rule is very similar to the idea behind the rules against torture. Deliberately hurting people, no matter who they are or what they have done, is a violation of their rights. It is a crime—that is, it breaks the rules without a good reason. Children should also understand that not all rules and laws are good ones, and that sometimes laws need to be broken to be fair and not hurt people. Laws that separated black people from white people in the United States and South Africa were such rules. When the people realized how hurtful such laws were to the whole community, some refused to obey them and many worked to change them.

While all the language used here is not totally suitable to these early grades, the concepts are essential to the first and subsequent stages of a developmental human rights learning sequence. Concerned teachers will find the appropriate words for instructing their students in these concepts.

Later Childhood and the Middle Grades

The later childhood ages of 9–11, grades 4–6, are the stage at which it is possible to introduce concepts of community and social values. While these concepts can be defined in abstract terms, their application should be described in clear social and behavioral language, relevant to the children's own lives and to the society in which they live. The notion of rules as guidelines to prevent harm and assure that all people in a group have a chance to achieve (to learn in class, to win a game) can now be developed to include the notion of *law* to assure social order and protect the members of society. Like rules, laws are standards of behavior (speed limits, prohibitions against theft and bodily harm) intended to prevent bad things from happening and make it easier for good things to happen. Laws, like rules, are also intended to protect our rights and remind us of our responsibilities.

At this level children are usually offered an introduction to some form of civic education and the concept of *citizenship*. There should be very clear instruction that a citizen has both *rights* and *responsibilities*, and that the enjoyment of rights depends on the fulfillment of responsibilities. We all have responsibilities to ourselves, to do and be all that we can; to others, to respect their rights and prevent or halt the violation of rights, our own and those of others; and to our communities (from classroom to the world), to do what we can to make them places where all members can enjoy their rights and fulfill their responsibilities.

Community is an essential concept for understanding citizenship and the significance of rights and responsibilities. Community can be defined for the children as a relationship among people who have something in common that they value. It can be the place where they live, their neighborhood or country, even the whole world. It can be a language or a religion, or any of the things that bring people together to live and work in ways that recognize that they need each other, just as we need each other in the classroom to learn together. The classroom is a learning community. The classroom rules are like the laws of their local town, or their home state, or native country, or the whole world. Communities that provide the best lives for their members are ones in which people are free and secure, where their needs are met and they are treated fairly. Laws help communities to do all these things for their people. Human rights laws are to assure that communities are just, to try to make sure that the relationships that constitute the community are fair to all.

The children should learn that in communities the people usually have many of the same values, that is, they think a lot alike about what is good and what is bad. Often they tell, or "declare" to the world or other communities, what their values are and what they want their communities to be like. Such descriptions can help children to understand what a *declaration* is. In these grades they will be taught in history or in lessons on national holidays about the Declaration of Independence, with which the founders of the United States told the world why they were breaking away from England and what they thought a good government should provide. Most important, this declaration said that governments should assure rights. So from the very beginning rights have been important in the United States. Other countries have made similar statements. Some of these are called *charters*. Some South African citizens put forth the 1955 African Freedom Charter in which they listed rights and responsibilities, and their hopes for a country free from racial discrimination. Some declarations are statements of value goals people hope to achieve. Most are drafted in the hope of *freedom*, the ability and opportunity to exercise rights and responsibilities.

The Declaration of Independence was a statement of value goals. The Constitution of the United States, like all *constitutions*, is the set of principles the founders designed to achieve those goals. For the American colonies of England the Declaration of Independence in 1776 and the Constitution in 1789 were developments in a struggle for rights among English people that began many centuries ago with the Magna Carta, which declared that even the king must obey the law and not violate the rights of his subjects. French speaking countries have a similar history. The Declaration of the Rights of Man and Citizen told the world why there was a revolution against the king of France in 1789, the same year the Constitution became the basis for the government and laws of the United States.

People in the colonies of France came to believe that they too had those rights, and eventually became independent of France in their quest for the freedom those rights proclaimed. The same quest brought independence to most colonized countries. The fact that the idea of human rights has spread throughout the world should be included in the human rights curriculum for upper elementary and middle school. It should be explained that, though there are variations in these rights and some countries emphasize some rights more than others, there are certain principles (ideas about rights) that are to be found in all cultures that value human rights. These ideas common to so many people were expressed in the Universal Declaration of Human Rights, one of the first value goal statements made by the United Nations. Set forth in 1948, it applies to people everywhere, men and women, grown-ups and children. This declaration means that the member countries of the United Nations are supposed to work for human rights. It is the most important rights declaration ever proclaimed, making possible all the other United Nations goal statements, guidelines, and rules on human rights. It calls everyone to take *personal responsibility* for human rights. Each of us has duties to our communities that require us to respect the rights of others. So we must be aware of *prejudice* and *discrimination*.

Early Adolescence and Junior High School

The ages 12 to 14 are years of rapid social development in which peer relationships are fiercely important. There is usually a great deal of in-group/out-group behavior, and the notions of "us" and "them," a significant factor in human rights violations, are often acted out both in and out of school. It is the time when prejudice and discrimination arising from ethnocentrism must be addressed as social problems for which communal solutions must be derived. It is also that stage at which students can be introduced to critical reflection on news media and culture, to help them become aware of the ways bias influences the information we receive and culture determines the ideas we have about others. Awareness of the nature and source of prejudice is an appropriate learning objective for this stage of development. In early adolescence there is a tendency in searching for one's own identity to be ready to exclude or denigrate what seems strange or socially undesirable (such as physical or behavioral) characteristics that set one apart from one's peers), or what the rest of society does not seem to respect (such as race or sexual orientation).

Prejudice as the breeding ground for human rights violations needs to be confronted in a way that can help students to understand the phenomenon in general and to apply that understanding to various situations and circumstances. It is especially important that adolescents study the global problems of racism and sexism through which millions of people are systematically denied their rights on the basis of personal characteristics in no way related to the victims' behavior, or to acts of choice. How prejudice operates in the students' own lives should also be addressed. It is best if the students themselves introduce the subject. Teachers should be very sensitive to the possibility of "preaching" on this issue; this is an age when adults tend to preach a great deal to children, who are strongly resistant to "lessons" presented in this way. Rather than forcing the issue, teachers should try to structure learning sequences that offer opportunity for the students to raise the issue or to encourage discussion. Raising non-threatening questions or using films and literature are two possible avenues to opening discussion of personal prejudice and discrimination.

The core concepts of *justice* and *equity* can be introduced by building on the concept of fairness introduced at the previous level. The distinction between equity and equality should be made. The value of *equality* calls for people to be treated the same, such as when they are accused of a crime. The value of *equity*, however, calls for different treatment so that real equality, having the same chance, can be achieved. Special facilities for the physically challenged or fair employment regulations to avoid racial or sexual discrimination are examples of different treatment for the sake of equity.

Problems of poverty are an appropriate topic for the early adolescent who is developing a sense of the nature of society, and the capacity to understand social problems. The concept of justice might be dealt with as *social justice* (fair treatment) and *distributive justice* (adequate access to the goods and services available in the society). It should be indicated that, because all rights carry responsibilities, the assurance of justice in a society calls for *social responsibility*. The attitudes, personal behavior, and public actions of the members of a society will in large part determine the degree of justice the society enjoys. This is true for all human society from the local community to the entire world. So in today's world we must exercise *global responsibility*.

Attitudes, behavior, and actions are influenced by the *social* and *political values* of the society. Some times these values are in harmony with what the society has declared to be its values and goals, sometimes not. An important aspect of social responsibility is continuously to examine the values and the actual social circumstances. Responsible citizens raise questions about how the society is doing in living up to the values it has declared. They also question the values to see whether they are, indeed, still what the society aspires to achieve. It is such questioning, and the action that often follows when the questions reveal that the society is failing to live up to its values, that lead to social change and sometimes produce new laws like those that abolished slavery and segregation in the United States and apartheid in South Africa.

It is also the process that led the United Nations to adopt a series of *covenants* and *conventions*, treaties that become *international law* in the countries that agree to them, to strengthen the world's capacity to achieve the fulfillment of human rights. The conventions of special relevance to this developmental level are the ones on racism, apartheid and discrimination against women (see the appendices for a list of important international human rights legal instruments, including these conventions).

This is also an age at which the possibilities for social and political action as a means to advance the cause of human rights can be introduced into the curriculum. The laws and institutions that exist for this purpose might be the subject of some learning units. National and regional court systems such as the Inter-American Court of Human Rights and the European Court of Human Rights, and the conventions they are authorized to interpret and apply, are good vehicles for teaching about such concepts as national and international law, covenants, and conventions. They can also be used to begin taking into account the nature and extent of human rights violations in various parts of the world. Introducing specific rights violations and possibilities for remedies at this level can help set the stage for more serious study of major human rights problems at the high school level.

Youth, Young Adulthood, and High School

The last years of secondary school are those that are most significant in the political education of young citizens. Many young people of this age have already been catapulted into adult responsibilities, such as care of their own children or of siblings, military service, or low wage employment; far too many have had direct experience of crime and the legal system. Many are disaffected from education and cynical about the possibilities for justice in their own and other societies. For such reasons, as well as for the efficacy of the curriculum itself, human rights education of youth at the senior high school level must deal directly with the realities of their lives and of the world they are entering.

Of course, teachers must exercise sensitivity in dealing with some of the very harsh material on gross violations of human rights. They should be alert to the possibilities of how it will affect the students, and indeed, how some of them may already have been directly affected by similar situations. Many students in schools today in the United States and Europe have come as refugees from such violations, and many suffer violations of their own rights in their own communities, families, and schools. Such conditions must be taken into account when units on these horrendous problems are undertaken. However, it is also important for the teacher to point out that, unless these situations are confronted and addressed as fundamental social and political problems that violate the ethical standards of human rights, there is little chance of their being resolved or eliminated. They should note that public awareness is almost always one of the first essential steps in the process of remediation of human rights abuses such as that outlined in the reconstructive approach. It is thus equally important to deal with the many efforts by citizen groups, major nongovernmental organizations, national and international institutions, and individuals to overcome specific and systemic violations of human rights.

It is at this stage that analysis of causes for human rights abuses might be integrated along with the various remedies that have been proposed and tried. One of the most helpful concepts for this purpose is that of *moral exclusion*, the psychological process of considering persons and groups outside the bounds in which the rules of fairness apply (Susan Opotow 1991). This phenomenon applies to various types of harm-doing, and can help to explain problems ranging from subtle discrimination to genocide. The concept that can be used to complement moral exclusion and open discussions of values, ethical choices, and alternatives is that of *moral responsibility*, both social and individual. This concept refers to the responsibility one bears to take social action consistent with the positive values of society, and to influence the society to be guided by those values; it includes also the responsibility for one's personal behavior. It brings a personal and ethical dimension to concepts of social responsibility developed in the early grades and brings to its most significant level the process of values assessment and choice-making to be woven throughout a developmental sequence. This process is in fact, equally relevant to adult education as a lifelong struggle toward moral development.

The international standards that are most relevant to teaching about these concepts are the Nuremberg Principles regarding individual responsibility, the convention on genocide, and the convention against torture. Discussion of the events and conditions that led to these standards cannot avoid the questions of risk and sacrifice often involved in the exercise of moral responsibility. The histories of those who have taken such risks and made great sacrifices in the struggle for human rights most certainly should be introduced, as should the great successes that have been achieved by individuals and social movements. Sample 26 provides one approach to this topic.

Groups of students might also investigate possibilities for being part of movements dealing with the particular human rights abuses that most concern them. The organizations listed in Chapter 7 provide some such possibilities, and students can organize their own efforts on local, national, or international human rights issues. They may even wish to become involved in the movement to have their country ratify some of the human rights conventions still not adopted as the law of the land, or to engage in mobilizing to define and codify new standards, such as the right to peace or to a sustainable environment. All these processes can form the basis of fruitful instructional units and satisfying experiential learnings that recognize the capacities of secondary school students to make moral choices and take social action.

The concepts suggested in this developmental sequence for human rights education are, of course, limited. They are put forth as suggestions to encourage teachers to think through a set of appropriate concepts as the basis of their own lesson plans, and to choose subject matter not so much by topic but according to some fundamental notions of what needs to be learned to develop the necessary values, skills and knowledge for students to be prepared to be responsible citizens in a global society seeking to bring forth a just world order.

Chapter 3
The Early Grades: Laying the Foundation for an Appreciation of Human Dignity—Kindergarten to Grade Three

Children begin the learning that determines their attitudes toward others with their very first breath. How infants are regarded by their families and the nature of the care-giving they experience will insruct them in how they are valued, about their human worth, and what they can expect from the world. This experience has a profound influence on how the child views the world and those who inhabit it. Children learn love and care through being given love and care. Teachers of the early grades should love and care for children.

That children's need of nurturing is stated as a right in both the Declaration and the Convention on the Rights of the Child is ample recognition of the need and significance of meeting it to the fulfillment of human rights in general. Children who do not appreciate their own human worth are not likely to appreciate that of others, nor to grow into citizens concerned about, much less active on behalf of, human rights. Thus education for *care giving* should be included in human rights education. Instruction and experience in care giving should be part of the earliest socialization of children, and should be included in their first formal education in kindergarten.

The development of respect for others, appreciation of human commonalities, and honor of human differences should also be intentionally cultivated from the earliest socialization experiences. In kindergarten the development of these attributes should become part of the explicit, intentionally planned learning sequence to be followed through the early grades. Through their own behavior as well as through particular learning activities, teachers should communicate to students that all human beings have innate worth and the right to be treated with respect. We are all part of one species or family with the same physical and emotional needs: we are in many ways the same. The human family is also richly varied, as will be specifically demonstrated in units for the kindergarten and the third grade included here: we are also very different. Human differences make life interesting and help us to achieve much more as a human family than would be the case if we were all the same in every way. *Appreciation of diversity* and *respect for differences* are value concepts to be woven throughout human rights education from this beginning stage to the more advanced levels of senior high school. As noted in Chapter 2, they are core concepts for the development of an attitude that values human rights, and are fundamental to the approach to human rights education described and exemplified in this teaching resource.

The following learning activities for the early grades are intended to instruct five- to eight-year-olds in these concepts regarding human commonalities and differences and are directed toward facilitating the development of *respect for others*, for *fairness*, and for behavioral restraints for the sake of the *community*. In these early educational experiences children may also be instructed in the need for *limits and rules* to maintain *social order* and assure *fairness*. And they may be helped to understand that being a member of a community entails *rights and responsibilities*. The complementarity between rights and responsibilities, assumed here to be essential to a good society, is also a theme crucial to the foundational learning experiences and to subsequent learning as it becomes more complex and more directly involved with the human rights issues and problems addressed in the upper grades.

Another essential aspect of the approach to human rights education outlined here is "ecological thinking," an holistic approach based on understanding the concept of living systems fundamental to the learning process. Ecological thinking derives from reverence for life. *Reverence for life* is a necessary complement to the core value of human dignity and integrity as it is realized in a sustaining and sustainable environment. Thus it is a concept introduced with the first descriptions of what it is to be human.

The best general curricular source for this early level of development is *Human Right for Children: A Curriculum for Teaching Human Rights to Children Ages 3–12*. It provides a variety of lessons compatible with those included in this resource and readily adaptable to a number of approaches to education for human rights and peace. It is the best single source to complement and extend the approach and samples presented here. It is highly recommended to those considering focusing on human rights issues throughout the full teaching year, and it will provide adequate material. See Chapter 7 for the source from which it can be ordered, annotations, and other curricular resources for the K–3 level.

Kindergarten. What Is a Human Being?—Reverence for Life

In our planetary age, an holistic approach to human rights education assumes the need for ecological thinking. Ecological thinking emphasizes interconnectedness and uses living systems metaphors. As human dignity is the core value of human rights, respect for life is the core ecological value. The two are inseparably interrelated and thus are the basic conceptual foundations upon which we build the very first sample learning experience in this resource.

The following lesson is intended to initiate in these youngest of learners an awareness of humans as self-conscious, reflective beings who are part of the living system of the Earth, and to start them on the way to understanding human responsibility for the quality of life of the planet and all who are part of it. On the foundation of this understanding, human rights education also seeks to build an appreciation of the human capacity to carry out this responsibility.

Learning Objectives. Students will:
- be introduced to ecological thinking;
- begin a process through which they become increasingly aware of their humanity;
- begin to see themselves as related to others and the living system of the Earth.

Learning Sequence. Note: Each introductory activity here is intended to take about ten minutes. The following may be done over two sessions, and all four steps may take a full week. Review the previous discussion each time you start a new talking circle.

Step 1. Have the children sit on the floor in "a talking circle," so that every child can see all the other children. Tell them that these talking circles are for "discussions," or talking about very important things. Teachers could also explain that "talking circles" are the way Native Americans speak their concerns on occasions of important ceremonies.

Step 2. Tell the children that everyone in the class is a human being. If there are fish or other animals in the class this can be stated as "almost everyone." All the people in the class—the teacher, the teachers' aides, if there are such, and all the children—are human beings. Then the question is posed, "What is a human being?"

Are we animal, vegetable, or mineral? Here the teacher can point out what a mineral is and that minerals are all around us and even in our bodies. For instance, our bones and teeth are made of minerals, and minerals are in the soil that grows vegetables. We also need air to breathe. Next, explain that "vegetable" means more than carrots and peas. We are also vegetable in part because we need food and so much of the food we eat is vegetable. We, like vegetables, also need water and air. The air is all around, and we all breathe it. So human beings are part of all the world and all the world is part of us.

But, it can be asked, are we really vegetable? Why not? Are we really mineral? Why not? Then are we animal? Why? What kind of animal are we? Here there can be a discussion of the physical characteristics of humans and some of the similarities and differences with other animals. In schools that are organized by particular religions or adherents to a particular philosophy, this discussion could include the ethical and spiritual considerations about human beings that are integral to their respective beliefs.

Step 3. During another "talking circle" session, review the previous discussions.

This discussion should consider the major differences between humans and other animals. The two the teacher should be sure to emphasize and include in the discussion, if the children themselves do not, are first, that human beings communicate to each other with words, not just a few sounds. We have lots of words and we call them language. Second, we make choices. We can decide a lot more about our lives than other animals can. So that means we have to learn how to use words well and how to make good choices. Here you might mention choosing foods that are good for our bodies, like selecting an apple instead of a candy bar. Since we are part of the world, if we keep ourselves healthy we help to make the world healthy. Just as we can contribute to a healthy world, so a planet well cared for helps to keep us healthy, too. Human beings in groups like kindergartens try to use words and make choices that are helpful and good for the whole group, and now they need to think about what is good for the whole world, too. Here, the teacher might ask the children to say why this might be so, encouraging them to consider interdependence, cooperative relationships, and responsibility for the Earth.

Step 4. Again form a "talking circle" and review the previous discussions.

This fourth discussion is intended to lay the ground work for a sense of human universality and social responsibility. Teachers may or may not choose to make this explicit, depending on the degree to which they think the children might comprehend it. But they should in their words and manner *make it clear that there is a universal humanity,* that we all need food to grow and live and clean air to breathe. Such understandings are the ground work for study of the right to food in later years and of the proposition of the right to a clean and safe environment. The discussion can be concluded by asking the children; to prepare for the next round of talking circles, to think of ways in which human beings are alike and different. Note that the focus on words is intended to build respect for language and ultimately for the significance of the language of human rights, especially as expressed in the landmark human rights declarations (see Chapter 7 for a list). The focus on choice-making is the foundation for the valuing processes essential to *social, global,* and *moral responsibility.*

Kindergarten. Human Beings Are Alike and Different

Human rights concepts and standards are based on the acceptance of a universal humanity, a universality that complements and is enriched by human diversity. The recognition of common human capacities for joy and pain is the origin of *empathy*, a capacity essential to the development of *concern* and *responsibility* for human rights, and an understanding of the consequences of *exclusion* and *harm doing*. These central concepts are the basis of the following kindergarten unit, a foundation for the development of attitudes supportive of the universal realization of human rights.

Learning Objectives. Students will:
- identify for appreciation human differences and commonalities as a step toward an understanding of human universality and diversity;
- be encouraged to think about the feelings of others and those who suffer harm.

Learning Sequence

Step 1. Review the talking circle discussion (Sample 1) in which they were introduced to the idea of the common needs and characteristics of human beings, and our relationship to the planet.

Step 2. The teacher asks how human beings are alike and different. Children will likely point out physical differences in size, hair color, and so forth, and indicate racial or gender differences. The teacher should encourage the children to think of as many differences as possible, communicating the attitude that the greater the variety the better, and that the more they can recognize the more they will understand how wonderful the whole human family is.

The teacher should be alert for opportunities to bring up culture and language. If race or ethnicity is mentioned, steer the conversation to geographic origins and how human beings live in more places on the Earth than most other animals. All animals can move from one place to another, but only human beings think and talk together about where they will go. Ask if any of the children or some of their families have come from other places in the world. Every classroom from kindergarten up should have a globe. Show the children on the globe where they are now and where they or their relatives, neighbors, or friends came from. Ask about the languages they know about, and explain how human beings not only use language to talk to each other, but that they have many different languages, showing how good human beings are at inventing many ways to do some of the same things.

Step 3. Ask what human beings do when they are happy. If children want to jump, clap, dance, or sing a song to demonstrate expressions of happiness, encourage them to do so. Explain that all human beings have music, songs, and dances, and that all celebrate. The songs and dances are different in different places and in different languages. Some of the celebrations are about the same things, like birthdays and naming days. Some are different like national holidays. Give examples of national holidays. In sum, reinforce that the differences among people are the result of the richness of the human family, the varieties of ways we humans have invented to do what we need to do and that we have had different things happen to us. We call these things "history." So human beings also have different histories, the stories of their countries.

Step 4. Next (if necessary, because of attention span, this step can be taken at a later time) move to what the most important commonalities are. Remind them of the previous discussion and steer the talk beyond physical commonalities and basic needs to feelings and emotions. Ask them how they felt when they fell down, or were hit by another child. Point out that all people feel pain when they are hurt. Ask them how they would feel if they thought they were lost. Point out that all people feel fear sometimes in scary situations. Grown ups who care for children try to protect them, to keep them from being hurt and scared. Since we know that all people, children and grown ups, can be hurt and scared, we try to prevent it. We try to talk and behave so that we don't hurt or scare other people. Most groups of people have rules to try to keep people from being hurt and scared. That's one of the reasons we have rules in school, because when you are hurt or scared it's hard to learn. School is for learning. One thing we will try to learn is how to work and be with others, so all of us can learn and grow to be the wonderful people we can be when we try our best.

Observe that most of us would like to be treated as the wonderful people we are. So we should try to treat others as we would like to be treated. If we are tall or short, have one color skin or another, wear glasses, or use a wheel chair, we all should be treated with *respect*. Respect means we appreciate how people are alike and different, and all are human.

Step 5. The next day briefly review some of the human differences the children identified and explain how the differences enrich the human family. Talk about commonalities and how they bind us together, and make us careful not to hurt and scare others because we know how it feels. Explain that the class rules will prevent the children from being hurt and scared and make the classroom a fair place.

These are themes that should be woven through all planned instruction and guided play. The teacher should keep always in mind that respect for human dignity and integrity needs to be cultivated as do the other fundamental human capacities and social attributes toward which early childhood education strives. Building respect for human dignity and physical integrity as the avoidance of harm to others is, at this age, the foundation for the avoidance and rejection of the human rights violations of child abuse, sexual assault, harassment, and torture in later years.

First Grade. Rules Are for Protection and Fairness

The concept of law as a social mechanism for assuring justice and protecting human rights can be introduced as children are being instructed in the limits on behavior that accompany the shift from supervised and free play to more formal instruction in the first grade. It is important for children to understand the reasons for these limits. The teacher should take care that rules do not seem to be the arbitrary whims of adults, enforced by their larger size or greater strength. While a respect for law and authority represented at this level by the rules and the teacher is a socially positive attribute to be cultivated for the sake of order, the insinuation by instruction or implication of blind obedience to authority, even at this young age, will impede the development of individual responsibility as it weakens the possibilities for authentic democracy and reflective choice-making. The following exercise is one possibility for communicating the positive functions of limits as guarantors of the rights of the members of a group.

Learning Objectives. This activity introduces the fundamental concepts of fairness and reinforces the prohibition against harm-doing that is essential to a just and nonviolent social order, the kind to which human rights standards aspire.

Learning Sequence

Step 1. Ask the children whether they know what rules are and what they are for. Work with their responses to the latter part of the question to develop a list of what rules are supposed to do. Print the list on newsprint and put it up on the wall or bulletin board, then read the whole list to them, pointing out how much they already know about rules. Be sensitive to the possibility of notions such as the enforcement of power. Emphasize game rules in which fair play is the actual purpose.

Step 2. Next, explain to the children that all the things they said related to two big ideas. These ideas are *fairness* and *protection.* We have rules for games so that the games are fair to all the players, and to help prevent people from being hurt in games. Rules also help us to know how to do things with others when we don't already know.

Rules can help us to be polite, like not talking when others are already speaking and not breaking into lines. Rules can help us to keep our places neat and in good order like picking up our crayons and toys and not throwing papers and trash in the streets. Rules can help us to learn in school, play in our neighborhoods, and get along with people.

Step 3. Explain that good rules make things good for people, so it is important to make good rules and keep them. It is also important to change them if we find out that they are not good rules or that they aren't working any more. The best rules are the ones that people make for themselves. The teacher will help make a set of rules for the class because grown ups have had lots of experience with rules. First read again the list of what rules are supposed to do.

Ask what kind of classroom they would like to have so that everyone could be happy and learn as much as possible. Then invite them to think of the rules that they will need to have that kind of classroom. The teacher can then write the rules on poster paper and post them next to the list of what rules are supposed to do. Read the rules over and ask the children to think about examples of the rules.

Step 4. Ask whether these rules do what rules are supposed to do. "Do we want to make any changes? Do we all agree to these rules, teacher and all students?" Discuss until you have general agreement.

Inform the class that "In our next lesson on how to have a classroom of fairness and order, we will make drawings of the rules that will hang in our classroom so that we can always tell what the rules are even if we can't yet read the list the teacher has made."

First Grade. Respecting the Rules— Making a Compact

An appreciation of the notion of the "social contract" contributes to the development of social and political responsibility and to an understanding of the need for the social limits set by rules and laws. From the earliest age children can be helped to understand that the nature of positive social relations rests on the recognition of limits set in the common good, and an agreement by the members of a social group to behave so as not to harm others or their environment, and where possible to enhance the common good.

As we consider the needs of education for a democratic society, we have to reflect upon ways to introduce the notion of the social contract that underlies the charters, constitutions, and conventions that make up the system of human rights standards and provide for democratic social orders. The following unit is intended to introduce these concepts. It also introduces a process of cooperative learning with the undertaking of group drawings.

Learning Objectives. Students will:
- reflect on the need for and the function of rules to guide social behavior;
- develop a "social contract" for their own class in the form of a compact, a pledge people who are dependent upon one another make to uphold the common welfare.

Materials. Set of rules for a fair and orderly classroom; drawing materials.

Learning Sequence

Step 1. Read the class rules to the children and ask them to decide which one they think is especially important. Read the rules again one at a time and ask for a show of hands after reading each one to indicate that they think that rule is so important that they want to do a drawing of that particular one. Talk about why each rule is important for a happy and productive classroom.

Step 2. Group the children according to the rules they have selected. Try to have one group per rule. The groups should first talk again about why they think the rule is important. The teacher should circulate, helping groups to focus their talks if necessary. Then they should work together on a drawing that illustrates the rule and why it is important. When the drawings are completed they are to be hung up around the list. Each group should explain their drawing, how it shows the rule, and why it is important. The teacher can say, "Tomorrow we will see if we can remember the rules and which drawing represents which rule."

Step 3. On the day following the making of the drawings, ask how many of the rules they can remember and which drawing represents which rule. Number the rules on the written list, then put the respective number on each of the drawings that represents it. (On subsequent days the numbers and the rules can be reviewed, providing instruction in numbers as well as in the rules.)

Step 4. Once all the rules are identified and the drawings numbered, tell the students that rules are also a kind of promise that all in the class make to be fair and polite to show that they respect each other. Tell them that such promises are sometimes called compacts or covenants, like the Mayflower Compact. Tell the story of the Mayflower Compact (this exercise is appropriate to include in a history unit on the Pilgrims and the settlement of New England by the Pilgrims).

Ask whether they know of any other stories of promises, compacts, or covenants. Some children may know the story of Noah and the Rainbow Covenant. (See Reardon, *Educating for Global Responsibility*, listed in the References at the end of Chapter 1, for a unit on the Rainbow Covenant.)

Step 5. Together with the children, make up a promise statement and hold a covenanting ceremony. The children make this promise to each other: "to use the rules so that all are treated fairly and to change the rules if they seem to be unfair."

This lesson communicates the fundamental principle of the social contract upon which human rights standards are based. Although the children may not comprehend these ideas at an abstract level, they should be able to understand that the quality of their life together in the class depends a good deal on living up to the promise of fairness that the rules represent.

Second Grade. Wishing a World Fit for Children — Understanding Human Needs

Second grade children are separating themselves from early childhood and see their own infancy in the very dim past. Many have infant siblings, some care for other younger children, and most find babies interesting. They can be taught a good deal about what is good for children and the good society by thinking about what would be the best things for a baby to have.

The following exercise, based on one designed by Stanley B. Smith while he was associated with the Martin Peace Institute at the University of Idaho, calls for children to think about just such things in the form of wishes for a newborn baby. With this exercise teachers can introduce the youngsters to the role that wishes and hope play in the way people live, and how visions function to make the world better.

The teacher can start by saying that some very wise people think that the best the world could be is a world fit for children. Ask them to start thinking about what the best world would provide for a new baby and what the baby might expect as she grows up in such a world. They might think also of what they might want to see for all children, including themselves. Later they can think about what needs to be done so those wishes can come true, and what they themselves can do to make that happen. This reflection can provide background for study of the Declaration and the Convention on the Rights of the Child. Tell the children that all through history people have worked for human rights to make the world better for everyone. Declarations about human rights are also wishes for a better world; they are descriptions of what the writers of the declarations wish for all people so they can have a good life. Tell the children that when we make wishes we use our imaginations. When we imagine good things and a better world, we actually begin to make the world better. Grown-ups call these wishes for a better world visions (pictures in our heads) and plans (ideas about how to make the visions real). Pretending is an important way to learn and to change the world.

Learning Objectives. Students will:
- be encouraged to reflect on the fundamental human needs of children;
- be prepared to learn about the Rights of the Child;
- envision a good childhood to understand the nature of a just society; appreciate the universal needs of all children; and take account of differences among various parts of the world.

Learning Sequence

Step 1. Preparation. The project should be announced several weeks prior to October 24, United Nations Day, a good day to celebrate being a member of the human family. Students are to make a gift for a newborn baby and wrap it in a "wish" for the child. The teacher during this time might use music, stories, or bulletin board to focus attention on the world the child will be born into and what childhood is like in various parts of the world.

Step 2. Explain to the students: "You are all special people with so much creative energy. I want you to help me plan a surprise party for a baby who will be born into the human family this year. Lets look at the globe together and select where the child will be born. The teacher can give some background about the area chosen. "If we were to visit that baby's home, what is the most important or wonderful gift you might bring? We will have a party to celebrate the birth and to share with one another our gifts and wishes for the baby."

Step 3. Students are asked to make a gift for the baby and wrap it in a wish. They should make something to represent the most important thing a new baby should have and then think of a wish for the baby to go with the gift. Students should be encouraged to draw a picture, write a poem, decorate a single word, make something out of clay, or present the new baby with a question that they hope the child one day will be able to answer.

The gifts should represent something the baby will need: a bed, clothes, a desk, some food, or whatever they think the baby should have for healthy infancy and childhood. The wishes should be for something in the child's world that would help provide a secure and happy life: other children to play with, good schools to go to, peace in her country, jobs for her parents. The teacher can "prime the pump" with suggestions, but let the children come up with their own ideas.

Step 4. The teacher encourages the students to describe to the class the gifts they have made and their wishes for the baby. They should explain why they chose that particular gift and made the wish they did. Display the gifts and post the drawings.

The teacher leads the class in a discussion of the many gifts the children have made for the new baby: which ones are necessary for the baby's health, which for the baby's happiness, and which will help prepare the baby's future. What does the baby most need? Also list their wishes for a better world for the baby. What could the world be like if their wishes came true?

Once a class consensus is reached about needs, students should be encouraged to use this information to make a list of "Needs of a Child" in every land. The teacher could write out and post the list of needs on the bulletin board. Make a similar list of "Wishes for a Better World" and post it, too.

Step 5. How does the baby grow? Ask the students to tell stories of how the baby is cared for and grows up to be seven years old. What part of the world does the child live in? Point it out on the globe. What food does the child eat? What kind of home does the child live in? What games do children play in that part of the world? How is the life of the child the same or different from their own lives? The teacher will need to provide some information, perhaps using illustrations, to enable the students to respond to these questions.

Step 6. Review the list of "Needs of a Child." The teacher could observe that many children are without these things. Perhaps this is especially true in the area of the world they have chosen for this child. They do not have the things we think they have a right to. Part of what we need to learn is how to change the world so all children can have these things. Going to school is supposed to help to learn how to make our wishes for a better world come true. If they do their best to learn, they will be helping to make a better world for that baby and for themselves. Suggest that the students "Look at the list of wishes for a better world and think about what we need to learn to make a better world."

Second Grade. Taking Responsibility to Stop Hurt and Harm

In building a sense of empathy, we also seek to develop in children the capacity to intervene to prevent or halt suffering and to nurture the desire to avoid inflicting hurt and harm. If we hope to help students develop the capacity to take action on behalf of human rights, we need to provide them with learning experiences which integrate an action element. Participatory exercises in the classroom and community related activities in and out of school are recommended as an integral part of human rights education.

The unit below is a participatory, role-play lesson based on one of many such role-plays written by Yvonne See, who represents the Women's International League for Peace and Freedom among the non-governmental organizations associated with UNESCO in Paris. The key idea is that we must be responsible, intervene, and take part when we see hurting or harming.

Learning Objectives. Students will:
- see how individual behaviors affect others;
- see that it is possible to prevent hurt and harm;
- recount events in which they did intervene or could have intervened to prevent or halt harm.

Materials. A flyswatter.

Learning Sequence

Step 1. Select the actors for the role play or ask for volunteers, three students to play two children and one fly.

Step 2. Set the scene with the flyswatter. The opening of the window can be mimed. Before the role play explain that the fly is a symbol. It can be seen as representing a dog, a bird, a human being, or any living creature.

Step 3. Give the students the script, and organize them into groups to read one role and help each other with the reading. Each group is to select someone to play the role they read. Then conduct the role play.

Chris: (mimes pulling the wings from the fly).

Pat: (to Chris) And what would you say if someone pulled both your arms out?

Chris: (laughing) Well, I don't have wings anyway. And I told you before, mind your own business.

Pat: No, I won't! I can't stand seeing a creature get hurt just for fun.

The fly: Yes, it sure does hurt.

Pat: (to Chris) If you go on like that, I'll get the flyswatter and kill the fly. At least it won't suffer then.

Chris: No way! I'm having fun and I haven't finished. (Pat leaves)

The fly: What's he [or she] going to do to me now?

Pat: (enters with the flyswatter) Stop right now or I'll kill it!

Chris: You just try!

Pat: (swatting about) Wham! Bang!

Chris: (furious) You stinker! It's flown away now!

Pat: I missed it! I'm glad I did, very glad!

The fly: Well, so am I! Oh dear! I've got a bit of wing missing and I'm flying all crooked, but I'll be all right. Thank you, Pat!

Chris: (to Pat) I'll pay you back for this. Just you wait. You'll wish you'd minded your own business, you stinker.

Pat: You're the stinker.

Chris: Say that again and I'll beat you up.

Pat: (making flying movements with his arms) Or pull out my arms?

Chris: You're the dirty fly!

Pat: But you did the dirty work.

Chris: That's my business.

Pat: (opening the window for the fly) You're free, now, lucky you. Now get away quick!

The fly: Goodbye! And try to play other games, Chris!

Pat: Bye fly! And now that you're free, don't come and bother us! Don't land on our noses or eat in our plates!

The fly: You know, I'm just like you. I've got a sense of responsibility, and if a fly bothers you, I'll make sure it stops.

Chris: Even if it's none of our business.

The fly: Of course.

Pat: (to Chris) You see, the fly agrees with me: you should never let people do harm without doing anything to prevent it.

Chris: Well, all right. (They both watch the fly fly away.) All that trouble for one little fly.

Pat: Well, you know, it would be just the same for any other creature.

Step 4. After the role play, have the students reflect on these questions: Do they agree with the conclusions? Is it better to do nothing than to do something? What is responsibility? Do they agree that to be a responsible human being one needs to behave in a humane manner, to prevent or stop people or things that hurt and harm people, animals, or any part of our environment?

Step 5. Discuss other types of intervention to prevent hurt and harm. Give examples such as sending food where there is hunger. Point out such places on the world map or globe. Ask the children to bring magazine or newspaper photos of areas of famine, drought, or torn by war, earthquakes, or other disasters. Ask them to give examples of "interventions." Explain that it means people or organizations like the Red Cross or the United Nations taking action where there is hurt or harm. Ask them how people can help and what the best outcomes of help would be. Try to lead them to at least two understandings: that the harm should be ended, and efforts should be made to keep it from happening again. How can Chris and Pat agree that what happened in the role play will not happen again? What standards or rules might be established? How should the standards be made to work? What might each child do to reduce the hurt and harm suffered in their world?

Step 6. Some teachers may want to use this role play and discussion to introduce the concepts of moral exclusion and inclusion, employing the notion of fairness. Ask the students to compare and contrast the two characters' ideas about fairness. Then ask to whom should we be fair? Why? If some people think they don't have to be fair to you, what would you say to them? What are their own ideas of fairness? Are the standards or rules fair that they thought of to prevent hurt and harm? Explain that these are what grown ups sometimes call "the big questions." They are hard for everyone to answer. People everywhere have asked these questions for a long, long time. We continue to try to find really good answers, but the important thing is to keep trying. If we stop trying to answer these hard questions, we can't ever be sure that we can stop all the hurt and harm. Trying, though, can be an exciting adventure, better even than some of the best games we know.

Step 7. This exercise could then be extended to "human rights heroes," stories of people (including children) who have tried their best to stop hurt and harm. Many more possibilities could be designed.

Third Grade. Learning to Value Global Diversity

At the age of about 8 years, children in industrial societies have usually acquired a great deal of information about the world, mainly from television. They are also very likely to be aware that all the people of the world live on one single planet, Earth. However, few will have acquired knowledge about the geography of the planet and the distinctions among various countries and cultures. They will be aware of differences among people, and can be quite vulnerable to ingesting without question the social prejudices of the adult world they inhabit. When this occurs without some experience enabling them to comprehend human differences as the enriching variety that characterizes the human family, then prejudice may take root. Uprooting social prejudice is a difficult and painful process, for the society and for those who harbor and those who suffer the prejudice. Given the great variety of nationalities and ethnicities of children who enter our public schools at every grade level, learning activities to prevent prejudice should be integrated into human rights education at every stage, so we continue to emphasize this learning goal throughout the samples provided here.

The following exercises can be adapted to any grade from the latter period of the second through the fifth. They were designed to involve third and fifth graders together. In schools with more homogeneous populations this grade mixing is a good device to assure some differences in the learning group, if only on the developmental level. It also introduces the notion that students can help each other to learn, the older ones can help the younger ones and the ones with one special talent or aptitude can help others with different talents and aptitudes, increasing the general pool of learning talents in the group and reinforcing cooperation as a learning mode. These differences in talents and aptitudes can also be pointed out by the teacher to indicate that the variety of human characteristics can always be used for socially constructive purposes, and what a waste it is when differences become the cause of conflict or unfair treatment.

This unit was designed by Julie Whitmore for a class in human rights education at Teachers College, Columbia University, in consultation with third and fifth grade teachers for use in their Massachusetts classrooms.

Learning Objectives. Students will:
· recognize and identify human difference;
· explore where various groups and nations live in the world;
· discover characteristics of various cultures.

Materials and Setup. Collect photos and drawings of people of different ethnic groups, countries, ages, reflecting as many human differences as possible. Post a large smiling sun on an upper corner of the bulletin board to indicate that learning about human diversity is a happy activity, and that all the people of the world live "under one sun."

Set a long table under the bulletin board. The table includes the following materials for exploration, analysis, discussion, research, and development. (The children may add to the initial group of articles placed on the table.)

- artifacts from peoples around the world
- video-tapes on peoples around the world
- audio-tapes on peoples around the world
- a decorated bin for newspaper articles
- magazines
- bumper stickers (e.g., Visualize World Peace)
- books (see bibliography)
- a world map posted near the bulletin board

As the unit progresses add students' work, ideas, etc. to this collection on display.

Learning Sequence

Step 1. Bring third and fifth grade classes together in one room. Set the stage for the whole unit by welcoming both classes. Inform the group that this unit was put together jointly by the third and fifth grade teachers and that everyone will be meeting together at least twice a week for a few weeks.

Using a globe in the front of the room discuss the following topics:

- People live all over the globe.
- Where have your family, friends or neighbors lived or visited?
- Can you show us where you or they visited?
- Are there children there?
- What language do they speak?
- Do they go to a school? What is the school like?
- What do they eat?
- What do their homes look like?
- What do they play?
- Continue discussion as per class input.

Step 2. Organize students into small groups of four or five children (mixed third and fifth graders).

Hand out a copy of *People* Magazine or a set of the collected photos and illustrations to each group. Ask children to:

- explore the book and/or illustrations together;
- choose a country that the group is interested in and explain that they will be learning more about their chosen countries through books, people, articles;
- dress a figure representative of their chosen country with the ethnic dress, hair styles (explain the meanings of ethnic and national).

Mingle among the small groups to answer or ask questions.

Step 3. Hand out adhesive backed paper like "Postits" to each child. Ask the groups to write the name of the country they chose on their Postits and then to write their names on them. On a blank outline of a world map have the children attach their Postits to the area where their chosen country is located. (Note: This helps children learn geography in a fun way and increases the children's commitment to the lesson/unit as they all put their names up on the map.)

Step 4. With the entire group of two classes together, debrief the small group activity discussing each group's country, and why they chose it. Ask the students to look at the map, and see if there are areas with no Postits. Ask whether all the Postits are in the right place. Involve them in changing the Postits if necessary. Some may change countries so all world regions are represented. (Note: all the students will then see Postits all over the map with country names on the appropriate locations.)

Step 5. Re-group all children after the Postits are placed. Start the children thinking about working as a group. Praise them for coming to a group decision and explain that sometimes it is difficult to have everyone agree because each individual has his or her own good ideas. However, sharing and working together often leads us to the very best ideas.

Step 6. Pose the following questions to the students:
- Was it difficult or easy to choose a country?
- How did you make the group decision on your countries?
- Did you all agree right away?
- Did you change your mind?
- Did you all voice an opinion?
- Did you vote on the country you chose?

Ask the children to think about *how* decisions are made in:
- your group;
- your classroom;
- your school;
- your family;
- your town;
- your state, country, world.
- What benefits do you get from sharing and considering different ideas?

Everyone's talents and ideas are valuable and worth considering. Working together as a group gives us the opportunity to work with and enjoy many types of talents, ideas, and resources.

Step 7. Explain that we will all be "celebrating people under one sun" together for the next few weeks (hence the sun bulletin board).

Next time we will start researching and talking about your group's country. Try to find out about:
- What food is eaten in your country?
- What do they wear in your country?
- What language do they speak?
- What do the people look like?
- What coins or money do they use?

You can discover these things by:
- finding a friend who comes from that country;
- finding books;
- talking to your family members, and other teachers.

Ask the group how else can we learn about these countries. Continue the process until the countries of each group have been studied.

Step 8. As a culminating exercise ask the children to list the ways the people in their countries are different from and how they are like others. Ask them how the differences make the world more interesting and can be helpful to everyone in the world.

Third Grade. Expectations and Obligations—Responsibilities Go with Rights

The concept of responsibility as the capacity to respond, intervene, or intercede in situations of harm-doing and rights violations can be complemented by the notion of obligations to one's society within the context of the social contract. While all societies acknowledge both duties toward and obligations from their members, most standards and documents on human rights do not enumerate the responsibilities and obligations of individuals to the society. A notable exception to this is the Declaration of Duties of States and Persons of the Association of Southeast Asian Nations, a document well worth the attention of all human rights educators. However, the essential aspect of the fulfillment of social responsibility to the realization of human rights, and to a just as well as orderly society, should be introduced when the concept of "rights" itself is first presented to learners. Children should know that society expects its citizens to be responsible. This expectation provides continuity and harmony. It is the assumption upon which we build our legal systems. The following learning sequence is based on excerpts from three curricula, Lillian Genser's *The Declaration of the Rights of the Child* and *The Child's Declaration of Rights and Responsibilities* published by the Center for Peace and Conflict Studies at Wayne State University (see Chapter 7) and a unit published by the United Nations Association of the United Kingdom (see Chapter 7). It provides an introduction to the relationships between rights and responsibilities.

Learning Objectives. Children will:
- become acquainted with the Declaration of the Rights of the Child (1959);
- identify specific responsibilities related to particular rights;
- identify examples of obstacles to rights;
- suggest ways to overcome obstacles.

Materials
- large print copies of "Responsibilities of the Child" and "Rights of the Child," reproduced by the teacher from the lists on p. 48
- markers and newsprint to record (1) the rights the students identify in Step 4 as implied by the "Responsibilities of the Child"; and (2) "Our Own Declaration of Human Rights," derived in Step 6 based on the rights listed in Step 4 compared to the "Rights of the Child"

Learning Sequence

Step 1. The teacher can explain another purpose of rules and manners. In addition to assuring fairness, they help us to know what to expect. When we are a member of a group or live in a community or country, we expect certain things. In our community, for example, we expect to go to school. If we have an idea, we expect to be able to tell people about it. Some of these expectations are called rights. We expect our community to provide us with opportunities to learn and to say what we think because we have rights to education and free speech.

People in communities also have obligations or duties. They must do certain things and behave in ways that fulfill the expectations of others that they will be treated fairly. In the United States people in a community are obliged to see that there are schools, so they pay taxes and set up school boards. They are obliged to let others speak their minds. They are not supposed to prevent others from saying or writing their own ideas. In the newspapers there are special columns and letters sections for people to express opinions. On the radio we have "call in" shows that allow people to enjoy their rights of free speech. Societies, that is, all the people who think of themselves as one group, have expectations and obligations. These are called rights and responsibilities when they are written up as the laws or rules of societies.

In 1959 members of the world community decided that it was important to make a list of the expectations children should have. So the United Nations put out the Declaration of the Rights of the Child. These rights were not written as laws, but they are an important list of what children should be able to expect from society. If children have rights, they must also have obligations or duties. Read to the class the list of "Responsibilities of the Child" prepared by Lillian Genser.

Step 2. After reading the list of "Responsibilities of the Child," post it on the bulletin board. Ask the children to think about what rights may go with these responsibilities.

Step 3. Next read each responsibility separately. For each one, ask the children to give a "for instance," an action that would be an example of that particular responsibility.

Step 4. Read the responsibilities for a third time and ask the class to say what right they think would go with each responsibility. Write them as a list on newsprint as "Rights That Go with Responsibilities," using the numbers that go with the "Responsibilities," and post the list on the bulletin board next to the "Responsibilities."

Step 5. Read the list of "Rights of the Child" and post it beside the other lists. Ask the children to state the rights in their own words and put the re-stated rights next to the previous lists. Invite the children to review the list, reminding them that it was put forth many years ago, in 1959.

Step 6. Ask the students to compare the two lists of rights, their own and the ones in the 1959 Declaration, and make up from them a declaration they think would be the best one possible. Post this list with the title, "Our Own Declaration of Our Human Rights."

Step 7. Ask the children to choose partners, then choose a right. With their partners they are to think of what might be an obstacle to the right they have chosen.

Step 8. Ask the partners to think now of a way to remove the obstacle.

The following two examples, adapted with permission from Lillian Genser's booklet, can be used as models for study and discussion of social expectations and obligations, and to start students thinking about actions for change.

1. *Right.* I have the same rights as every child, no matter whether I am black, white, brown, or yellow, boy or girl; no matter what language I speak, or what my religion is; no matter who my parents are, or whether they are rich or poor.

Responsibility. I should treat all people, no matter who they are, as I would want them to treat me: in a way that is fair, friendly, and helpful.

The Way It Is. Johnny and his neighborhood friends have a baseball team. They play another team whose members live a few blocks away. Tony, the best pitcher on Johnny's team, moved away last week. A new child moved into Tony's house.

What Do You Think. Does the new child have a right to play on the team? What if he is not a good player? What if he speaks another language? What if he is of a different color? What if the new child is a girl? Just how do people in this world differ from one another? How are they really alike? In what ways is it good for people to be different from each other? Why? In what ways is it good to be alike? Why? What would be a fair way to decide if the new child should be asked to play on the team?

2. *Right.* Rules and laws should be passed so that all children have the chance to grow up healthy and safe, and in a good place to live.

Responsibility. I should cooperate with people who protect the safety and health of children. I should know and remember the safety rules I have been taught, and I should observe them in school, on the playground, at home, and wherever I go.

The Way It Is. Linda has to cross a very busy street to get to school. So many children have been hurt at the corner that her parents asked those responsible to have a traffic light put there.

What Do You Think. What should be done if a traffic light is not placed at the corner? If you were a member of the safety patrol, what would you do about children who do not follow your signal to cross the street? What are some good rules for children who play on the playground? Where are other places you might get hurt, and what can you do to be safe? Some children have brought guns to school thinking the guns will make them safe. What about the safety of other children when guns are brought to school? What should be done to make schools and all places safer for children? What can children do? What do grown-ups need to do?

Step 9. Review the rights and obstacles identified in steps 7 and 8. Ask what they themselves can do
    (1) to remove the obstacle;
    (2) to assure that everyone fulfills his or her obligations from the list of responsibilities.

Emphasize that it is what they themselves can do. Teachers and parents can help, but children are responsible, too.

Step 10. Provide an opportunity for students to try some of their action suggestions.

Responsibilities of the Child

1. Treat everyone in a way that is fair, friendly, and helpful.
2. Know, remember, and obey safety rules.
3. Study to become a good citizen and learn about other countries.
4. Take care of our bodies and the places where we live, study and play; not do thoughtless, dangerous things.
5. Be considerate of people who have special problems.
6. Love and respect our parents, and those who take care of us and teach us.
7. Keep our school and playground a safe place.
8. Try our best to take care of ourselves and each other.
9. Learn the skills and habits to be a good worker when I am fully grown.
10. Learn ways to use our energies and talents to serve friends, family, community, and people everywhere.

Adapted with permission from Lillian Genser, *The Child's Declaration of Rights and Responsibilities* (Detroit: Center for Peace and Conflict Studies, Wayne State University, 1979).

Rights of the Child

1. The right to equality, regardless of race, color, sex, religion, or national or social origin.
2. The right to develop physically and mentally in a healthy manner.
3. The right to a name and nationality.
4. The right to adequate nutrition, housing and medical services.
5. The right to special care if physically or mentally challenged.
6. The right to love, understanding, and protection.
7. The right to free education and to play and recreation.
8. The right to be among the first to receive relief in times of disaster.
9. The right to protection against all forms of neglect, cruelty, and exploitation.
10. The right to be brought up in a spirit of tolerance and peace and as a member of the universal human family.

Prepared by the United Nations Association of the United Kingdom.

Chapter 4
The Middle Grades: Introducing Standards and Principles — Grades Four to Six

As children come to later childhood they become more aware of social relationships and more interested in social interactions. While most of this developmental process centers on the society of their peers and a good deal on gender relations, they also pick up on the cues of the larger society, the unspoken-attitudinal and the spoken-behavioral indicators of social values. They are, as well, more aware of the world and are likely to know something of public events, social issues, and problems. Indeed, they are in need of guidance in interpreting the larger world, and in understanding and developing social relationships and their own place in the world.

Among the core concepts especially important at this level, as noted in the conceptual development framework, are *fairness* and *freedom*. It is a stage at which children can be helped to understand *unfairness, prejudice, discrimination,* and various actual rights violations, both historic and contemporary. They are able to understand information in more of the actual social context, and toward the end of this stage, to gather data and to engage in some of the abstract thinking of interpretation. It is thus important that the values aspect and the application of ethical principles to interpretation of information and to social relationships be explicitly dealt with. This is a crucial stage at which the reasoning in values application or rejection of a reasoned approach in favor of a specific ideology or other systematic form of prejudice can take hold in the political socialization of the child. Teachers should encourage children to give reasons for their opinions on social and human relationships, help them to articulate their opinions and reasons, and require that they listen respectfully to those of their classmates.

This age of more abstract conceptual capacity is also an appropriate one to introduce some of the particular international standards of human rights as the problems that violate them are considered. The students may also be helped to reflect on their own rights and those of their classmates: how they may be obstructed or fulfilled. Children of the late elementary or middle grades can be helped to understand that constructive human relationships and humane societies are built upon ethical principles, and that human rights standards are an attempt to apply such standards to everyday life, social institutions, and personal behavior.

The following units provide opportunities for teachers to guide students into the habit of values reflection and reasoned choices on issues of human relations and human rights, while providing them with significant information on problems and standards.

For teachers seeking more extensive curricula for the middle grades, *New Tools for International Understanding* is most appropriate. It takes an approach that assumes peace to be the consequence of relationships that strive for social justice and honor human dignity and integrity. See Chapter 7 for the address from which it is available and additional curricular suggestions for the middle grades.

Fourth Grade. The Convention on the Rights of the Child—The Metaphor of the Tree of Life

At about the age of nine children tend to become aware of new dimensions of their social selves. The expectations of society in regard to a variety of issues are part of the context of their learning. Some fourth grade curricula address social problems and topics related to civic education such as the Declaration of Independence and the Constitution. The fourth grade then is an excellent stage at which to introduce the international instruments for the protection of human rights intended to be legally binding. By far the most appropriate one is the Convention on the Rights of the Child, adopted by the United Nations General Assembly in 1990.

The following unit could be introduced by the story of the Convention from the 1959 Declaration of the Rights of the Child, through the Year of the Child in 1979 and the ten year effort to formulate the Convention as a list of the fundamental human rights of children everywhere. Materials on this history and background are available from such United Nations agencies as UNICEF and nongovernmental organizations such as Defense for Children International (see Chapter 7 for addresses).

In telling the story, teachers might stress the role of individuals, child advocacy groups, and citizen's organizations in this effort to come up with a list of rights that all the members of the United Nations would accept, and the efforts of these groups to convince the leaders and all the people of the great importance of the rights of children. They should be told of the heroes of human rights such as Michael Jupp, a citizen of Great Britain who as a very young man did military service in South Africa where he saw the terrible consequences of apartheid to Black Africans and came to believe that we all have a responsibility to struggle for human rights. He was probably the person who most influenced the success of the Convention. The world lost a real human rights hero when he died only days before national leaders signed the convention at the United Nations. The Michael Jupp story could be the beginning of many such stories, a number of which are to be found in excellent children's books.

The unit that follows introduces the convention and provides an opportunity to demonstrate how human rights issues relate to other world questions such as the health of the environment, and how symbols and folk art can express human experience and meaning. The tree of life is a wonderful metaphor for use in human rights education. Metaphors of living systems also help to introduce learners to holistic and ecological thinking, the preferred mode of the approach to human rights education advocated here. This unit was designed by Susan Lechter, a Canadian graduate of Harvard University and Teachers College, Columbia University. She prefaces the unit with this statement:

This curriculum focuses on the rights of children all over the planet, drawing examples from the Convention on the Rights of the Child. The goal is to provide children with an awareness of human rights as they relate to them personally as well as to others. Thus, the intention is to build within the child a moral framework and to foster an understanding of his/her place in the world. Further, the child should become aware of those in vulnerable circumstances and develop an appreciation for the necessity of the Convention on the Rights of the Child and an understanding of how it is intended to serve children all over the world. (Susan Lechter. Introduction to "Curriculum on the Rights of the Child," unpublished)

Learning Objectives for the Entire Unit. Students will:
- acquire information about children's rights through study of specific articles from the Convention. They will also be introduced to information about some obstacles to the fulfillment of these rights;
- recognize some denials of the human rights of children and participate in a group project aimed at helping to overcome these denials;
- develop a sense of their own individual places in their world, and develop respect and concern for others around them and for children who are victims of unfortunate and dire circumstances.

Each theme elaborates on two or three articles of the Convention. Two important elements are stressed. (1) Each provision should be explained in very simple terms so children can grasp the basic nature of the issue and reflect on it. (2) The activities in which the children can actively participate are essential to the learning experience, because they contribute to the affective development of the students. The activities bring out the emotional and affective aspects of human rights violations and related injustices. Further, they involve the behaviors and skills crucial to relating to others, to perceiving injustices, and to taking initiatives against human rights violations.

Note. It is essential that the teacher be thoroughly familiar with the Convention on the Rights of the Child, and review the materials about it published by UNICEF and Defense for Children International. (See Chapter 7 for sources.)

Unit 1. The Convention Is Essential to the Lives of Children

Learning Objectives. Students will:
- learn to distinguish between wants and needs;
- identify basic survival needs;
- become acquainted with the principles and provisions of the Convention on the Rights of the Child.

Materials. A large piece of cardboard, assorted markers, colored construction paper.

Learning Sequence

Step 1. Discussion about what children need to be happy and healthy. Write on the blackboard two columns: "WANTS" and "NEEDS," and list elements under each.

Compare and contrast these and distinguish personal from universal needs. "Wants" are what make us happy. "Needs" are what makes us healthy.

Step 2. Draw the Tree of Life on a large piece of cardboard and have students color it. The *roots* can represent the *four basic needs of children* outlined in the convention. Tell the children that the tree will not survive without having its basic needs fulfilled and being protected, and neither will the children. Ask what trees need to survive and grow; note why trees are important to our life and the life of the planet. The future of the Earth depends a good deal on healthy trees and living forests. It also depends on healthy children and peaceful communities. Ask what children need to survive and grow. A theme to stress is that unless the children's needs are fulfilled they cannot grow, learn, and develop.

The *trunk* is the *entire Convention* from which the branches, twigs and leaves grow. The *branches* may represent the *basic principles* of the Convention on the Rights of the Child. Explain that principles are ideas about what is good and important, guidelines for what needs to be done. The Convention extends these ideas out into the world for all to know, just as the branches extend the tree and its leaves into the air providing us with oxygen. When children enjoy health and well-being the whole community is better off, just as we have a healthier environment when there are lots of healthy trees.

The *twigs* can be the *individual articles* of the Convention. The teacher can select an appropriate number of the articles most relevant to the topics to be emphasized as the basis of some of the lessons suggested here. Leaves can be added to the twigs. Each *leaf* may represent a *child in the class*, one leaf to be made by every student during lesson 2. This Tree of Life will be a symbol to draw on throughout the classes to follow.

Step 3. On separate pieces of large paper print a summary of each Convention article selected for class discussion. Divide the children into learning groups. Each group is to receive one summary. As you distribute them read each aloud to the entire class. Then allow a few minutes for the children to discuss the article while you pass out drawing paper.

Step 4. In groups students will do drawings representing one article of the convention. Put the number of the article represented on each drawing, and put them all around the classroom. The teachers will then put the number on a twig on the Tree of Life.

Step 5. Announce that students will do drawings of the articles at the end of each lesson until all the articles are completed. Repeat this exercise until all articles studied are on the Tree of Life. *Note:* The children need not try to remember all the articles, but should discuss them so that their purposes are understood.

Unit 2. Children Need Identity, Dignity, and Nourishment

Learning Objectives. Students will:
- become aware of their uniqueness and identities as individuals (Articles 7 and 8);

- recognize the importance of nutrition, clothing, and shelter for all children (Articles 6 and 27);
- understand the necessity of universal health care (Article 24).

Materials. Globe or world map, drawing paper, crayons or markers, leaf cut-outs, pictures of children from various parts of the world, writing paper.

Learning Sequence

Step 1. The Talking Circle: "Our Names." Students sit in a circle and they each talk about their own name: its origin, what it means, if the name is or was shared by another member of the family, how many names they have, and what countries and languages their names come from. Ask, "Why are names important?" Consult the world map or globe to point out where names come from. The students can design pictures by writing their names and making picture posters out of them. Compare stories about celebrations of naming ceremonies, name days, and birthdays and how they differ from family to family and country to country.

Point out that some children do not have names given to them by their families, because they have no families. Ask what it might be like to be called "Shoe Shine Boy" or "Hey You." Ask why people everywhere value their names. Each child should be given a leaf cut out and crayons to print his or her name on one side and the country the name comes from on the other side of the leaf. Ask the children to select an article of the Convention they wish most of all for the children of the world to enjoy. Attach each of their name leaves to the Tree of Life on the twigs that represent the respective articles they each have chosen. Announce that it is now their Tree of Life, a symbol of the community of their classroom and their hopes for other children. They will care for their community and each other as they care for all children, all trees, and the whole Earth.

Step 2. If there are sufficient resources, organize a lunch activity for "citizens of the world to attend a meal at the Restaurant of the World." This activity, designed by UNESCO, is fairly extensive. Children pick a card out of a hat; each card has a picture of a child from some other part of the world and a description with name, age, and country that becomes that particular student's identity for the day. Ask them to find their countries on the globe, and tell whether they knew this name before. Tell them what languages the names represent. The number of cards for each world region should correspond proportionately to its percentage of the world's population. The children are then invited to a special lunch where they sit according to geographic regions. The North American and European "representatives" sit at beautifully set tables; African "representatives" have plenty of space while Asians are overcrowded; and so forth. There is an unequal distribution of the food, with North America, Europe, Australia, and Japan receiving the most, and only those from wealthy countries receiving dessert. The children are asked to react to this experience. The post-"lunch" discussion about how they felt during the lunch and if they thought it fair is most important. The teacher then explains that this "game" represents the real situation of food distribution in the world, and asks which rights of the child are violated by this situation. Whose rights are violated? Point out that even in "rich" countries there are hungry children. How should we respond to this situation? Finally all students should be served dessert as a celebration of the hope that all the world's children will soon have enough food.

Step 3. Have the students write poems or stories or design art work about what it means to have or to be deprived of the basic needs of food, shelter, or clothing. Invite them to recite their poems, read their stories, or explain their pictures.

Step 4. Revisit the Tree of Life. Discuss the survival needs of the tree and what is needed to keep the tree living. Ask what could harm or weaken the tree. Note that the growth of the tree depends on the fulfillment of its needs. You can also talk with the children again about the needs of the planet; how it needs trees to produce and clean the air, and how the tree stands for its own life, our lives, and the life of Earth.

Unit 3. Children Need Protection from Hurt and Harm

Learning Objectives. Students will:
- recognize the importance of protecting children and providing them with a safe and secure environment (Articles 20, 33, 36);
- understand that all children regardless of race, ethnicity, religion, refugee status, or disability are entitled to protection (Articles 2, 22, 23, 30);
- know that no child should be the victim of cruel treatment or abuse of any kind, nor should he or she be used and taken advantage of in any way (Articles 36 and 37);
- realize that children need special care and protection to grow into healthy and responsible adults (Articles 2, 22, 23, 30).

Materials. Lists of names of sixth grade students who will participate in a "caring buddy system," materials for making puppets, drawing materials.

Learning Sequence

Step 1. Present a scenario where a child is prevented from or unable to participate in a class activity. Children can act out the scene or may dramatize it by making puppets and role-playing the puppet characters. Discussion should follow on their feelings of exclusion, anger, powerlessness, and about appropriate behavior and ability to change the situation. How can activities be planned to assure that all participate? What if some children are physically challenged or "differently abled"? In what ways can they help their classmates to be fair and "inclusive"? What responsibilities do all class members have in regard to the limitations of others? What responsibilities do the "physically challenged" have?

Step 2. Discuss students' thoughts and feelings about refugee children are homeless and the concepts of having no home and no security.

Step 3. A "buddy system" may be implemented in the school between older and younger classes so that older students can experience a sense of responsibility for their younger "buddies" and younger students experience being cared for. This care may be defined in terms of an older "buddy" looking out for the best interests of the younger student with respect to his or her adjustment and comfort at school in both the academic and social arenas. The buddies should be encouraged to meet once a week and work on homework together, or perhaps team up with other buddies for recreation. Monthly meetings can take place in large groups with the teachers exploring what the children have done and learned in their buddy dyads. The children can then organize into groups, the older children in one and the younger in another. The older students can discuss the concept of responsibility for their "buddies." The younger children may share their feelings of being cared for or looked out for by the older ones, and think about how they might look out for still younger children.

Step 4. Revisit the Tree of Life. Write out and decorate the articles covered in this section and attach them to the tree.

Step 5. Choose several different cultures and present them to the class. Describe how the Tree of Life may be different for the children of the different cultures. For example, the children of the Kung tribe of hunters-and-gatherers of Southern Africa's Kalahari desert will have similar and different wants and needs from their own. Discuss the universality of the basic needs of children.

Step 6 Closure. Have children draw individual Trees of Life as representations of their own lives and what they consider to be important roots, activities and relationships. The roots can be their basic rights and needs as learned throughout the previous sessions. The branches may represent their interests and goals. The twigs can be their studies and actions for human rights, and the leaves can be labeled with the names of their families and friends who are helping them to achieve their goals. All the trees can be the forest of the world in which they hope to live. When their trees are completed, ask the class to describe their hopes for the forest, the world, and their future.

Fourth Grade. Confronting Prejudice

An education that elicits exercise of judgment and reasoned reflection is essential to the development of a culture respectful of human rights. The achievement of such a culture requires the recognition and reduction of both individual and social prejudice. Prejudice tends to be strongest in persons and societies where reasoned judgment is weak. Teachers need to be aware of prejudicial attitudes and behavior among their students and to be able to facilitate reasoned reflection on the prepackaged beliefs most societies inculcate. Handling incidents of prejudice can be a sensitive matter. The children who demonstrate prejudice must themselves be treated with respect, and not made to feel that they are being censured. Prejudice should be treated for what it is, lack of knowledge and reflection, and therefore a problem for schools to address.

Fourth grade is a significant stage in the social development of children, when it is necessary to deal with social and cultural prejudices. While youngsters of nine and ten may not comprehend the *concept* of *moral exclusion*, they can certainly understand the *process* of denial of the right to fair treatment. Excluding individuals from their social groups in school grades or out-of-school activities occurs frequently; the first stages of "in-group" "out-group" behavior characteristic of early adolescence often occur at this stage. Children of this age are well aware that they are "leaving out" and "scapegoating" other children. We know that for the excluded these experiences sometimes inflict wounds that never heal. Those who do the exluding may affirm and strengthen prejudicial attitudes that will impede their own moral development and severely limit the capacity of the society to assure justice and equality. Religious, ethnic, ideological, and economic prejudices may be the most obvious bases of this exclusionary behavior communicated by the society. However, prejudices related to physical and personality attributes or particular social or family circumstances are just as powerful in any specific group of children such as a grade school class, and should be of concern to educators committed to the central value of human rights, universal human dignity. Thus prejudice itself is an important topic for human rights education in the middle grades.

This unit on religious prejudice can be a good starting point that can be adapted to other forms of prejudice. It is excerpted from *New Tools for International Understanding: A Peace Education Curriculum for Elementary Schools* by Dale L. Hudson (see Chapter 7 for address).

The unit begins with the statement of some of the fundamental assumptions of the designers; it is reproduced here because examination of the assumptions underlying curricula is important for all educators selecting and designing learning materials.

Certain generalizations are basic to this unit.

1. One of the barriers to peace and human rights is religious prejudice (an opinion formed without taking time and care to judge fairly; people show religious prejudice when they dislike other people because they belong to a different religion). Point out to the students how this is similar to other forms of prejudice.

2. Religious prejudice can be lessened or eliminated by education which leads to a sympathetic understanding of others and to an appreciation of the beliefs and values of other faiths.

3. No education that sets out to inform children about the world in which they live, past and present, can ignore religion. Religion is a most significant influence on how people view the world, each other, and social relations and responsibilities.

Learning Objectives. Students will:
- be introduced to the major world religions;
- be informed of the contributions of many faiths to world culture;
- see their own religious identity in relation to other faiths.

Materials
- handout prepared from the list, Facts About the Faiths of the World (p. 60)
- old magazines
- chart paper
- pictures of various holy places throughout the world
- religious symbols to color
- encyclopedias, maps, books, videos that explain various faiths
- Draft Convention on the Elimination of All Forms of Intolerance (available from the United Nations, see Chapter 7)

Resources. Community resource speakers who would be willing to talk about their religions.

Learning Sequence

Activity 1. One of the best methods for children to become familiar with various religions of the world (also providing a spring board for further study) is to celebrate some of the festivals of each faith. Local community members willing to share what they know about a festival may be invited to the class. Authentic food, music, and dance may be prepared and performed by the children. Traditional costumes may be worn. Children may make, color, and attach religious symbols to a world map of religions. The teacher may show videos, slides, pictures, and read books about festivals to the children. Various collages may be constructed out of small pieces of paper torn from magazines and pasted on a piece of art paper to represent a particular religious festival.

The following religious festivals, chosen because they are especially festive and meaningful, are presented in alphabetical order. They are merely suggestions. The final choice, of course, is left to the classroom teacher, but nevertheless will require additional research and planning. Additions or deletions are expected, and lessons on particular festivals may have to be given on dates other than those noted here.

1. The Baha'i Faith. The Feast of Naw-Ruz (March 21). This is the Baha'i New Year and is a time of rejoicing. People exchange presents and give parties.
2. Buddhism. Obon (mid-August). This is a Japanese festival when 27 lanterns are lit to guide the spirits of the ancestors back to their homes for their annual visit. It is also a family reunion time. Food is offered to the spirits and the festival ends with folk dancing in celebration.
3. Confucianism. New Year's Day (February). The evil spirits of the old year are frightened away by firecrackers and the good new spirits welcomed with incense. Children receive presents of money either tied up in packets of red paper or laid out in the pattern of a dragon (a good omen) at the foot of their bed. The traditional food is a type of dumpling.
4. Christianity. Christmas (December 25), the celebration of the birth of Jesus Christ whose life and teachings inform this faith, is usually popular with children because gifts are exchanged and several generations of families gather for festive meals and church services.
5. Hinduism. Divali (November). This is the New Year festival. Homes are filled with lights so that Lakshmi, the goddess of prosperity, will visit them.
6. Islam. Id-Ul-Fitr or "small festival" (a cyclical feast not at a fixed date). This marks the end of Ramadan, several weeks of fasting and assessment of one's life. Parties are given, and cards and presents are exchanged. The children receive presents of money and new clothes. The family sit down together to an especially good meal which should include a dish called "sheer," made with suet, milk, and sugar.
7. Judaism. Passover or the Feast of Unleavened Bread (usually March). This festival celebrates the deliverance of the Jews from slavery in Egypt. After the four symbolic foods are tasted at the seder, the evening meal, the youngest child asks four traditional questions to which the oldest man present — usually the father or grandfather — replies with the story of the escape of the Jews from Egypt.

Activity 2. Provide children with the handout. Assign a research project in which they interview each other and friends of various faiths and record the information on the charts. Share the results in class.

Other Activities

1. Older children may wish to research assigned questions that ask for specifics about a particular religion (give an example of how religion influences society).

2. Some children may wish to make a brief oral presentation about their own religion or a religion they wish to know more about.

3. Teachers may wish to have the older students research various topics within a religion and compare, contrast, and generalize the data using a chart similar to the handout.

4. Visitors representing faiths of which there are no adherents in the class may be asked to come and tell about their beliefs and festivals.

5. "Friends of Many Faiths." Have the children first make lists of their friends and their faiths, and then make themselves a greeting reminder calendar of their friends' religious festivals, so they can extend special greetings on the appropriate

days. Have the children make an appropriate greeting card for each one. They can make a list of all the faiths to which they have some connection through friends and families.

6. Hold a discussion on religious prejudice. Ask whether the students know of any examples. Show places on the map where there have been religious wars or severe religious discrimination. Tell about the United Nations Draft Convention on Elimination of All Forms of Religious Intolerance and about religious freedom as a fundamental human right.

7. Ask why religion is important to people and discuss how people have developed religions to understand their lives and make them more meaningful. Ask why it is important to respect religious beliefs, even if we do not share them and do not believe as others do. Why has religious belief been protected by law and human rights standards? You might also discuss religious freedom as a principle of American society, protected by the Bill of Rights; how it was listed as one of the "Four Freedoms" so important that President Roosevelt said it was sought by people everywhere; and how it became one of the principles of the Universal Declaration of Human Rights and of the United Nations.

FACTS ABOUT FAITHS OF THE WORLD

	Buddhism	*Hinduism*	*Islam*
Holy book			
When it began			
Where it began			
Where it is practiced			
Founder/prophet			
Present calendar year and date new year begins			
Important festivals/holy days and what they commemorate			
Teachings/beliefs/values/laws			

Note: This chart can be extended to include as many faiths as are of interest.

Fifth Grade. The United Nations— Establishing Rights

Ten-year-olds often have a lively interest in how and why things happen, so fifth grade is a good level at which to introduce lessons showing the evolution of the concepts and means of protection of human rights. Certainly, human rights education should include consideration of the United Nations and the crucial role it has played in defining human rights and establishing standards for their protection. Education for global citizenship requires that the United Nations and its work in confronting major global issues be central to the social education of all students. The United Nations Association conducts a vigorous citizen education program, and through its affiliates has produced a number of resources for use in elementary and secondary classrooms. The following unit prepared for the United Nations Association of Minnesota by Dorothy Hoffman and Mary Eileen Sorenson is excerpted from a full three-part curriculum for the upper elementary, or middle grades. This curriculum is a very useful resource for educators who wish to teach more about the United Nations.

This extract was chosen for inclusion here because it provides an excellent introduction to the concepts of rights and international instruments to protect them. It deals with the sources of rights and the differences between declarations and conventions, and reprises the notion of basic needs fulfillment as fundamental rights presented in Samples 9 and 13.

Learning Objectives. Students will:
- generate a definition of a "right";
- be introduced to the Universal Declaration of Human Rights and the Convention on the Rights of the Child;
- match instances of denial or assurance of rights to the article in the Convention that identifies the specific right in question;
- locate and share with classmates an incidence of assurance or denial of specific rights of a child or children.

Materials
- Handout #1, Preamble to the Charter of the United Nations
- Handout #2, Universal Declaration of Human Rights (see Sample #16, Handout #2)
- Handout #3, History of the Convention on the Rights of the Child

- Handout #4, Convention on the Rights of the Child (abbreviated version from Appendix)

Chapter 4

Learning Sequence

Step 1. Write the word "right" on the board and have students think about the primary ways in which the word is used (right as the opposite of wrong, "Right now!" "You have no right," right hand, etc.). Bring focus to the way the word is used in "You have no right" or "I have a right." Have students volunteer sentences using this meaning of the word and record, orally or in writing, their responses. Pose the question, "From the responses of our class, what is 'a right'?" Discussion of this question can be conducted with the whole class, pairs, or small cooperative groups given the task of generating a definition of a "right." Share ideas and definitions. Make a list of examples of rights.

Step 2. Ask, "On the basis of our ideas and definitions, in your opinion, should children have the 'right' to all the items we reviewed? Why? From where do you think the ideas came that humans should have 'the right' to some things?" After some discussion suggest that it is perhaps from the human desire for dignity and respect for self and others. "Do you think this is a new idea?" Discuss the questions.

Step 3. Say, "Most of us can say quite comfortably, 'I have my rights!,' and 'You have no right to do that to me.' From where do we *get* our rights? In the United States, the Bill of Rights, ratified in 1791, is intended to assure certain rights to all United States citizens. Does this mean everyone's rights were guaranteed immediately after ratification? In this country, how are people's rights protected?

"The U.S. Bill of Rights is a very important document. Other countries have similar documents and means to protect rights of citizens. Can people's rights be protected in places where there are no written documents describing rights and the means to their protection? A concern for the basic rights of humans exists in most social and political systems of most cultures. In cultures where there is no written language, people's rights can be known and protected through customs or laws in the oral tradition. Listen to what Eleanor Roosevelt had to say about the importance of universal human rights."

Where, after all, do universal rights begin? In small places, close to home—so close and so small that they cannot be seen on any maps of the world. Yet they are the world of the individual person; the neighborhood he lives in; the school or college he attends; the factory, farm, or office where he works. Such are the places where every man, woman, and child seeks equal justice, equal opportunity, equal dignity without discrimination. Unless these rights have meaning there, they have little meaning anywhere. Without concerned citizen action to uphold them close to home, we shall look in vain for progress in the larger world. (Eleanor Roosevelt, "The Great Question," speech before the United Nations, New York, 1958)

Ask, "What, essentially, is Eleanor Roosevelt saying about the need and concern for human rights?" Give students time to study the quotation, to formulate their ideas, and to share them with their classmates. Have students summarize their thinking about the universality of concern for human rights over time and culture."

Say, "Perhaps it is the human capacity for empathy and compassion that is at the core of this concern for others—people's will to live their lives with dignity and to provide the same for their offspring."

Step 4. Say, "This human capacity for empathy and compassion lies at the core of the United Nations Universal Declaration of Human Rights. But first, what is the United Nations?"

Distribute Handout #1, the Preamble to the Charter of the United Nations. Discuss the purposes described in the Preamble to the UN charter. Then ask, "Why might the United Nations work very hard to try to ensure protection of human rights?" Next, distribute Handout #2, the Universal Declaration of Human Rights, and ask, "Do you think we will find in this document any of the 'rights' we listed?"

In pairs have the students read and discuss the Preamble to the Universal Declaration of Human Rights. Then read it aloud to all the class and ask why human rights are important to peace. List the reasons on a sheet of newsprint and post it on the bulletin board.

Step 5. Explain, "We're hearing terms here like 'declaration,' 'bill,' and 'convention.' It is important that we are clear on the meanings of these words so that we are all talking about the same thing when we discuss them."

Write the following definitions on the blackboard or on newsprint to post on the bulletin board.
- *Declaration:* a general statement of principles which is not legally binding, that is, not an international law. (Explain "legally binding.")
- *Convention:* a legally binding treaty or agreement among nations that have agreed to it, that is, an international law.
- *Ratification:* formal approval of a treaty or a covenant by a sovereign state (that is, one nation).
- *In force:* when enough nations have ratified a convention to make it an international law applicable to all nations and persons.

Step 6. Tell students there is a document that deals only with the rights of children. "Why do you think a separate document was created for children? How do the needs or rights of children differ from those of adults?" Distribute Handout #3, "History of the Convention on the Rights of the Child," and discuss it. Ask students to form pairs and share ideas about why there might have been a need for a declaration and convention on children's rights. List the reasons on the board, discuss them, and keep on the list those that are actually reflected in the Convention.

"What does the United Nations want to have happen with the Convention? The Convention was adopted by the General Assembly in 1989 and with ratification by over 20 nations, it has become international law. In those nations where the Convention has been ratified, it is presently considered law of the same status as other national laws. How can such laws be used to help children?" Discuss the use of law to assure that positive rights are enjoyed, such as education, shelter, food, and protection against physical abuse, and economic exploitation. Select and read several articles of the simplified version of the Convention to illustrate these assurances and protections.

A productive homework assignment might be: "Find a picture, article, headline, story, poem, etc. dealing with some aspect of the rights of the child. It can tell about children getting or having their rights, or being denied their rights. Bring your example to share with the class and to become part of our classroom display on the United Nations Convention on the Rights of the Child. Be prepared to talk about how you feel about what is symbolized or reported in the article, picture, story, or whatever you have contributed to the display, and which article of the convention and what particular right of the child is concerned." Distribute Handout #4, the condensed Convention on the Rights of the Child.

Step 7. Ask the students to relate the materials they brought to class to a particular article of the Convention. Then ask what can be done to assure that the right is fulfilled for the children of our town, country, world. Can they themselves do something for children's rights? Make a list of "Actions for Children's Rights." Post it and periodically discuss what the students or others may be doing to carry out these actions. One such activity might be to write to the embassies of various countries and to the United States Department of State asking if they have ratified the Convention and the reasons why? Explain, "There is no end to this lesson. We must always be alert to human rights abuses and to the special needs of children. We will check on what we are doing to help throughout the time we are together in this class. We can be very powerful defenders on human rights."

Sample 11, Handout 1.
Preamble to the Charter of the United Nations

We, the peoples of the United Nations, determined to save succeeding generations from the scourge of war, which twice in our lifetime has brought untold sorrow to mankind;

And to reaffirm faith in fundamental human rights, in the dignity and worth of the human person, in the equal rights of men and women and of nations large and small;

And to establish conditions under which justice and respect for the obligations arising from treaties and other sources of international law can be maintained, and to promote social progress and better standards of life in larger freedom;

And for these ends to practice tolerance and live together in peace with one another as good neighbors, and to unite our strength to maintain international peace and security, and to ensure, by the acceptance of principles and the institution of methods, that armed forces shall not be used, save in the common interest, and to employ international machinery for the promotion of the economic and social advancement of all peoples;

Have Resolved to Combine Our Efforts to Accomplish These Aims.

Sample 11, Handout 3.
History of the Convention on the Rights of the Child

The Convention was adopted unanimously by the United Nations General Assembly on November 20, 1989. It is the most complete statement of children's rights ever made.

Milestones in the development of the document

1. One of the first acts of the General Assembly at the time of the creation of the United Nations in 1945 was to establish the United Nations Children's Emergency Fund (UNICEF).

2. The Universal Declaration of Human Rights (1948) recognized that children must be the subject of special care and attention.

3. In 1959 the United Nations adopted The Declaration of the Rights of the Child, specifically addressed to the protection of children's rights, and providing a moral framework and a guide to private and public action.

4. 1979 was designated the International Year of the Child, to give impetus to the desire to write a convention that gave the force of treaty law to children's rights.

5. On January 26, 1990, 61 countries signed the Convention (a record first day response). Signature is accepted as a sign that a country will seriously consider ratification.

6. On September 2, 1990, one month after the twentieth state ratified it, the Convention became international law and national law for those countries that ratified it. For other states, the Convention becomes law thirty days after they ratify it.

From *The Rights of the Child*, Fact Sheet 10, United Nations Center for Human Rights (see Chapter 7).

Fifth Grade. Making a Difference— Your Right to Action

It is important that programs in human rights education not only emphasize the responsibilities that adhere to rights, but also offer opportunities to carry out those responsibilities and take actions on behalf of human rights. At every grade level it is possible to provide students with the opportunity to determine for themselves actions they can take to extend and strengthen human rights protection and realization. Such actions are essential on several grounds. First, students must not be left feeling that the problems are too great to be addressed by ordinary citizens. It must be stressed that most of the great steps toward the acceptance and advancement of human rights have been initiated by individuals and small groups of citizens. Everyone can do something for human rights. Indeed, it is our civic responsibility to do so. Second, it is evident that participatory and active learning is often the most effective educational experience. Finally, it is important for students to see the connections between what they are studying and the world outside the school.

The next learning activity, which comes from the United Nations Association of Minnesota curriculum, provides guidelines for learning suitable to the fifth grade level. At this point children are able to see connections and take social action, and should be encouraged to do so.

Learning Objectives. Students will choose a project that:
· makes the intent and content of the UN Convention on the Rights of the Child known to others;
· includes deeds that are in the spirit of the Convention;
· reinforces the connections between rights and responsibilities;
· emphasizes the interconnection and interdependence of all humans in all countries on Earth.

Learning Sequence

Step 1. Inform the students that the Convention proclaims that "States [that is, the governments of the member nations of the UN] should make the Convention's rights widely known to both adults and children." Then raise some questions: "Why do you think this directive is included in the document?" "How important is it to have the rights proclaimed by the Convention widely known to both the adults and the children of the world?" Try to encourage the expression of as many opinions as possible. Make a list of the reasons offered.

Ask, "Whose responsibility is it to make the rights widely known?" Here help them mention as many potential agents as possible for the fulfillment of the Rights of the Child. "Is this something in which you can play a significant role? Why might you want to?"

Step 2. Display and read the following quote from Thomas Hardy and ask students how this quotation relates to their study.

"The human race is one great network which quivers in every part when one part is shaken, like a spider's web when touched."

Ask students to speculate about how many of the children of the world enjoy most or all of the Rights of the Child. What about the children in the country in which they presently live? What about the children in their town or city? (UNICEF's annual *State of the World's Children* can provide data about the actual conditions.) Where do they think children enjoy the most rights and why? What do they think of this situation?

Here the teacher can introduce problems related to poverty. Sample #13 on hunger might be introduced. If it has already been studied, it can be reviewed.

Step 3. Raise the following questions.

"Why have we studied the Convention so thoroughly?" "Now that we know more about the Convention than almost all adults of the world, do we want to do anything with this knowledge?"

Step 4. Read (and perhaps display) the following quote from Alice Walker: "Helped are those who find the courage to do at least one small thing each day to help the existence of another—plant, animal, river, or human being. They shall be joined by a multitude of the timid" (Alice Walker, *The Temple of My Familiar*, p. 289).

Then ask what *our* choices are. What problems do we face? What problem can *we* do something about? What do you think of the following possibilities?

(1) Educating adults in local, state, and national governments about the Convention.

(2) Educating other children and adults about the "State of the World's Children" in relation to these rights.

(3) Choosing a particular area of rights (survival, development, protection, freedom) and teaching others of the issues related to each area.

Step 5. Now begin a brainstorming process about what the students themselves can do. Small groups choosing particular areas to brainstorm, followed by each group sharing with the whole, would likely yield a greater diversity of ideas. Some possible projects:

(1) Contacting local, state, or national governments, and sharing concerns and suggestions about the fulfillment of children's rights at these levels.

(2) Conduct a Model United Nations meeting, focusing on the area of rights students are concerned about.

(3) Take one right such as the right to a name and nationality and conduct a school-wide awareness effort about it, so everyone in the school becomes aware of that right, what it means, and why it is important.

(4) Identify groups in their community that work for one of the rights stated in the Convention and interview some of their members. Have them come to speak to classes, or have students volunteer for community service with these groups.

(5) Food drives are always valuable. Identify a local organization that distributes food to children in particular.

(6) A school can "adopt a country" to raise money for UNICEF's program of immunization of all infants born during that year (see Chapter 7 for address).

(7) Adapt the rights to the family level. How can I, as a family member, help ensure the rights to development of a younger brother or sister by being a kinder sibling? If I am being denied rights to protection, how can I get help?

(8) Students will generate many other valuable ideas.

Encourage students to work on their action projects either individually or in groups, whichever they find suits their goals best. Suggest that they keep the projects manageable, and that they should be able to see a time when the project, or at least this stage of the effort, is completed.

Assign a date on which they will be expected to report to the class on the status of their projects. A project description handout might be useful to help the students organize their projects and the means to report them.

Step 6. Closure. Discuss the projects with the class. How meaningful were they? How significant is what was learned from them? Will the projects have an impact on the students' personal futures? Did their projects suggest further projects?

Tell the students, "You have spent a great deal of time in this study. Take a minute to think it through from the very beginning to the completion of your personal action project. Think also about what the Convention means, could mean, should mean, to the children of the world. Think of how to condense this meaning into a symbol, a story, a wish, a poem, a dance, a sculpture, a picture that captures the spirit of the Convention. Picture in your mind this symbol. Image it clearly. Add color (think of how you can add color to a poem, dance, a wish, etc.) and texture."

"Put your 'mind picture' in some form to show it to others. This creation is your tribute to the Convention, a picture of your responsibility to it, and your feeling for it. Make yourself a promise to do something for the rights of children."

Additional Resources for Teacher Preparation and Adaptation to Classroom Use

1. U.S. House of Representatives Select Committee on Hunger. The major voice for hungry people both domestically and internationally on Capitol Hill, working to identify both the root causes of and the solutions to hunger and hunger related diseases. For updates and information on the Committee, contact the Chairman, House Select Committee on Hunger, US House of Representatives, Room H2-505, House Office building Annex 2, Washington DC 20515, 202-226-5470.

2. Model United Nations. Preparatory book, newsletter, calendar of MUN conferences; annual teacher in-service program in New York. Contact: UNA/USA (Model UN Program), 485 Fifth Ave., New York, NY 10017, 212-697-3232.

3. Super Cupboard. A step by step guide for a six- to eight-week course offering people life skills along with their food packages. Contact Pennsylvania Coalition on Food and Nutrition, 128 Locust St., Harrisburg, PA 17101, 717-233-6705.

4. UNICEF. *State of the World's Children.* Annual report. It is also distributed in a pamphlet abstract with some of the graphs and charts that illustrate the report.

5. UNICEF. Halloween Boxes. For the UNICEF Field Office nearest you and the contact number for ordering UNICEF Halloween boxes, contact US Committee for UNICEF, 333 East 38th St., New York, NY 10016, 212-686-5522.

6. United States Ratification of the Convention on the Rights of the Child. For information on what you can do to support ratification, contact: Anne Keeney, Interaction, 1815 H Street, NW, 11th floor, Washington, DC, 20006, 202-822-8429.

7. World Declaration on the Survival, Protection, and Development of Children. A declaration and plan of action signed by over 71 world leaders (including President George Bush) at the World Summit for Children (September, 1991). Contact UNICEF House, World Summit for Children, Three United Nations Plaza, New York, NY 10017.

Sixth Grade. Children and Hunger— A Violation of Equity Rights

Sixth grade children begin to think of themselves as approaching their teen years and more grown up than other elementary school students. By this age they are "big kids" and they feel it. This is especially so in schools where sixth is the highest grade. In middle schools where they are the youngest it may be less pronounced. All, however, are likely to be able to engage in more abstract thinking and understand more of the multiple elements of problems and problem solution. They are ready to face some of the realities of significant rights violations and the global problems of poverty, largely accountable for the denial of children's rights. When introduced to the Convention on the Rights of the Child, they learned the concept of basic needs; they should be ready now to contemplate and comprehend the concepts of *deprivation* and *poverty*. In undertaking such themes teachers should take into account the degree to which some or all of the students may be deprived and poor. An adaptation of Sample 21 for younger students would be most appropriate for such classes. This sample should be preceded by some study of the Convention on the Rights of the Child.

The most severe and widespread deprivation of a basic need is hunger, a problem which to some degree plagues almost every nation of the world. It is the greatest single obstacle to the most basic and fundamental of human rights, the right to survival, which many argue includes the right to food. The following lesson is excerpted from a curriculum designed by Kaaren St. Armour Gray, a teacher at St. Vrain Valley Schools, Longmont, Colorado. It is intended to support World Food Day activities and was produced by the Office of Global Education in cooperation with the Center for Teaching International Relations (see Chapter 7 for addresses). Its tone indicates that it is intended for students unfamiliar with hunger. Teachers should be sensitive to the possibility that some students in the class may not have adequate nourishment.

Learning Objectives. Students will be helped to:
- understand the who, where, and why of world hunger;
- work cooperatively in solving problems;
- practice communication skills;
- practice mapping skills and analyze characteristics of geographic locations.

Materials
- Videos or filmstrips
- Articles from newspapers, news magazines, etc., or videotaped television news

or documentary programs on hunger supplied by the teacher or researched by students. This taping must be assigned at least a week before the day of this lesson
- Chart prepared for use during the lesson, with headings: WHO? WHERE? WHY?
- Overhead transparency of a world map
- Overhead marking pens of various colors
- Large projection of the world map on chart paper made by using the overhead transparency
- Small pieces of drawing paper (approximately 3" × 3")

Learning Sequence

Step 1. What Does it Mean to be Hungry? Begin by asking students what they think hunger is. Write student responses on the chalk board. Ask, "How do you feel when you are hungry?" Elicit such responses as: you have a headache, you feel weak, you have a strong desire for food, etc.

Step 2. Looking into the Face of Hunger. Display photos and news articles on the bulletin board and allow time for students to review and think about the images. Show the video tapes and have students react to them in pairs.

Step 3. Discussion of the Images of Hunger.
 1. Ask students what pictures or stories were most important to them. How did they feel, and what surprised them?
 2. Write the meaning of real hunger on chart paper or on the board. (Real hunger means people living days and days with no food, or not eating the right balance of food, or living years and years with not enough food.)
 3. Begin to fill out, with student responses, the previously prepared chart (based on information gained from the video, film, or news articles). WHO (poor people in poor countries, poor people in rich countries).
 4. WHERE (all over the world, but especially in Africa, South and Central America, and Asia). Turn on the overhead projector and project the world map. Based on what they've learned so far, have the students take turns highlighting with marking pens areas of the map where they think there is hunger.
 5. Return to chart. Fill in WHY (war, drought, too much rain, cash crops instead of food crops, poor land management, poor distribution, poverty).

Step 4. Mapping World Hunger.
 1. Organize students into cooperative groups of four or five members. Have them select a discussion facilitator, a reporter, and artists. Each group will meet together and decide on and design a way of showing each of the causes of hunger to glue on a world map. All group members should contribute to the art work done on small pieces of paper. Give each group five to seven small pieces of drawing paper. Allow time for students to discuss and draw.
 2. When the groups appear to be finished, call the class together again. Each group's reporter will tell about the art work the group has produced. Tell students to think about a place in the world where this problem might be happening and accordingly place art work on the world map in an area of the world where there

is hunger. The group can decide together on appropriate placement, but teacher guidance might be needed. (Consult overhead world map transparency used in Step 3.4.)

3. Investigate the finished map for clustering of causes. If clustering appears, analyze why this occurs.

Step 5. Follow-up. Ask the following questions:

1. What articles of the Convention on the Rights of the Child are violated when children go hungry?

2. What do you think it is like to be a hungry child? What do you think hungry children think about? What do you think they worry about?

3. If you were a hungry child what kind of help would you want from others? What kind of help would benefit you immediately? In the long term? Which of the causes of hunger would be addressed by each type of help?

4. What could we do as a class to help the hungry? What might we do to contribute to ending the global problem of hunger? How could we "interrelate" our local and global ideas and actions?

5. Make a class action plan to help either locally or internationally with hunger relief and action toward the elimination of hunger. Elicit student suggestions and make a list of possible projects. Decide on the one or two projects the class will do, and form task forces to conduct and report on them regularly. Hold periodic assessments of the success of the projects in terms of the goals set when they were undertaken. Encourage students to pay attention to TV news and other sources of news they have access to, so they can tell the class from time to time about on-going problems of hunger and anti-hunger programs.

6. Is hunger a human rights issue? How could the recognition of access to food as a human right help us to solve the problem?

Note. In pursuing the discussion in response to the queries in Step 6, teachers may want to review learnings from Sample #11 on human rights as international law. They would also find it useful to consult Sample #21 on the right to food.

Some agencies to contact about actions against hunger

UNICEF
United Nations Plaza
New York, NY 10003
212-754-7229

Interfaith Hunger Appeal
475 Riverside Drive, Suite 635
New York, NY 10015
212-870-2035

Church World Service
Box 968
Elkhart, IN 46515
219-264-3102

Inter Action
200 Park Avenue South
New York, NY 10017
212-777-8210

Sixth Grade. Apartheid Is a Crime — The African Freedom Charter

The fifth grade unit, Sample 11, on the United Nations as the source of the international standards for human rights offered some definitions of the types of documents that state these rights, and indicated that some have become international law. Civic education for a global age should familiarize citizens with these laws and the fact that violations of some of them are international crimes. Since the sixth grade is often the beginning of civic education, it is the appropriate age at which to introduce the concept of crimes against human rights. It is also an appropriate level at which to study another major human rights issue, the legalized racism of apartheid. Though the formal structures of the system in the Republic of South Africa have been abolished, the consequences of apartheid and similar aspects of colonialism in various other countries continue to be at the heart of many human rights problems. Given the post-apartheid developments in South Africa, it is also important that students become aware that there have long been visions of socially just, non-racist societies, among them a non-racist South Africa. Such a vision informed the earliest freedom struggles in that land. As the vision of a just global order is found in the Universal Declaration of Human Rights, the vision of a socially just South Africa is found in the Freedom Charter of 1955. Drafted by a multi-racial group of South Africans, it became the major policy statement of the ANC, the African National Congress, the main South African opposition to the apartheid system. Both the charter and the ANC were "banned" (forbidden) under apartheid, but the ANC won in the first multi-racial elections in 1994.

The following unit is adapted and constructed from several sources: a unit that appears in an extended curriculum resource prepared by Paula Bower, a New York City elementary school teacher, and distributed by Educators Against Racism and Apartheid (see Chapter 7 for address) entitled, "Apartheid Is Wrong"; *The Whole Child*, by UNICEF–UK (see Chapter 7); and material used by Margaret Carter in her Birmingham, Michigan seventh grade class.

Learning Objectives. Students will:
- review and reflect on legal systems of racial segregation;
- study the characteristics of the apartheid system;
- review the African Freedom Charter;
- compare the Freedom Charter, the Universal Declaration of Human Rights, the U.S. Declaration of Independence and the U.S. Bill of Rights.

Materials
- Universal Declaration of Human Rights (see Appendix and Sample 16, Handout #2), U.S. Bill of Rights, Declaration of Independence
- Handout #1, African Freedom Charter
- Handout #2, "Killed for Expressing His Opinion"
- Comparison retrieval charts

Learning Sequence

Step 1. The teacher should provide background information on the apartheid system and Handout #1, the African Freedom Charter. The teacher should also make available books and biographies about Mohandas K. Gandhi, Nelson Mandela, Stephen Biko, Helen Suzman, and such South African anti-apartheid groups as the women of the Black Sash. Teachers might also use parts of some feature films such as *Sarafina*, *Cry Freedom* and *A Dry White Season*, which have scenes depicting the 1976 Soweto massacre of school children who demonstrated for the cause of education in the English language. Handout #2 on that event can be used to complement or substitute for the films.

Tell the students, "On June 26, 1955, the African National Congress held a Congress of the People in Kliptown, South Africa, at which black and white South Africans, the elected representatives of the popular organizations—trade unions, youth, women, etc.—of that country, came together to adopt a manifesto that has become known to the world as the Freedom Charter. It contains a vision of a 'non-racial South Africa' that inspires the on-going struggle for justice and equality in that nation."

Step 2. Distribute comparison retrieval charts with horizontal and vertical bars to make sixteen spaces. Label the columns (1) Freedom Charter; (2) American Declaration of Independence; (3) U.S. Bill of Rights; (4) Universal Declaration of Human Rights. Label the rows (1) Reason for making this statement; (2) Political rights; (3) Legal rights; (4) Economic, social, and cultural rights. Also provide a simplified version of each of the four documents. Report the results to the class so that all may make their own comparison charts. Discuss the similarities and differences. Consider the historical circumstances in the American colonies, early United States, the world of 1948, and South Africa of 1945 and today. (*Note*: Such charts can also be used to compare the various rights charters and regional human rights systems.)

Step 3. Distribute Handout #2, "Killed for Expressing His Opinion." Have the students read it and then discuss the questions posed on the handout sheet.

Step 4. Have the cooperative learning groups research the present situation in South Africa and share their research with the entire class. The teacher can provide newspaper and magazine articles for the students to use and encourage them to seek out other sources. Then have the groups make proposals on "How to Achieve the Goals of the Freedom Charter." Recommend that they use the Universal Declaration of Human Rights to strengthen and extend the Freedom Charter. Note that all members of the United Nations are supposed to abide by the Declaration, and that South

Africa regained its membership in the organization in 1994. Each group should elect one of their members to present their proposals in a panel on the topic. After the proposals have been made, have the panelists respond to questions and comments from the rest of the class, and defend their proposals in accordance with the Freedom Charter and its implementation of the Universal Declaration of Human Rights. Then have the panelists conclude one common proposal based on all the comments on the various proposals made by the cooperative learning groups.

Step 5. Research other cases such as the U.S. civil rights struggle against segregation and contemporary ethnic conflicts. Use similar procedures for proposing solutions based on principles of justice, ethnic equality, and the rights enumerated in the Universal Declaration of Human Rights. Discuss the relationship between the ideas in the Universal Declaration and the Declaration of Independence and the Bill of Rights. Are the principles and rights enumerated enjoyed equally by all who live in the United States? Does everyone in the United States have what is called for in the Freedom Charter? What thoughts do the students have about the words used in these documents? Would they express the ideas differently?

Sample 14, Handout 1.
African Freedom Charter

We, the People of South Africa, declare for all our country and the world to know: that South Africa belongs to all who live in it, black and white, and that no government can justly claim authority unless it is based on the will of all the people;

And therefore, we the people of South Africa, black and white together—equals, countrymen, and brothers—adopt this Freedom Charter. And we pledge ourselves to strive together, sparing neither strength nor courage, until the democratic changes here set out have been won.

The People Shall Govern!

Every man and woman shall have the right to vote for and to stand as a candidate for all bodies which make laws;

The rights of the people shall be the same, regardless of race, color or, sex;

All bodies of minority rule shall be replaced by democratic organs of self-government.

All National Groups Shall Have Equal Rights!

All people shall have equal right to use their own languages, and to develop their own folk culture and customs; . . . groups shall be protected by law against insults to their race and national pride; The preaching and practice of national, race or color discrimination and contempt shall be a punishable crime;

All apartheid laws and practices shall be set aside.

The People Shall Share in the Country's Wealth!

The national wealth of our country . . . shall be restored to the people;

The mineral wealth shall be transferred to the ownership of the people as a whole. . . .

Adopted by a Congress of the People, Kliptown, South Africa, June 26, 1955.

The Land Shall be Shared Among Those Who Work It!

Restrictions of land ownership on a racial basis shall be ended, and all the land redivided amongst those who work it to banish famine and land hunger. . . ;

Freedom of movement shall be guaranteed to all who work on the land. . . ;

People shall not be robbed of their cattle, and forced labor and farm prisons shall be abolished.

All Shall Be Equal Before the Law!

No one shall be imprisoned, deported, or restricted without a fair trial;

No one shall be condemned by the order of any government official. . . ;

Imprisonment shall be only for serious crimes against the people, and shall aim at re-education, not vengeance;

The police force and army shall be open to all on an equal basis and shall be the helpers and protectors of the people;

All laws which discriminate on grounds of race, color, or belief shall be repealed.

All Shall Enjoy Equal Human Rights!

The law shall guarantee to all their right to speak, to organize, to meet together, to publish, to preach, to worship and to educate their children;

The privacy of the house from police raids shall be protected by law. . . ;

All shall be free to travel without restriction. . . ;

Pass Laws, permits, and all other laws restricting these freedoms shall be abolished.

There Shall Be Work And Security!

All who work shall be free to form trade unions. . . ;

The state shall recognize the right and duty of all to work, and to draw full unemployment benefits;

Men and women of all races shall receive equal pay for equal work. . . ;

. . . a forty-hour working week, a . . . minimum wage, paid annual leave . . . , sick leave and maternity pay;

Child labor . . . and contract labor shall be abolished.

The Doors of Learning and of Culture Shall be Opened!

All the cultural treasures of mankind shall be open to all;

. . . [e]ducation shall be to teach the youth to love their people and their culture, to honor human brotherhood, liberty, and peace; education shall be free . . . and equal for all children. . . ;

The color bar in cultural life, in sport, and in education shall be abolished.

There Shall Be Houses, Security and Comfort!

All people shall have the right to live where they choose, be decently housed, and to bring up their families in comfort and security; . . .

Rent and prices shall be lowered, food plentiful, and no one shall go hungry;

A preventive health scheme shall be run by the state;

Free medical care and hospitalization shall be provided . . . ;

Slums shall be demolished, and new suburbs built where all have transport, roads, lighting, playing fields, crèches, and social centers. . . ;

Fenced locations and ghettos shall be abolished, and laws which break up families shall be repealed.

There Shall Be Peace and Friendship!

South Africa shall strive to maintain world peace and the settlement of all international disputes by negotiation—not war;

Peace and friendship amongst all people shall be secured by upholding the equal rights, opportunities and status of all.

Sample 14, Handout 2.
Killed for Expressing His Opinion

Hector Peterson, aged 13, was shot dead by police for demonstrating against a new ruling by the Minister of Education, in June 1976.

Hector lived in Soweto, a black township outside the city of Johannesburg in South Africa.

In 1976 secondary schools in Soweto were full to bursting, with students going to school in shifts, a shortage of textbooks, and underqualified teachers. The Minister of Education announced that half of all subjects taught at school, including math, history, and geography were in future to be taught in Afrikaans instead of English.

Many of the white people in South Africa are of Dutch origin and Afrikaans is their language. But it is a language that is not spoken or understood anywhere else in the world. School children saw no point in learning a language that would only be of use to communicate with their white employers. English is the common language among the black inhabitants of South Africa, who often also speak an African language.

On June 16, 1976, a mass demonstration by school children was held in Soweto in support of education in English. As they marched through the streets, the police responded with tear gas and bullets. Hector Peterson, aged 13, was the first child to be killed. Hundreds of children were shot and arrested. A full list of those killed, between 25 and 100, was never issued.

This was only the start of many demonstrations and boycotts (refusal to go to school) by black children in South Africa. An unknown number of children were killed, imprisoned, and tortured by the police. These children made great sacrifices for and contributions to the abolition of the apartheid system in South Africa.

• Could you imagine school children in this country having a mass demonstration?

• What issues might they demonstrate about?

• What do you think would be the result?

• What do you think about the South African children wanting their education in English? How would you respond if you were told you had to learn in a new language? Do you know of other instances in which children cannot or could not learn in their own languages?

From *The Whole Child*, prepared by UNICEF-UK (see Chapter 7).

• Do you think the language of education should be considered as a human rights issue? Why? How should it be decided?

• What actions for education rights do you think would be most appropriate and effective?

• Why is education an important human right?

• Are there cases in other countries where children have been deliberately killed by police or with the apparent consent of the government?

Chapter 5
Junior High School: Reflecting and Valuing—Grades Seven to Nine

The pre-adolescent and early adolescent years are crucial in the development of personal and social identity. The need to "belong," to be accepted by a peer group, can lead youngsters to values dilemmas for which they have not been prepared. Early and pre-teen peer groups often tend to be exclusive of those who don't "fit in." The seeds of moral exclusion, placing others outside the moral community and the bounds of fair treatment, find fertile ground in the twelve- to fourteen-year-old age group. Consequently it is an important stage at which to deal with the phenomenon and explore its consequences. Recommended as background reading for teachers is the work of Susan Opotow, who edited a special issue of the *Journal of Social Issues* on the topic (Vol. 46, No. 1, Fall 1990). Her own research on the notions of moral community held and applied by adolescents is enlightening and helpful to teachers of human rights seeking to educate toward moral inclusion and universal respect for human dignity. The essays in the special issue describe the phenomenon and give illustrations of some historical events that it produced such as the Holocaust and the exclusion of Haitian refugees from the United States.

The intellectual capacity most in need of nurturing at this stage is the capacity for reflective valuing. Young people of this age should be encouraged to think about what values they hold and how the values affect their personal relationships and the social groups to which they belong. They should also be helped to reflect on the values that seem to guide the society and how social values relate to their personal values. Most important to human rights education is their reflection on the social and political consequences of actions taken in accordance with their personal values. They should be helped to reflect on questions of consequence. Would the whole society benefit from the proposed action? If not, who would suffer negative consequences and why? Would their values lead to a socially just society? Would their values help to achieve universal human dignity? The samples offered in this section can be used as the basis to encourage such an inquiry and to develop the students' capacities for reflecting and valuing.

Teachers looking for a good general curricular resource for the junior high level might consider *Taking a Stand Against Human Rights Abuses* (by Michael Kronenwetter) because it offers a Western historical overview and emphasizes social responsibility (see Chapter 7). It will enable teachers to guide students in the development of social responsibility as they reflect on their own personal and social values, paving the way for the more sophisticated exploration of cultural and political values that should be included in human rights education at the senior high school level.

Note. While students should be encouraged to express their values and be required to give reasons for the opinions and positions they articulate, their privacy should be respected. Sharing of ideas and values should be on the basis of the individual student's willingness to do so. Privacy is important to all human beings, especially to adolescents.

The following samples were selected for grades seven through nine, designated here as junior high school. The ninth grade material is equally applicable to four-year, grades nine through twelve, high schools.

Seventh Grade. Why Study Human Rights—Presenting a Rationale

In early adolescence students are entitled to know why the curriculum they are required to study was selected. They should also be encouraged to provide reasons for their actions or opinions and expect the same from their classmates. Reasoning on the basis of values and facts is a skill a human rights curriculum can help to develop. It is thus appropriate to introduce the formal study of the general field of human rights and the international standards with the fundamental question, "Why should we study human rights?"

There are various ways in which a discussion of the rationale for human rights education might be initiated at this or any grade level. The following unit, one brief and fairly simple way to do so, is the introductory lesson from a unit published by the World Affairs Council of Philadelphia used in that city for several years after its publication in 1979. The two seventh grade samples presented here are interrelated and can be presented as a sequence, or used independently.

Learning Objectives. Students will:
- reflect on the significance of human rights;
- note the relevance of human rights to their own lives;
- speculate on the role of human rights in bringing about the kind of world they want to live in.

Materials
- Preamble to the Declaration of Independence
- Handout #1, Human Rights: What's in It for You and Me

Learning Sequence

Step 1. Provide the Preamble to the Declaration of Independence and the Handout to all students and assign the reading of both as homework. Have the students begin a human rights journal by writing their reactions to their readings.

Step 2. Form cooperative learning groups of four to six members. Present each with the following activities. After each activity have the groups report the results to the entire class.

Activity 1. Ask the students to discuss how the Declaration of Independence expressed a vision of a better world for the initiators of the American Revolution. List the basic human rights it proclaimed, and explain the relationship it described between government and rights. How do citizens play a role in that relationship? Is education important to that role?

Activity 2. Ask the groups to discuss and prepare responses to the questions that are included in the handout. They should prepare two sets of responses: their own, and the responses they would imagine the writers of the Declaration of Independence would give.

Activity 3. Make a list of human paradoxes, things that seem contradictory about people. Example: "People are selfish and care only about themselves. People are self-sacrificing and do much for others." Point out that such contradictory characteristics can be found with a single human group or even one person.

Conclude the discussion of the first activity by observing that broad generalizations about human beings and groups of human beings are misleadingly one-sided and that stereotypes prevent us from really understanding others.

Activity 4. Ask students to do the following. Name three things that could make the world better. Compare your list with your classmates'. Explain why you named the three you did. Are your reasons different from your classmates'? What values led you to decide on these three things? Who would benefit most from your changes? Would anyone be less well off? Which things would you change on your list?

Conclude the discussion of this activity by having the class make a list of what all could agree might make the world a better place. Note which of these things are related to human rights.

Step 3. Assign students to look for and clip human rights stories from newspapers and other available sources. They should be especially alert to stories that reflect their list of changes that would make a better world. Discuss the clippings and post them on the bulletin board under the headings of the changes they relate to.

Activity 5. Ask the students to reflect on the clippings and the stories they tell about the human experience. Suggest that they write their reflections in their human rights journals: either concerns, hopes, or ideas of what could be done and who could do it. Explain that the journals are private. They are tools for helping us think. Sometimes we are not ready to share our thoughts. When we are ready, sharing them is a wonderful way to learn. In discussions we can clarify our values and our ideas so we and others have a better understanding of problems and possibilities for solutions. So we can keep journals for our private thoughts and have discussions for sharing our ideas.

At the end of the two seventh grade units the class can return to the list and decide on some actions they could take to make these things happen.

Sample 15, Handout 1.
Human Rights:
What's in It for You and Me

Human rights is a very important topic these days. The news has been filled with stories about the plight of the Kurds struggling against the government of Iraq that has killed and displaced them; people in American cities, concerned about homelessness and violence; refugees fleeing famine and dictatorships, some of them drowning at sea. The worldwide struggle for freedom, and many cases in which people suffer mistreatment from others, sometimes their own governments, is often on TV and in the papers. We hear a lot of talk about human rights issues.

We also get a lot of different reactions. Some people say that politicians see these questions as a chance to make themselves popular. So they make a lot of statements in favor of human rights. But does anything really happen? Others say it's sentimental nonsense. They say no-one with an ounce of common sense thinks the questions can be answered, and that the soft-hearted "do-gooders" just like to think they can. But there are a lot of people who take human rights very seriously. They are working very hard, day after day, to make even a little progress. At times it almost seems hopeless. But they don't give up. Why not?

There are lots of reasons why people struggle for human rights. Some people have been victims of torture and unjust imprisonment themselves. They don't want it to happen to them again. Others feel a concern for other people whose rights have been violated. They don't want these things to happen to anyone. Still others see it as a matter of principle—that it's just the right thing to do. They believe that we should work for a world where everybody's rights are respected. There are a growing number of people who hold this belief, many of them Americans. Mostly they are people who really believe what it says in the Preamble to the Declaration of Independence. It says that rights are what we are entitled to just because we are people. Why not have a look at it yourself? Do you believe in the principles of the Declaration of Independence? But why bother to study about human rights? What's in it for you and me?

First, the easy answers. We never know when we could get into some trouble. In any case, it pays to know your own rights. If you get arrested, you had better know what your rights are. If you are a victim of injustice, you might help yourself if you know about human rights. So, it could be a matter of self-defense.

Excerpted with permission from *Human Rights* (Philadelphia: World Affairs Council of Philadelphia, 1979). The first paragraph has been revised in terms of contemporary conditions.

But what about others? Suppose it's a friend or someone you care about. It would be good to be able to know how to help. Yet many of the stories in the news are about people and events pretty far away. Why care about that? What's it got to do with you? Here's where the harder answer comes in.

The fact is that we live in a world where everything is connected with everything else. We are all in the same system. And sooner or later what happens in one part of that system is going to affect all parts, you and me included. So if we want the best chance for ourselves, we have to think about others too. That's what human rights is all about—a better chance for everybody, including you and me. It's funny, but not too many people have caught on to that idea yet.

There's another reason too. It's human beings themselves. They are all alike, and they are all different. All of them have the same universal needs. And each one is a totally unique individual. That's what human rights are all about. How can we have a world where everyone's needs are met, but also where all people are free to be their unique selves? That's another thing about human beings. They like big challenges. Who can resist a double dare?

92

Seventh Grade. The Relationship Between Rights and Responsibilities— The Universal Declaration of Human Rights

The following unit is based on one of various simplified versions of the Universal Declaration of Human Rights. Some teachers do their own simplified versions in the particular vocabulary of their own students, some in other languages or in the slang or everyday speech that makes the content more real and vivid to the learners. This particular version was chosen for inclusion here because it is followed by a list of responsibilities that complement each of the rights. Since we have advocated social responsibility as one of the main developmental concepts for these grades, we believe that the introduction of specific rights standards should be accompanied by equally specific responsibilities, so that students see that both rights and responsibilities are actual behaviors and circumstances, not mere abstractions. They should be helped to understand that personal behavior has social consequences.

By early adolescence students should begin to exercise social responsibility and reflect on standards. The Universal Declaration of Human Rights is the most appropriate set of standards for assessing social responsibility on the part of individuals and society. This unit, extracted from the curriculum published by the World Affairs Council of Philadelphia, is one way to make these points in a seventh grade class on human rights. We recommend that this unit be presented in early December in observance of Human Rights Day, December 10.

Teachers will find an excellent visual introduction to the Declaration in a video entitled "The Universal Declaration of Human Rights," which uses students' own words and illustrations along with visuals produced by an international group of animators. It is available from Amnesty International and the United Nations (see Chapter 7 for address). Also available from Amnesty and the United Nations is *The Universal Declaration of Human Rights*, a presentation of the Declaration in the six United Nations languages, illustrated by Jean-Michel Foulon.

Learning Objectives. Students will:
- review and reflect on the specific rights enumerated in the Universal Declaration;
- review and reflect on the responsibilities related to each of the rights;

- assess the Universal Declaration and make suggestions for revisions, additions, and deletions;
- give reasons for their suggestions and compare their reasons with those of their classmates.

Materials
- Handout #1, Ideas About Human Rights Differ
- Handout #2, Some Rights Listed in the Universal Declaration of Human Rights
- Handout #3, Human Responsibilities

Learning Sequence

Step 1. Provide the students with Handout #1, "Ideas About Human Rights Differ," and assign it as homework.

Step 2. After the students have read the handout, present the following topics for discussion.

If you did the previous sample lesson, ask the students to review the list of things you determined would make a better world, especially the items related to human rights. Do these items fall in a particular category of rights? Does one category seem more important than the others? Why or why not?

Ask students to research the changes that have taken place in the way of life in Eastern Europe since 1990. How do these changes affect human rights? Which categories of rights are not affected? Other areas of the world could also be discussed.

Step 3. Distribute Handout #2, "Some Rights Listed in the Universal Declaration." Allow class time for reading the list of rights.

Step 4. When the students have read the list, pose the following questions for discussion:
- Do you agree that all the items listed in the Declaration should be considered rights? Why or why not? Are there rights that should be added? Which rights? Why?

Step 5. Distribute Handout #3, "Human Responsibilities," and allow the students time to read.

Step 6. When the students have studied the list of responsibilities, pose the following questions:
- Do all the responsibilities listed seem reasonable and necessary? Why or why not? Does everyone in the class agree on what human responsibilities we have?
- Are there some responsibilities you think are too difficult for you to fulfill? Which ones and why? What might make it easier for you to do so?
- How might these actions contribute toward achieving a better world? (Refer to the things that would make the world better that you previously listed.) List an action that you and your classmates might take to fulfill each responsibility.

Conclusion. Explain that human rights is a two-way street. We all should work to fulfill our own rights, and defend the rights of others. Democratic governments are based on the idea that citizens have responsibilities as well as rights. We can't expect the government to do it all. We must make an effort, too. It's really the best way to work for human rights.

Sample 16, Handout 1.
Ideas About Human Rights Differ

The best set of guidelines for a good society is the Universal Declaration of Human Rights. The Declaration is a list of thirty rights to which every person in the world is entitled. The list was unanimously adopted by the General Assembly of the United Nations on December 10, 1948. Ever since then, December 10 has been celebrated as Human Rights Day. And the Declaration has served as a set of ideals to work for. Even though all the member nations of the UN agreed to them, these rights are not yet universally guaranteed. The Declaration is, nevertheless, an important statement about the human needs society should meet.

Rights are another way of expressing human needs. They are the things the society agrees everyone should have. Not all societies make these things available in the same way. In socialist societies, the government agrees to meet the basic and social needs recognized as human rights. In capitalist societies there are different ways of meeting the needs. Some are met by business and industry, which produce material goods for basic needs. Some are met by private groups like churches, citizen organizations, and theatrical companies, which help to meet social needs. Most countries agree that certain needs should be met by the government. Mainly these are protection needs. So all governments have armies and police.

But countries have differed in the importance they place on types of rights. Western countries have traditionally placed most importance on political rights. The first ten amendments to the United States Constitution, the Bill of Rights, list political rights. Freedom of speech and assembly are thus very important to these countries. The Eastern European countries under socialism formerly stressed economic and social rights. The right to work and to education were generally stressed in socialist countries. In some developing countries, there seems to be equal emphasis on political, economic, and social rights. In poor countries the stress is usually on basic needs that are fulfilled through economic rights. Most countries, however, agree on the rights in the Universal Declaration as a general list of human rights and there is a movement toward a more holistic approach which views all categories of rights as interrelated and inseparable. The 1993 World Conference on Human Rights reflected this view when it declared that human rights were universal and indivisible.

Excerpted with permission from *Human Rights* (Philadelphia: World Affairs Council of Philadelphia, 1979). (This is also Sample 11, Handout 2.)

Sample 16, Handout 2.
Some Rights Listed in the
Universal Declaration of Human Rights

Because the actual wording of the Declaration is difficult for the average person, here is a list in everyday language of some of the 30 rights. As you read them, think of the particular needs which are contained in each right. Do you believe these are needs that society should meet?

• Everyone should be free and have equal rights.

• Everyone in every country, no matter of what race, nation, sex, belief, whether rich or poor, is entitled to all the rights in the Universal Declaration.

• No one should be tortured or treated cruelly, even when being punished for committing a crime.

• Everyone accused of a crime should be considered innocent until proven guilty in a fair and public trial.

• Everyone has a right to privacy and to a good reputation.

• Everyone should be able to live where he or she pleases, and to go from one place to another within his or her own country. People should also be able to leave and return to their own countries.

• Everyone should be able to escape persecution by going to another country. This does not mean that criminals have the right to flee from punishment.

• All adult men and women have the right to marry and start a family. No one should be forced to marry against his or her own will.

• All people have the right to their own opinions. They should be able to express their opinions and to exchange ideas with others.

• All people have the right to participate in their own governments. Everyone has an equal right to public services. No government should exist against the will of its citizens. Fair and democratic government should be assured by elections. Elections should be held periodically on the basis of universal suffrage.

• Everyone is entitled to "social security." In other words, governments must try to assure that people have their basic needs fulfilled, treat each other with respect, and have as much chance as possible to develop their personalities.

• Everyone has a right to work; to choose his or her own work; to good working conditions; and to protection against unemployment. Everyone has the right to equal pay for equal work. All people have the right to be paid fairly for work, so that they and their families can live in dignity. Everyone has the right to form a union and to join unions to protect their rights as workers.

• Everyone has the right to rest and to free time, including paid vacations and reasonable working hours.

• Everyone has the right to education. The purpose of education is to help people develop as fully as possible. It shall promote understanding among different nations, religions, and races. It should also aim to achieve respect for human rights and peace. Parents may decide the kind of education their children receive.

• People are entitled to live in a country and a world where the rights listed in this Declaration are fulfilled.

• People should fulfill their duties to the community in order to complete their personal development. The only limits on human rights are fairness to others, respect for their rights and the good of the community, and preserving the purposes of the United Nations.

Sample 16, Handout 3.
Human Responsibilities

The Universal Declaration was also based on the idea of human responsibilities. Here is a suggested list of some things citizens should do. Do you agree with them? What other suggestions would you make?

• Everyone should treat others with respect and defend the rights of others.

• Everyone should try to prevent discrimination against others because of race, nationality, sex, and so on.

• No-one should force another to work without pay.

• No-one should permit the torture of another person, nor treat others cruelly in any way.

• All people should try to prevent illegal arrests and expulsions from their countries.

• No-one should consider or treat those accused of crimes as guilty until their guilt is proven in a fair trial.

• Governments and people should not enter homes, listen in on telephones, or open mail without the permission of the persons concerned. No-one should slander another person.

• People and governments should not force people to live where they don't want to. No-one should prevent others from traveling or leaving their own countries.

• People and countries should offer asylum to those who are persecuted.

• Everyone should belong to the nation he or she wants. No one should take his or her nation for granted.

• Men and women who marry should respect and defend each other's equal rights. Parents should care for their children and teach them to be responsible citizens.

• Everyone should respect others' rights to their own opinions and their own religious beliefs. People and governments should not interfere with religious freedom.

- Everyone should respect and defend others' rights to freedom of expression.

- Everyone has the responsibility to vote in elections.

102

- Employers should provide workers with adequate time off. In the home, work should be shared so one person is not overburdened.

- Everyone has the responsibility to get an education.

- People should work to make cultural life and scientific information available to everyone.

- Everyone should work to achieve a world of peace and freedom.

- Everyone should try to make it possible for others to enjoy all human rights and achieve personal fulfillment.

Eighth Grade. Refugees and Racism— The Problem of Discrimination

The early teen years are a time in social development when young people often are discriminatory and morally exclusive. Prejudicial attitudes, if reinforced by peers, family, and society, can become deeply rooted and continue to pose a severe impediment to social justice and human rights. Thus this is an important time to reprise some of the instruction directed toward moral inclusion and fundamental respect for human dignity that was advocated as the central content for human rights education in early childhood. At this stage, however, it is essential to be direct, to name the problems and confront them as they exist, not only in society, but in school and in athletic and social settings where young adolescents learn about social relationships. Moral exclusion, racial and ethnic prejudice, and discrimination comprise major human rights problems. These problems become more severe in the climate of rapid global change, and must be addressed by education.

Refugees are one group who suffer discrimination and exclusion. Global problems of poverty, environmental destruction, political repression, ethnic conflict, and war have driven many people from their native lands. Refugees and migrants are now living in communities that not very long ago were homogeneous. Often their presence is evident because their physical appearance differs from that of the traditional population. For refugee and immigrant school children the differences in culture and custom may also set them apart from their classmates. They frequently suffer the consequences of intolerance and ignorance of human diversity, and so become the victims of moral exclusion among their peers as well as in the larger society.

The study of prejudice, discrimination, racism, and ethnocentrism should be a significant component of human rights education at this level, whether or not there is ethnic diversity in the community. These forms of moral exclusion should be presented as manifestations of the central problem of the denial of human dignity that make possible such severe forms of human rights violations as torture and genocide. Students should be helped to see how individual behavior as well as public policy can contribute to or interrupt this humanly destructive cycle.

Because of the growing number of immigrants and refugees in schools and the increase in tensions and hostility between ethnic and racial groups, anti-prejudice education is especially urgent. The following materials, a diagram and excerpts for discussion from Betty Reardon's *Discrimination: The Cycle of Injustice* (Sydney, Australia: Holt Saunders, 1977) and a collection of student writings, *Winning Ideas to Stop Racism*, published by the Department of Canadian Heritage (see Chapter 7), which sponsored a contest on the topic of racism, demonstrate the cyclical process of systematic discrimination and the personal pain caused by racial prejudice. It is also recommended that teachers include the United Nations Declaration on the Elimination of Racial Discrimination and other relevant Conventions when units on prejudice or racial and ethnic conflict are offered.

Learning Objectives. Students will:
- reflect on the process and characteristics of discrimination;
- review the emotional and social consequences of racism;
- consider actions to reduce prejudice and overcome racism;
- review the international standards to combat racism.

Materials
- Handout #1: Chart on the Cycle of Discrimination
- Handout #2: The Problem of Negative Discrimination
- Handout #3: Racism—A War to be Eliminated
- Handout #4: Student Statements on Racism

Learning Sequence. Several of these learning steps can be adapted to a performance mode. Art forms, role playing, and recitations are excellent tools for learning about issues covered here.

Step 1. Introduce the concept of racism and discrimination by distributing and discussing Handouts #1 and #2. It may be necessary to allocate two homework assignments to the reading. The students might define and give examples of the key concepts presented in the readings: discrimination, prejudice, structural violence, genocide, anti-semitism, ethnocentrism, sexism, racism, colonialism, exclusion, ethnocide, exploitation, oppression, stereotyping, human equality, and global community. The teacher should review the cyclical process of discrimination so that the students understand how such events and circumstances as the Holocaust, the internment of Japanese Americans during World War II, racial segregation in the United States, apartheid in South Africa, and the forced removal of Native Americans to reservations came about.

Step 2. Provide background on the many world situations that have produced refugees. Point out on the world map where the refugees come from and where they took refuge. Distribute Handout #3. Ask for six volunteers to read Phuong Huyn's story aloud. Have the entire class read the last two paragraphs aloud together. If there are refugees in the class, speak to them privately to see if they would be willing to share their own stories. Try to be sensitive to how this lesson might affect them and their relations with their classmates.

Step 3. Pose the following questions for discussion:
- How did you feel as you read and listened to Phuong Huyn's story?
- Do you know of similar experiences? If so, what happened and how did the victims of prejudice respond?
- How should we as a class observe March 21?

Step 4. Distribute Handout #4. Allow time to scan the three readings and ask for two volunteers to read the brief account and the slogan aloud. Then have the whole class read "Racism Rap" together after a third volunteer reads it aloud once.

Step 5. Present the following tasks to be undertaken by cooperative learning groups of four to six students.
- Write a scenario of how Leilani came to like "being different."
- Write an anti-racism slogan.
- Write a rap on racism.

Step 6. Students who wish to do extra credit work could research and present reports to the class on the UNESCO Declaration on Racism, the Convention on the Elimination of All Forms of Racial Discrimination, and the Convention on the Status of Refugees.

The United Nations High Commission for Refugees publishes a periodical entitled *Refugees* which is an excellent teaching resource (see Chapter 7 for address).

Sample 17, Handout 1. The Cycle of Discrimination

THE CYCLE OF INJUSTICE

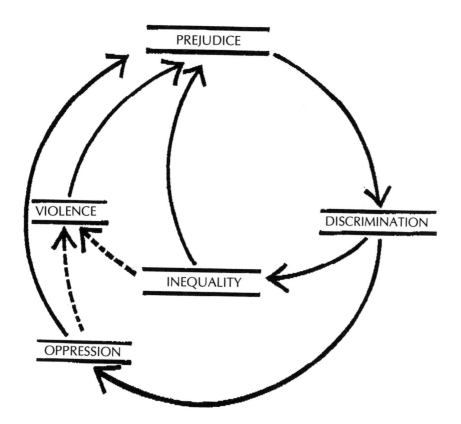

Adapted with permission from Betty Reardon, *Discrimination: The Cycle of Injustice* (Sydney: Holt, Saunders, 1977). This book was dedicated to the memory of Fannie Lou Hamer, whose struggle to break the cycle of discrimination inspires us to continue to strive for human dignity. Teachers may wish to provide background on Hamer, the Freedom Riders, voter registration drives, and other aspects of the U. S. Civil Rights Movement, or to show video excerpts from the PBS series *Eyes on the Prize.*

Sample 17, Handout 2.
The Problem of Negative Discrimination

Article 1. All human beings are born free and equal in dignity and rights. They are endowed with reason and conscience and should act toward one another in a spirit of brotherhood [Note: the phrase in "spirit of brotherhood" is intended to include both women and men. Some human rights advocates are working to establish the use of inclusive, gender neutral language in United Nations documents.]

Article 2. Everyone is entitled to all the rights and freedoms set forth in this Declaration, without distinction of any kind, such as race, color, sex, language, religion, political or other opinion, national or social origin, property, birth or other status. (The Universal Declaration of Human Rights)

What Is Discrimination?

Discrimination is a word with mixed connotations. When applied to personal taste in food, the arts, or fashion, it connotes something positive. Indeed, people are proud to be described as "of discriminating taste." However, when applied to social behavior, particularly towards certain identifiable human groups, it has a negative connotation. Few people would wish to be described as "discriminatory" in dealing with their fellow human beings. Yet *negative discrimination* is more the rule in human society than the exception: very few, if in fact any, human groups do not discriminate against other human groups.

In its simplest terms, discrimination means *acknowledging differences*. Clearly, there are many observable differences among people. Human diversity gives a great variety and richness to the human experience. Discrimination becomes negative when it is accompanied by a definition of differing *value* among and between people. When one group considers another group to be less important and less worthy than itself, it often denies that group basic human rights and access to the benefits of society. In these terms, discrimination is a *denial of human dignity and equal rights* for those discriminated against. This process denies human equality and imposes a life of problems and struggle upon some, while endowing others with privileges and benefits.

Discrimination takes many forms, from simple personal *prejudice*, a predisposition to respond favorably or unfavorably, to systematic political oppression. Many

Adapted with permission from Betty A. Reardon, *Discrimination: The Cycle of Injustice* (Sydney: Holt Saunders, 1977). As used here, "negative discrimination" is similar to "moral exclusion," placing persons or groups outside the boundaries of fair treatment. See Susan Opotow, ed., "Moral Exclusion," *Journal of Social Issues* 46, 1 (1990).

people believe that personal prejudice in social and political terms is no more serious than personal taste. However, the right of people to select their own associates has sometimes been extended to the right to choose their neighbors, which quickly infringes on other people's right to live where they please. Furthermore, individual prejudices can very quickly solidify into group customs, and finally into discriminatory laws and structures. An effective approach to discrimination must deal with individual prejudice, but it must also address the systems and structures which perpetuate unfair treatment.

Prejudice is the fertile ground in which custom, habit, and attitude take root and grow into systematic oppression. The political authority serves one human group at the expense of other human groups and allows a form of life for the oppressed that not only denies their human rights, but actually limits their right to life itself. Often as a result of lack of social services, minds are undeveloped, bodies are stunted, and personal fulfillment made impossible. Life is frequently shorter for the oppressed and always more painful.

This systematic discrimination by institutions is considered by some to be *structural violence*. Within this concept, violence is defined as deliberate or avoidable injury to life or health. Social customs and political institutions (such as apartheid laws of South Africa that segregated blacks from whites except when blacks provided labor and other services for whites) can make it inevitable that certain groups within a society will have limited life and health. These structures then impose violence as surely as opposing armies or any combatants do. Viewed in these terms, discrimination is a complex social problem involving attitudes, customs, and values, as well as laws and other social, economic, and political institutions.

Religious and Cultural Discrimination

In addition to its appearance in such generalized forms as prejudice and structural violence, discrimination takes many specific forms. Students of history are most likely to be acquainted with the manifestations and consequences of ethnic or religious discrimination. Extreme discrimination on these grounds has sometimes evolved into *genocide*, the deliberate attempt to murder an entire human group. Muslim Turks attempted to exterminate the Christian Armenians during World War I. In the Nazi death camps of World War II, millions of people, including two-thirds of all European Jews, were systematically murdered.

Ethnocentrism is a belief in the superiority of one's own culture and ethnic identity over other cultures and identities. It often results in discrimination because of cultural identity and physical appearance. The group that controls the society maintains its privileged position by discriminating against those groups that are different in identity, appearance, or lifestyle. The most frequent form of discrimination on these grounds is exclusion.

Exclusion is the practice of denying access to places, services, and experiences. It frequently prevents the victims of discrimination from overcoming the bases of other forms of discrimination. The adjective "exclusive" is often thought to be synonymous with "luxurious" or "excellent"—for example, when describing a school or club. Its actual meaning and its real consequence is denial of access to those who do not meet the criteria for entrance. Although these criteria may take into account such things as academic or athletic skills, the most important factors are usually economic means and human identity in terms of social class, religion, ethnic group, race, or sex.

We noted earlier that genocide, the murder of an entire people, can result from the escalation of discriminatory practices. The human species is thus deprived of some of its richness of physical variety. More frequently, we see a decrease in the variety of cultures, which could be called *ethnocide*. Western industrial society has been particularly guilty of this crime, sometimes by intention, sometimes by insensitivity to the human consequences of its drive for growth and "progress," and frequently by its imposition of conformity through discrimination.

Discrimination by Custom, Tradition, and Myths

Just as the cycle of discrimination that starts with prejudice can move from simple exclusion to ethnocide and genocide, so too the cycle begun by predetermined social roles on the basis of sex, race, or economic status can propel the human experience from simple "tradition" to exploitation and oppression. *Exploitation* consists of taking unfair advantage of the social, cultural, or physical circumstances of certain people. For example, women who give birth are also expected to carry the full burden of childrearing and homemaking. In agricultural societies, women do these chores in addition to raising crops. In industrial societies, they often perform factory or office jobs as well as homemaking tasks that are seldom shared by men. This form of labor exploitation has also been suffered by some racial groups, particularly those blacks whose human freedom was denied them throughout the centuries of slavery. They were offered little or no hope, or any chance of escape. So also the poor often find it impossible to escape from poverty. When exploitative conditions seem irreversible and the exploited are denied opportunities to change or flee from their exploitation, then oppression exists. *Oppression* can be maintained openly by repressive institutions, such as the military, the police, and unjust laws. But it can also be enforced by custom and tradition. Indeed, slavery was once believed to be within the "natural" order, just as today, the subservience of women is still thought by some to be "natural."

One of the chief reinforcements of discrimination by tradition is *stereotyping*: holding a fixed, simplistic, usually negative image of an entire group of people. Stereotypes tell us that women are less rational and less responsible than men; that blacks are lazier, more sensual, and physically stronger than whites; that the poor are dirty, lack ambition, and expect the government to take care of them. Stereotypes are examples of negative discrimination, for they deny both human diversity and human equality. We can lump many individuals into one inaccurately described general category, allowing us to deny their humanity and therefore their rights to fair treatment. Stereotypes help to perpetuate discrimination and exploitation, as well as such systems as colonialism.

The stereotyping of former colonial countries persists even in the present, providing a rationale for continued discrimination against and manipulation of the "less developed countries." In the Western culture of the industrial countries, "more and bigger" are positive concepts, but "less" is a negative one, usually meaning "less value" or "less importance." Language is a crucial element in stereotyping and so a significant instrument for discrimination.

The Most Common Forms of Discrimination

The three most common and widespread forms of discrimination practiced in the world today are sexism, racism, and colonialism. The daily life of every one of us is negatively affected in some way by each of these.

112

Sexism is probably the most subtle as well as the most universal form of discrimination and therefore may be the most crucial. Irma Mazelis, in an unpublished paper in 1975, described sexism as "deeply rooted attitudes, values, beliefs, customs and practices based upon the belief that women are inferior to men because they are born with different physiological, psychological and spiritual characteristics, which lead them to carry out a specific type of work which is marginal to the processes of production."

Racism is the belief that racial differences carry with them superior and inferior human capacities. It leads to discriminatory social customs and cultural separation of groups according to race, physical characteristics, and ethnic identity. Social benefits are then denied to the separated people. Racism is the most apparent form of discrimination, and frequently captures public attention in the media. It is the subject of many strong protests and sentiments within nations and throughout the world.

Colonialism is the control and exploitation of weaker groups by stronger groups through the establishment of political authority or economic dominance. The dominant group can then determine the rules and terms by which society is guided and decisions are made. These rules usually reflect the assumption made by the stronger group of their own superiority, and result in the attribution of more rights to this "superior" group. Colonialism in its various manifestations—from discrimination against entire nations in the world economic system to discrimination against groups of the poor within societies—is the most systematic type of discrimination. It pervades the social, political and economic institutions of present world structures.

Why Is Discrimination a Global Problem?

We each perceive and identify problems from the perspective of our own values. However, we should all place a very high value on human equality. This can best be achieved in a society in which no human identity is given greater value or enjoys more benefits than any other, whether that identity is designated by sex, race, culture, social, political, or economic function. The world society of the future should be based on the value of human equality; social benefits could then be enjoyed by all the world's people. This new world society would form a *global community*.

A real community is characterized by an equitable sharing of all the benefits available: economic, social, political, intellectual, aesthetic, or spiritual. The core value of any community, local or global, should be the value of human equality. All human beings should be nurtured, cherished, and fulfilled as far as possible. The function of the community is to provide this nurture, to educate its members to cherish life, and to create opportunities for fulfillment. Discrimination as it exists today throughout the world at all levels of social organization is clearly an obstacle to human community.

Sample 17, Handout 3.
Racism—A War to Be Eliminated

Reader 1

I was born on October 9, 1974, in Saigon, Vietnam, to Hien Huynh and Lieu Tran.

My family were among twenty-three people to escape from Vietnam and the V.C.s, March 25, 1979, in a boat built and piloted by my father. We spent a dangerous five days in the sea of Indo-China, where we ended up being robbed by "modern day pirates" and forced to land at Malaysia.

The life in Malaysia was SO dreadful! It was like being in a prison, with not enough food or water to keep anyone alive, and we had to spend six months in the refugee camp at Pilau Bigong.

Reader 2

We arrived in Regina, Saskatchewan, on September 26, 1979. A special thanks to the Dannevirke Lutheran Church for sponsoring us, or we wouldn't be here today.

As soon as we came to Canada, I had to start school immediately. Honestly speaking, I was scared to death! I had to meet a whole new group of people who spoke a whole different language. I knew nothing. Everyone could talk and laugh with each other while I couldn't communicate with anyone. It was like I was in my own world, away from everybody. Here, I stood out like a rotten potato with no one to comfort or understand me . . . not even my kindergarten teacher. I was only five and already categorized as "the outsider."

Reader 3

I had to go through a couple of years of teasing. At this age, I was too young to know why people were doing this to me. I didn't know or have any idea of what RACISM was. The only thing I knew was that the words stung and hurt me more than anything I know.

The teasing got to the point where I began to feel VERY ashamed of my nationality. I was embarrassed that I stood out, and I thought it was a disgrace to do so. I also began to have poor self-esteem, and little pride and dignity, which caused me to become shy, quiet, and withdrawn from others.

I did have friends who understood how I felt and who always stood by my side through thick and thin. Then, there were the ones who called us discriminating, unfeeling names like "chink" and "ching-chong."

Honorable Mention, personal story by Phuong Huynh, Redvers High School, Redvers, Saskatchewan. Adapted with permission from *Winning Ideas to Stop Racism* (Ottowa: Anti-Racism Campaign, 1992).

With one other family, we were the only Oriental families in the community of Redvers. We didn't understand all these name callings, nor did we understand why people were doing this. Often racial remarks are made unintentionally, without thinking of the consequences, yet they may deeply hurt a person.

114   *Reader 4*

As time went on, my brothers and sisters and I grew to understand what prejudice was, but we'll never understand why it's out there. We have been fighting a war for us to be accepted.

People may think that they're so cool, but once, just once, I'd just LOVE to see them stand in our shoes and feel how hurt we are. It's no big joke. . . . Can't they get it? WE ARE HUMANS TOO!

I cannot believe in someone who cannot believe in me.

Presently, I am 16 years of age and in grade 11. To tell you the truth, the people in my school seem to have an understanding of my feelings and have stopped their immature wisecracks. . . . HEY? It's a start!

Reader 5

Canada is made up of immigrants from all over the world. Everyone of all races built this country together. We are living in a multicultural society, and we should accept and learn about cultures different from our own. Bigotry, like an infectious disease, hurts the individual both mentally and physically. Once the hurt is out in the open, no matter how many apologies there are, the hurt will never go away. Discrimination against others is not something one is born with, but is taught. You can't go through life making fun and putting someone down who is different from you. It's just a waste of time. I guess, if you can't say something nice, why bother saying anything at all? No one was put on this earth to discriminate and hurt others. It really hurts to be alienated, and not to be accepted for who we are.

Entire class

Racism cannot be eliminated from this world overnight, but the dream will never go away.

Mark March 21 as the International Day for the Elimination of Racial Discrimination. Remember, racism hurts everyone.

Action Idea

Poems, stories, songs, plays, paintings, and drawings are all effective ways of identifying and communicating our feelings and those of others. Produce a class anthology on the themes of exclusion, discrimination, prejudice, racism, ethnocentricism, and sexism.

Sample 17, Handout 4.
Student Statements on Racism

"I Like Being Different"[1]

I know what it's like to get up every morning to go to school or to a job to be taunted, to be despised, to be hated. I know what it's like to be different, to have to laugh off or ignore racist comments, to have fear or sadness bottled up inside, ready to burst, trying not to burst. But I'm used to it, and I like being different. I like being me. I don't wish any more that I was white, or that I was like everybody else. After all, wouldn't the world be boring, if we were all the same?
Honorable mention: Leilani D. Cleveland, Windsor Regional High School, in Windsor, Nova Scotia.

Slogan[2]

"Membership in humanity has a fair fee. To join, treat others with dignity."

Racism Rap[3]

How do you know they're not exploding inside
Being robbed of their dignity
when you're destroying their pride?
So don't take away another person's right
'Cause all you're doing is instigating a fight. . . ."

Action idea

Organize a photo shoot on the theme of "Together We're Better" to demonstrate the richness of the human diversity in your school. Display the photos in the main hall, so visitors as well as students and teachers can see the pride you take in this richness.

Excerpted with permission from *Winning Ideas to Stop Racism* (Ottawa: Anti-Racism Campaign, 1992).
1. Honorable mention, Leilani D. Cleveland, Windsor Regional High School, Windsor, Nova Scotia.
2. Winner, Garmen Ko, part of the winning team from Doncrest Public School, Richmond Hill, Ontario.
3. Winners, Mike Boshevski and Jim Tsirgotis, part of the winning team from Doncrest Public School, Richmond Hill, Ontario.

Eighth Grade. Learning About Human Rights Through Creative Dramatics

The arts can be used in human rights education to explore the most human aspects of the issues in the struggle for human rights. The arts also stimulate the creative imagination essential to developing empathy for others and imaging and envisioning positive alternatives for human society. Bonnie Friedman designed a curriculum based on puppetry and theater arts to teach human rights in junior high school. It is adapted here as four lessons for use in the eighth grade.

Overall Objectives. Students will:
- become familiar with the United Nations Universal Declaration of Human Rights;
- become aware of the international standards on human rights;
- become aware of how these standards are used to define violations of human rights;
- formulate and creatively express their personal definitions of humanness and human rights;
- develop group process discussion and listening skills;
- develop cooperative learning skills by working in groups to write and perform puppet shows and skits expressing their solutions to problems posed in class.

Core Inquiry. Throughout the unit the following questions are posed as the central inquiry:
- Why is the question of human rights important?
- What does "humanness" mean?
- What does "human rights" mean?
- Do all persons start out "equal"?
- What does "equality" mean?
- How do human rights relate to caring for and respecting others?
- Is it important to you to feel cared for and respected?

Teaching Methods
- Webbing (a spontaneously drawn illustration of ideas and their interrelationships) and brainstorming (sharing the very first responses to a theme or problem) will be used to organize and reflect on ideas and questions.
- Creative dramatics exercises, role play, and working with puppets will be used as described in each lesson.

- Students might be instructed to interview their parents on definitions of human rights as a beginning research project and a way to connect the ideas of the lessons to their lives.
- These procedures have been selected to reflect a pedagogy of experiential and cooperative education methods that emphasizes teaching human rights by modeling a respect for student's human rights in the classroom. The combination of visual, auditory, participatory, and kinesthetic approaches is designed to reach as many different "learning-types" as possible.

Preliminary Observations
- Start out as specifically as possible, with situations relating to the students' lives. Make global connections where you can, but do not push those connections on students. The teacher needs to be sensitive to the realities of the students and the possibilities that they themselves may suffer from lack of care or abuse.
- Be prepared for questions of gender and race to arise, along with possible resentment toward you and among students.
- Know your students. Who are they? Where do they come from? What is it like for them when they go home at night? How do they view you?
- Early adolescents' concepts of human rights may often be rooted in a very two-sided analysis of basic questions of "good" and "evil." Often their conclusions are based solely on their personal experiences and how they are treated. Teacher input is required, focusing evaluation of information based on wider and more reasoned reflections such as, "How can we use this information? What does it mean in your daily life?"
- Establish with the class why it is important to care about and respect others, and make that point the focus for all discussion and activities. Emphasize how listening is one way of caring.
- As teacher, keep in mind the interaction of attitude and circumstances: talking about human rights may bring up painful connections in your students' lives. How can you accept and acknowledge the reality of those circumstances and also offer a sense of hope, a way for them to deal with those circumstances so they can fulfill their potential as individuals as well as be connected to their immediate community and the broader human society?
- Take a long hard look at your own life: your attitudes, advantages, values, how you believe you became who you are, got where you are. What is your sense of responsibility to yourself and the human community which surrounds you, and how did this sense develop?

Exercises to relax the students and tap into their creative energies. Start each lesson with some exercises. The two described here are samples of various possibilities.

Loosening-up exercise. A leader stands in front of the group so all can see him or her, and begins to make movements and sounds—simple at first, more varied as the exercise progresses—which others in the group attempt to imitate, thus achieving the same energy level. Easy starters are stretching movements; using background music helps. Move from fairly safe to sillier, bolder movements (such as making faces, animal sounds, and the like). This is a bit like "Simon Says" but the movements are more active and flowing, and should build up in a way that stimulates circulation and raises the energy level.

Mirror exercise. This exercise involves two or more people mirroring or copying each other's movements and sounds. Start in pairs and expand to the whole group by combining pairs. Each person is leader and follower, and thus all have to work out a pattern of cooperation among themselves and develop sensitivity to each other if the exercise is to come off. People often find it easiest to start off with one person taking the initiative, with one movement leading into the next, letting the movements rather than the people lead. The key to developing such a flow is for partners not to focus on the parts of the body that may be moving, but to look into each other's eyes. Though the exercise is difficult to describe, in practice it is clear to the partners when the mirror works spontaneously.

LESSON ONE
Objectives
- to introduce the importance of cooperative learning and learning as dialogue;
- to establish an atmosphere of trust and creativity in the group;
- to outline and explore the direction of the lessons to follow by creating an experiential base for the group to work from.

Materials. Puppets or materials for making puppets

Learning Sequence

Step 1. Ask why (if) class members think the issue of human rights is important; make web drawing of their answers on blackboard.

Step 2. Use brainstorming to web class ideas of (a) definitions of human rights; (b) important questions of human rights on large sheets of newsprint (to be saved for comparison at end of lesson five).

Step 3. Engage the class in a version of the "loosening up" acting exercise (see above) to prepare them for puppet work.

Step 4. Engage the class in a version of the "mirror" exercise (see above) to help them experience the development of ideas as a synthesis that develops from relationships between learners, where no one is really the "leader." (Teacher participation in these exercises will aid in overcoming any possible embarrassment students may feel as well as model the concept of learning as dialogue.)

Step 5. Using assorted clean socks, sock puppets, or puppets made by students if possible, introduce students to puppets as a way of role playing. (Directions for making puppets can be found in Courtaney Brooks, *Plays and Puppets and Etcetera* (Claremont, CA: Belnice Books); see Chapter 7.

Step 6. Using puppets, enact a skit about a tyrant or bully, such as an unfair teacher or a student who abuses others.

Step 7. Discuss how this exercise illustrates violations of the human rights brainstormed earlier and how students felt during the exercise. Emphasize ways in which the human dignity of some of those portrayed in the skit may have been violated.

LESSON TWO

Objectives

- to illuminate class definitions of human rights with international standards and explore how ideas of human rights interact with the reality of limited material resources;
- to connect concepts of rights and responsibilities.

Materials. Copies of the Universal Declaration of Human Rights. (See Appendix for an excerpted version and Sample 16, Handout # 1 for a simplified version. Select one to be used as a handout.)

Learning Sequence

Step 1. Repeat "loosening up" exercise with a student leader.

Step 2. Repeat "mirror" exercise, expanding to groups.

Step 3. Discuss class ideas of what "values" are. Do we all have values? Where do our values come from? (Be prepared with your own summary of what values are to help give some direction to the discussion.)

Step 4. Review the Universal Declaration of Human Rights, emphasizing understanding the concepts and the values reflected in the Declaration.

Step 5. To help place the Universal Declaration within the context of the students' lives, do some role playing. Have students work in pairs to role play a time they felt their rights were violated. Have them play themselves and the one or ones who violated their rights, thinking about how the other person involved in the situation might have felt, and why. This means each pair does four role plays: two for each partner, so the person whose situation it is gets to play each side. To begin, partners must explain the details of the incidents to each other, then "script" them into role plays. If time allows, partners present role plays to the group, which can give feedback on what they think caused the conflicts involved.

Step 6. This exercise brings students back to the idea of human rights as relationships which may involve conflict. To focus on positive change, after the first round of role plays have students go back into their pairs and think about ways they could have helped the situation turn out positively, so that the human rights of all involved would have been more respected. Have them try role-playing both sides again, testing their vision of how it could have been changed.

Step 7. Teacher input to help explain that in practice there are two levels of human rights, human rights as defined by laws and general standards, as well as human rights in the sense of interactions that happen between individual persons, can help to clarify for students the possibilities and limits of the control they can have over perceived oppression in their own lives.

Step 8. So that students feel empowered rather than powerless, it is vital to emphasize how they can make things better in individual interactions and how they can work in groups for systemic change that protects and fosters human rights. The situations they bring up may not have easy immediate solutions—be prepared for cases as diverse as not wanting to do the family dusting to stories of police abuse.

LESSON THREE

Objective. Students will develop their own group consensus-based standards of human rights, informed by the standards they have learned about.

Learning Sequence

Step 1. Introduce this lesson by telling the students that the class will explore how they might apply what they have been learning about human rights to their own lives.

Step 2. New groups again; "loosening up" exercise again; "mirror" exercise again.

Step 3. Have the groups imagine each has the job of planning the rules for the global community; they must develop a document of human rights—with the provision that they do not know what they will be in the community (they don't know their gender, race, religion, country, economic status).

Step 4. Review the concept of "standards" and summarize the group's definition of what a "standard" is. Then have each group write its standards down, along with an explanation of how they expect to make those standards work on a practical level. Create a puppet show or role play drama which will express those standards in action to the rest of the class.

LESSON FOUR

Objective. To pull experiences together in the culminating activities of puppet show presentations and group consensus decisions on standards of human rights.

Learning Sequence

Step 1. Begin this lesson by raising the following questions.

Are the questions we've been exploring easy questions? Why or why not? How do we feel about human rights after trying to imagine a fair system of standards without knowing our own roles in the community? What does it mean to "be human"?

Step 2. Form the same groups.

Step 3. Start with "loosen up" and "mirror."

Step 4. Provide brief rehearsal and organizing time for puppet presentations.

Step 5. Puppet presentations, illustrating the human rights standards devised by the class members.

Step 6. Class combines standards presented to form a whole-class document created by consensus decision making. If class members are not familiar with consensus decision-making, explain. In consensus, group decisions are reached by democratic, respectful discussion. There is no voting. A chairperson can help make sure everyone has at least one chance to give input on the questions, and the decision reached must be acceptable to everyone in the group. The key to consensus is that the group stays focused on achieving the task, and that individual members, unless they feel very strongly about an issue and can explain why to the group, should ask themselves how important the point is and whether they can live with the decision of the group, even if it is not the exact decision they would have made.

Step 7. Class compares this document to original web chart from Lesson One and to the Universal Declaration of Human Rights, and discusses what it is that accounts for the similarities and differences.

Step 8. Conclusion. Discuss how awareness of issues is the first step to action, and explore what the ideas of human rights and global standards mean in their lives.

Ninth Grade. An Appreciation of Civil and Political Rights

As previously pointed out, the Western tradition of human rights has emphasized on civil and political rights. This resource takes a holistic approach centered in the fundamental value of human dignity, and holds all rights in inseparable relationship to that value. At times, however, particular aspects of human rights need to be the focus of attention. Two of the core principles of this book, preparation for global citizenship and the human value of freedom, both call for some such special focus on civil and political rights.

Political freedom and democracy have inspired some of the major recent changes within nations and in the international system, much of them impelled by citizen action and popular movements. Citizens' organizations have become a significant factor in both national and international politics. Organizations dedicated to the universal realization of human rights and freedom are among the most active and significant of these bodies, many of which are international in scope and operation. Such organizations have been the main factor in focusing world-wide public attention on human rights issues and problems. Thus their activities should be included in curricula on civil and political rights. Such organizations are also rich sources of information for curricular purposes. They also offer an opportunity for students to become involved in actual efforts to enhance the cause of human rights. (See Chapter 7 for a list of such organizations.)

Ninth graders have reached a level of development at which they are able to consider political aspects of social issues, and should be encouraged to reflect on political responsibility and the essential features of democracy. Some of them have already become active in various public issues and causes, and in the advocacy of democratic schools and student rights. The extracts adapted from Lori Martin's lesson plans that follow can help to extend such interest.

The unit Martin designed for her Tampa, Florida, ninth grade science class encourages reflection on political freedom and the characteristics of a democratic society. It is significant that such a unit was prepared for a science class. It reflects the growing emphasis on social responsibility among some science educators. Its general goals are to offer students an opportunity to perceive the contrasts between freedom and oppression and to learn about one of the most successful human rights organizations, Amnesty International, dedicated to obtaining the freedom of "prisoners of conscience." Specific objectives and materials are listed for the following lessons, designed for ten class periods.

LESSON THEME. A Day of Restricted Freedom

Learning Objectives. Students will:
- list rights and freedoms they may take for granted;
- compare life in Orzabalia to life in their own country;
- compare life in Orzabalia to life in other countries;
- develop a list of what they believe to be fundamental political rights.

Materials
- Handout #1. Proclamation of Public Order of the Republic of Orzabalia
- Optional, U.S. Declaration of Independence

Learning Sequence

Step 1. Day 1. Distribute the Proclamation of Public Order (Handout #1) and introduce students to a hypothetical country where they will be "living" for the next two weeks of class. Explain that over a century ago the Republic of Orzabalia became independent from the European country that had held it as a colony for about 200 years. Since that time its history has been one of struggle both among factions of the powerful ruling class, and between the ruling class and the poor peasants and factory workers, most of whom are descendants of the indigenous people who inhabited the area before European colonization. Several years ago a group of army officers took over the country, claiming that a disastrous civil war would destroy the country if they did not maintain public order. They established martial law upheld by the Proclamation of Public Order. Explain that, in fact, many former colonial countries came under military rule in the mid-century decades following World War II.

Step 2. Day 1. Announce that all class members are now students in this country and are to try to describe a typical day in Orzabalia. To do so they must familiarize themselves with the regulations of public order. Ask individual students to read the Proclamation aloud paragraph by paragraph. Ask the students to reread and think about the Proclamation in preparation for the next class.

Step 3. Day 2. Working in cooperative learning groups of four to six, students sketch one day's activities in their own lives and events in their town under the Proclamation. Circulate, checking the day's events, alerting students to any violations of the regulations of public order.

Step 4. Day 3. After all the groups have sketched out a full day's schedule, hold a class discussion, based on such questions as:
>   Was it difficult to outline a typical day? Why?
>   How do you feel about the experience?
>   What obstacles to "normal" life did you encounter?
>   What would you miss most if you had to live in a "police" state?
>   What reasons might the authorities of Orzabalia give for the restrictions imposed for "public order"?

Do you ever feel restricted or confined in your own lives? What reasons are you given for these restrictions?

Compare these reasons. Which seem reasonable or justifiable? On what grounds?

Step 5. Day 4. Working in the same groups, students are to compile a list of the unjust restrictions of freedoms they find in Orzabalia. Next they are to devise a list of what they believe to be the freedoms no one should be denied.

When the lists are completed, have each group read and explain its list of unjust restrictions. Do such restrictions exist or have they recently existed in some actual countries?

Next have each group read its list of basic freedoms. Why are these basic? Which of these freedoms are encoded in the laws of their country?

Note: Some students may include here a reading of the bill of particulars of the Declaration of Independence as the basis for a discussion of the claims of injustice made by the American colonists in declaring independence from England.

LESSON THEME. Fundamental Rights and Freedoms

Learning Objectives. Students will:
* summarize basic human rights and freedoms articulated by the international standards set forth in the Universal Declaration of Human Rights and the International Covenant on Civil and Political Rights;
* summarize the rights of children set forth in the Convention on the Rights of the Child;
* compare the international standards to their own lists of rights, and if the teacher so decides, the United States Bill of Rights.

Materials (see Chapter 7)
* Universal Declaration of Human Rights (see Appendix and Sample 16, Handout #2); Convention on the Rights of the Child (see Appendix); International Covenant on Civil and Political Rights (available from the United Nations, see Chapter 7; a simplified list might be prepared by the teacher)
* Comparison retrieval charts (see directions below)
* Optional, U.S. Bill of Rights

Learning Sequence. Explain that political freedom relates to participation in public affairs and government. Together they are the basis of democracy. Distribute or have students make comparison retrieval charts. Across the top of the chart the three human rights documents (perhaps four including the Bill of Rights) are noted. Along the sides, note such political rights as
* freedom of assembly
* freedom of religion
* freedom of expression
* freedom of political belief
* the right to vote
* the right to a fair trial
* the right to leave and return to your country
* freedom from arbitrary arrest

Step 1. Day 5. Distribute the Declaration and Conventions, and review the major articles dealing with political rights. The review is then summarized and students fill in the comparison retrieval charts with the relevant articles from each set of standards, adding rights identified in the review of the standards. Keep the charts for future reference.

Step 2. Day 6. Reconstitute the cooperative learning groups. Ask students to take out the lists they previously developed and compare them to the international standards. Are there rights on their lists that should be added to those enumerated by the standards? Which rights of the international standards are violated in Orzabalia? Be sure to review the Declaration, the Covenant, and the Convention. You might also discuss here how the U.S. Bill of Rights responded to the injustices noted in the Declaration of Independence.

Step 3. Day 7. Summary class discussion:
- What were rights common to all your lists?
- Are all people everywhere entitled to these rights?
- How can we guarantee that all rights are not violated?
- Should the people of other countries be concerned about situations like that in Orzabalia?
- Should children or any human group have particularly specified rights? If so, why and on what basis should the rights be specified?

LESSON THEME. Action for Human Rights

Learning Objectives. Students will:
- describe the purposes of such organizations as Amnesty International;
- discuss the role of Amnesty International and define "prisoner of conscience";
- interpret song lyrics on issues of human rights;
- orally express what they've learned this week;
- if they choose, write letters on behalf of Amnesty International "prisoners of conscience."

Materials
- Audio tapes of songs of social justice and human rights; videotape of Amnesty International Rock Concert
- Pamphlets and flyers on Amnesty International; various issues of student versions of Amnesty's "Urgent Action" notices (see Chapter 7 for address)

Learning Sequence

Step 1. Day 8. Have students bring in tapes of human rights music to present to the class. Each cooperative learning group is to introduce one song, explain what human rights issue it is about, and offer an interpretation of the lyrics. Have the students discuss what effect they believe the song has or could have on public opinion about the issue.

Step 2. Days 8 and 9. Distribute materials describing the work of Amnesty International and assign it for home work. The following day hold a discussion on Amnesty's purposes and how the organization goes about achieving them. Ask the students to reflect upon the concepts of social responsibility that underlies this work. (Some teachers may want to provide information about more than one human rights organization. The list in Chapter 7 can be consulted to select the other agencies.)

Step 3. Day 9. Show selected portions of the Amnesty International rock concert video. Hold a discussion similar to that about the audio tapes. Also discuss the purposes, values, and motivations of the performers who participated in the concert.

Step 4. Day 10. Form cooperative learning groups and distribute the "Urgent Action Notices." Have the groups discuss the case described in their "Urgent Action Notice." Identify the human rights violated in the cases of these "prisoners of conscience" and draft a letter, a copy of which each student will send on behalf of the prisoner to the officials cited in the notice. Some may want to join Amnesty and keep the class informed on the outcome of their cases and further cases.

Optional. A full-length film entitled *Forgotten Prisoners,* available in video stores, provides a good overview and introduction to Amnesty International. Selected portions could be shown for discussion in one period or the entire film could be shown over several class periods. Amnesty International also distributes several shorter videos. Other full-length films relevant to this unit are *The Handmaid's Tale, Animal Farm, 1984,* and those listed in Chapter 7 under "Political Repression."

Sample 19, Handout 1.
Proclamation of Public Order of the Republic of Orzabalia

By order of the Council of Public Security charged with the maintenance of public order and the welfare of the Citizens of the Republic of Orzabalia, the following regulations are proclaimed to be in effect as of the publication of this proclamation. Any infractions of these regulations will result in the immediate arrest and detention of the violator. Persons arrested and detained will be brought before a closed session of the Tribunal for Public Order, which will take action appropriate to the severity of the offense. There may be no appeals to higher tribunals of any cases involving infractions or violations of the Regulations of Public Order.

> General Felix L. Chien
> President of the Republic and
> Commander of the Armed Forces

I. Law and Civil Order

• The Constitution of the Republic of Orzabalia is hereby suspended for the period of this civil emergency. The current regulations will serve in place of the Constitution.

• The civil emergency will remain in effect until such time as the Council of Public Security deems the emergency to have passed.

• All representative governing bodies are hereby adjourned, to be resumed after national elections, the dates and procedures for which will be announced by the Council of Public Security under the authority of the President of the Republic and the Commander of the Armed Forces. The Council shall henceforth be the ruling civil authority of the Republic until the reconvening of the representative governing bodies, following the national elections.

II. State Security

• For the security of the state and its citizens, all citizens will be issued official identification papers, civil activity papers, and area permits. Citizens may engage in only those activities authorized by their papers. Persons may not leave the municipal areas designated by their permits without authorization from the Council of Public Security's respective precinct office. All papers and permits must be carried at all times. Citizens are reminded that their individual security, the security of their families, and that of their residential communities depends upon strict adherence to these and all security regulations subsequently declared by the Council to be enforced by the Precinct Office Police.

• A curfew will be in effect from 9:00PM to 6:00AM for all citizens over 21 years of age; and from 6:00PM to 8:00AM for all minors, except children under 12 accompanied by their parents.

• School buildings, universities, museums, theatres, places of worship, and all assembly halls will close daily no later than 5:00PM. During open hours security and order in all such public places will be maintained by the Precinct Office Police.

• Citizens may not possess or carry any form of weapon, firearm, tool, or appliance that may serve as a weapon. All such items must be immediately surrendered to the Public Security Precinct Offices. Weapons necessary to the responsibilities of Public Security Precinct Office police and military personnel will be issued by the state. Infractions of the weapons regulations, a severe threat to public security, may call for invoking the death penalty.

• Documents for travel inside and outside the country will be issued for the extent of the time and distance of the travel and are to be returned to the Public Security Precinct Office upon return. Travel documents will be issued only for emergency purposes for periods no longer than two weeks.

• Meetings of more than four persons may be held only by permit in places designated for this purpose.

• No more than four non-residents, including minors, may be in any residence without a permit at any time. Persons intending to entertain, consult professionals, receive condolence visits, or otherwise admit more than four non-residents to their homes shall apply to their Public Security Precinct Office at least 24 hours in advance for the required permit.

III. Information and Communication

• An Information Media Office has been established by the Council for Public Security. This office will be responsible for the editing and publishing of the *Daily Paper*, formerly edited by the staff of the World News Syndicate. All other newspaper licenses have been suspended until further notice from the Council.

• The radio station and television channel of the National Network are now under the management of the Information Media Office. All other broadcasting licenses have been suspended. The National Network Radio will broadcast programs from

7:00AM to 8:30PM and the television channel will transmit from 7:00PM to 9:00PM. Music and emergency announcements will be broadcast by radio on a 24-hour basis.

•   The Council has established the Truth Publishing House to publish all hard cover, paperback, and text books. All other publishing firms have suspended operation.

•   The Information Media Office will supervise the Ministry of Education and control curriculum content and teaching procedures.

IV. Public Services and Public Morality.

[As a possible additional activity students could draft sections IV, V, and VI of the Proclamation.]

V. Criminal Procedures

VI. Social Benefits and Economy Regulations

Ninth Grade. Recognizing Responsibility—Protecting Human Rights

As students begin to undertake the academic responsibilities of secondary school education, they might also be introduced to the responsibilities of global citizenship. The study of the possibilities for remediation of human rights violations and strategies for prevention of violations are excellent vehicles for this purpose. They could learn about actions on behalf of human rights, and how the rights defined by the Universal Declaration of Human Rights have been successfully claimed and defended. Such study could include actions and institutions ranging from individual acts of challenge to oppressive authority and courage in the face of severe violations, to international legal agreements and systems for the protection of human rights. Students should learn that everyone can contribute to the protection and fulfillment of human rights. Violators of human rights can be held accountable before the law, and victims can appeal to a range of organizations and processes. Citizens movements, actions, and the legal standards they have helped produce constitute the history of the struggle for human rights.

Teachers will find a succinct overview of the legal institutional possibilities in the protection and fulfillment of human rights in "A Guide to U.N. Human Rights Machinery" (pp. 20–21) and "Regional Human Rights Systems" by Patricia Mische (pp. 22–25), both in *Breakthrough* (Winter/Spring 1989). These articles, at least, should be read as teacher preparation for this and similar units. They might also be used for student material at the senior high school level. For the junior high level one resource now out of print, *The Struggle for Human Rights* (1977), designed some years ago, is still relevant to curricular needs and extracts are presented here as Handouts #1 and #2.

Knowledge of the historical origins of human rights is important to understanding the human rights movement as a dynamic, living human endeavor. The teaching of history can be greatly enlivened by the study of the conceptualization of and struggle for human rights.

Learning Objectives. Students will:
- review the evolution of national and international legal protections of human rights;
- reflect on the processes of social change and citizens movements that have resulted in these protections;

• assess the current state of human rights abuses and protections in various parts of the world.

Materials
• Handout #1, The Struggle for Human Rights
• Handout #2, Landmarks in the Struggle for Human Rights
• Optional, Handout #2 from Sample 17, Moral Exclusion
• Optional, Universal Declaration of Human Rights (see Appendix or Sample 16, Handout #2)
• Optional, U.S. Declaration of Independence

Learning Sequence

Step 1. Provide the students with Handouts #1 and #2 and assign them for homework. Then ask:
• What are the major principles and concepts of rights noted in the Declaration of Independence?
• What is the International Bill of Rights and what categories of rights does it seek to protect?
• What seems to be the historic scope of the development of human rights standards? Have individual students or teams research and report on each of the developments in the chronology from 1215 to 1948.

Step 2. Pose for discussion the following questions:
• Why would a government, even though it had signed human rights covenants, place its "national interests" above them?
• What advantage is there in trying to get nations to sign such covenants? Might there be any dangers involved in signing such covenants? If so, what might they be?
• What are the strengths and weaknesses of international laws to protect human rights? Explain your reasoning.

Step 3. Pose for discussion the following questions:
• What makes it possible for some people to violate the human rights of others? (Here the teacher might refer to moral exclusion and make use of Handout #2 from Sample 17. Handout #1 from Sample 17 can also be used to extend this inquiry with further background on discrimination.)
• In what ways have the laws of the United States or other countries been used to guarantee human rights? Have there been cases of unequal treatment under the law?

Step 4. Explain that many people in the United States now claim that their rights are not fully guaranteed. Then suggest some of the following research activities.
• Which United Nations covenants and conventions on human rights has the United States ratified? What are the reasons for failure to ratify certain of them? Write to U.S. Department of State, 2201 C Street, NW, Washington, DC 20520. Also write to the office of the United States Representative to the United Nations, 799 United Nations Plaza, New York, NY 10017.

- Where do your own representatives in the Senate stand on ratification? Write to your Senators at the United States Senate, Washington, DC, 20510.
- If you are a citizen of a country other than the United States, which UN covenants on human rights has your country ratified? If your nation has failed to ratify certain ones, what are the reasons? Write to your foreign minister and to your UN representative. (U.S. students might also research other countries.)
- Which nations have ratified the UN covenants and conventions on human rights? Write to the UN Human Rights Commission, Economic, and Social Council, 799 United Nations Plaza, NY 10017. Who is working for the ratification of human rights conventions? Write to some of the groups listed in Chapter 7. Ask each to state its purpose and the conditions which make its work necessary.

Step 5. Have the students:
- Start a human rights file or perhaps a bulletin board with one section for each continent. Divide each section into two parts: "Protection" and "Violation."
- Under each heading, place magazine and newspaper clippings that give examples of the protection and violation of human rights in that part of the world. For each clipping, note which rights from the Universal Declaration and the covenants and conventions are concerned. If you can, investigate the newspapers and magazines of other countries for different viewpoints on what is happening.
- At the end of a month, make an assessment of how well each area seems to be doing. You might want to continue this project for a number of months.

Step 6. Concluding discussion. Pose the following questions:
- What seems to be the state of human rights in the world today?
- What are the most encouraging initiatives and actions for the protection and fulfillment of human rights?
- What actions might you as an individual or we as a class take toward achieving a world in which human rights are truly respected?

Sample 20, Handout 1.
The Struggle for Human Rights

What Are Human Rights?

Rights are conditions or powers to which people are entitled by law or custom.

The first ten amendments to the United States Constitution, the Bill of Rights, are examples. The rights listed in this document are protected by law.

The Universal Declaration of Human Rights is another list of rights. It is not, however, a legally guaranteed list. Instead, it is a statement of belief. The members of the United Nations believe that certain rights and freedoms are worth protecting because their guarantee will help produce a better kind of world. The Declaration lists some thirty rights that the drafters hoped to have universally recognized and protected. The member nations of the United Nations have "pledged" to try to "promote respect" for these rights and freedoms and eventually "to secure their universal and effective recognition and observance."

Can Laws Protect Human Rights?

Rights can be and often are violated. During the past two hundred years many people have worked to have certain rights guaranteed by law. Handout #2 lists important landmarks in the struggle to guarantee human rights by law.

During the last part of the eighteenth century, two very important revolutions took place in the Western world—the American and the French. In both instances, a large number of people felt that they were oppressed, that their rights were being denied, and that the laws of the time were against them rather than for them.

The American revolutionaries, out of "a decent respect for the opinions of mankind," stated their ideas about government and rights very clearly in the Declaration of Independence. They declared that "All men are created equal," have certain "unalienable rights"—rights that cannot be taken from them. These rights, however, were seen at the time as pertaining only to white men, not to *all* men and women.

Then the Declaration stated: "To secure these Rights, governments are instituted among men" [sic]. Thus, according to the signers of the Declaration of Independence, a purpose of government is to protect human rights, and as the constitutional history of the United States unfolded, to extend equal rights to all.

Adapted with permission from Jack R. Fraenkel, Margaret Carter, and Betty Reardon, *The Struggle for Human Rights* (New York: Random House, 1976), pp. 13–23.

The colonists explained why they revolted against Great Britain. They said that if a government didn't assure human rights—or didn't enforce them—then the people could "alter or abolish" the government. This they claimed as "the right of revolution."

This idea has been very significant in many of the revolutions that have taken place during the nineteenth and twentieth centuries. A number of revolutionaries in other lands have modeled their own statements of purpose on the Declaration of Independence.

The new government established in 1789 guaranteed that, in the United States, certain human rights would be protected by law. In the same year the French Declaration of the Rights of Man and Citizen stated that the purpose of "all political organizations" was the assurance of human rights.

With the ratification in 1791 of the first ten amendments to the U.S. Constitution, the Bill of Rights became part of the law of the land. It specifies particular rights that the federal government must assure. In spite of such legal guarantees, however, many groups of Americans have felt obliged to protest on behalf of their own rights. These groups include Catholics, Jews, Italian Americans, African Americans, Native Americans, refugees, factory workers, women, disabled people, homosexuals, and many other groups.

In the eighteenth century, the American colonists believed that the right to abolish an unjust government was so important that they went to war to establish a more just government. In today's era of nuclear arms, nerve gas, and biological weapons, war is so potentially disastrous that it could destroy humankind. Highjackings, sabotage, and acts of political terrorism have produced an increased fear of violence.

Many people today believe, therefore, that violence is not the most reasonable way to exercise or achieve rights. The Universal Declaration says it is essential "that human rights be protected by the rule of law." Otherwise human beings would be forced, as a last resort, to seek "rebellion against tyranny and oppression."

Laws can be used badly or well. They do not necessarily guarantee that rights will be protected. In fact, laws can be passed which restrict people's rights.

Can Treaties Protect Human Rights?

In 1948 the United Nations General Assembly approved the Universal Declaration of Human Rights as a statement of goals. This Declaration was intended as the first stage of an "international bill of rights." All member nations promised to work toward the fulfillment of these rights.

In 1966 the General Assembly adopted two "covenants" as the second stage in the international protection of human rights. The covenants became international law in 1976 after 35 nations ratified or agreed to them. The purposes of these covenants are to describe specific human rights more clearly, and to get governments to agree to provide for the legal protection of these rights.

A covenant is a formal agreement between two or more parties. It is a form of treaty, and therefore part of the body of international law. When a government agrees to a treaty, it promises to observe its provisions. For instance, trade treaties set forth the terms or rules under which the nations involved will trade with one another. Treaties, however, are different from laws governing nations within their own borders. There is no world executive or police force to enforce a treaty or any other kind of international law. Nations obey international law only if they wish to. They cannot be forced to do so. There is nothing to prevent national governments from interpreting international law in ways to suit their own purposes. (For those interested in a perspective that envisions international law as enforcible by consensual agreement of the international community we recommend Roger Fisher's "Bringing Law to Bear on Governments" in *The Conquest of War*, ed. H. B. Hollins (Boulder, CO: Westview Press, 1989).

Even after ratification by 35 nations, it may still be difficult to enforce the two human rights covenants adopted by the UN General Assembly in 1966 and the other conventions adopted since then.

One of these is the International Covenant on Economic, Social, and Cultural Rights. The rights in this covenant cover jobs, working conditions, and opportunities to develop skills and choose one's own occupation. The second is the International Covenant on Civil and Political Rights. This is quite similar to the United States Bill of Rights.

These two covenants and others are international law. But some nations have placed their own government's interest above the rights protected in the covenants, and interpreted these covenants to suit themselves.

Human rights, then, are frequently violated. At present not even one human right—not even the right to life—is universally guaranteed. Whether any human rights will eventually be universally protected depends on all of us and the kind of world we want to live in. It depends on the ideas we have as to what is important, on what we value.

Sample 20, Handout 2.
Landmarks in the Struggle for Human Rights

1215   Magna Carta (England)

1689   Bill of Rights (England)

1776   Declaration of Independence (U.S.)

1789   Declaration of the Rights of Man and Citizens (France)

1791   Bill of Rights (first ten amendments to the U.S. Constitution)

1832   Reform Bills of 1832, 1867, and 1884 (England, extension of voting rights)
–1884

1861   Edict of Emancipation (Russia, frees serfs)

1865   Thirteenth, Fourteenth, Fifteenth Amendments to the U.S. Constitution
–1870   (abolish slavery and grant citizenship rights to former slaves)

1920   Nineteenth Amendment to the U.S. Constitution (gives women the right
       to vote)

1945   Charter of the United Nations (reaffirms faith in fundamental human
       rights)

1948   Universal Declaration of Human Rights adopted by UN General Assembly
       (declares that human rights are integral to peace)

1948   International Convention on the Prevention and Punishment of the Crime
       of Genocide adopted by UN General Assembly

1950   European Convention for the Protection of Human Rights and
       Fundamental Freedoms

1955   African Freedom Charter declared by the African National Congress

1959   European Commission of Human Rights established (under Convention for
       the Protection of Human Rights and Fundamental Freedoms)

1960   Inter-American Commission on Human Rights established by Organization
       of American States

1965   International Convention on the Elimination of All Forms of Racial
       Discrimination adopted by UN General Assembly

1966   International Covenant on Economic, Social, and Cultural Rights and
       International Covenant on Civil and Political Rights adopted by UN General
       Assembly

1967   American Convention on Human Rights adopted by Organization of
       American States

1970   UN Economic and Social Council asserts the right of the UN Human Rights
       Commission to hear and act on complaints by individuals of violations of
       the Universal Declaration of Human Rights

1973   UN Human Rights Commission issues draft convention designating
       apartheid as a "crime against humanity"

	1976	International Convention on the Suppression and Punishment of the Crime of Apartheid adopted by UN General Assembly
	1979	Convention on the Elimination of All Forms of Discrimination Against Women adopted by UN General Assembly
	1979	Declaration of the Rights of the Child
142	1981	African Charter of Human and Peoples' Rights adopted by Organization of African Unity
	1983	Association of South East Asian Nations Declaration of the Rights of Peoples and States (drafted by group of nongovernmental organizations)
	1984	Convention Against Torture and Other Cruel, Inhuman, or Degrading Treatment or Punishment adopted by UN General Assembly
	1989	Convention on the Rights of the Child adopted by UN General Assembly

Chapter 6
Senior High School: Confronting the Problems, Taking Responsibility—Grades Ten to Twelve

The last years of secondary school are a time of passage from adolescence to young adulthood, and for most citizens the last years of formal education. It is thus essential that the curriculum of citizenship education in secondary schools include study of current issues and problems of human rights, policy debates about what constitutes a human right, action strategies for remediation and prevention of violations, and citizens' movements to arouse public awareness and bring about policy action in regard to specific problems and cases.

Adequate preparation for global citizenship also requires familiarity with the international human rights standards, the problems and principles which gave rise to them, and the machinery and processes which exist for their implementation. Direct action and experiential learning in relation to social justice and human rights issues and movements are advocated as part of the formal curriculum. Such experiential education could be conducted in cooperative efforts between schools and the agencies and organizations that protect and advocate human rights (see Chapter 7). The samples that follow attempt to provide some direction toward such curricular possibilities.

For a varied and overall coverage of human rights issues and topics in curriculum materials for the senior high school level, we recommend *Teaching Human Rights*. This extensive collection of well constructed and clearly described units written by David Shiman of the University of Vermont is available from the Center for Teaching International Relations, University of Denver (see Chapter 7).

Tenth Grade. Is There a Human Right to Food?

Senior high school should offer students opportunities to deal with issues related to controversies in human rights, and with questions related to rights in the process of being defined and recognized by national societies and the international community. Preparation for taking part in defining and recognizing rights should be a significant and essential component of education for global citizenship. The international standards in human rights education can be used to facilitate discussion and learning about those issues of meeting human needs not specifically established as rights. Hunger poses such an issue: there are differences of opinion on whether there is a human right to food, and if the existing international standards could be used to claim it.

As students come to the senior high school years they should be encouraged to consider ways in which the existing standards can be applied to further develop social conditions conducive to the achievement of social justice on a global scale, and reflect on whether the fulfillment of basic needs requires the formulation of new standards. The following unit developed by Debora St. Claire for use in her tenth grade class at the Satellite Academy in Brooklyn, New York provides such an opportunity. There is no more fundamental human need than that of nourishment adequate to maintaining life; hence the issue of whether access to food should be assured as a right is a significant area of inquiry for human rights education.

This unit combined with Lori Martin's lessons on political and civil rights provides a basis for learning about the "International Bill of Rights" comprised by the Universal Declaration of Human Rights, the International Covenant on Civil and Political Rights, and the International Covenant on Economic, Social, and Cultural Rights. Teachers may also wish to review Sample 13, which deals with hunger.

LESSON THEME. Human Needs and Human Rights

Learning Objectives. Students will:
- differentiate between "wants" and "needs";
- define "basic needs";
- determine how the international human rights standards address the issue of hunger.

Learning Sequence

Step 1. Needs Versus Wants

1.1. Needs. In order to get the students thinking about needs, the lesson begins with the motivating question, "What do you need?" The teacher may begin the interaction by stating one of her *needs* (a pencil, for instance) to prompt student responses. Responses are recorded on the board with the heading "Needs."

1.2. Wants. After a number of students have expressed their needs, the teacher moves on to "Wants," asking, "What do you want?" The teacher may then state that she *wants* a mechanical pencil. Note responses on the board.

1.3. Review the lists asking why each item is needed and why each is wanted. "What do the reasons tell us of the nature of needs and wants?"

1.4. Next, compare the two lists by asking for similarities and differences between them. The class then reviews the lists, determining which are truly "needs" and which are actually "wants." If necessary, reclassify some items.

1.5. Develop working definitions of "wants" and "needs."

1.6. Then discuss the question: Are basic human needs universal? What does "universal" mean? How can we judge what needs are and are not universal?

Step 2. Basic Needs

2.1. Brainstorm. "What do we need to survive?" Follow brainstorm format: individually for 2 minutes, and in pairs for 3 minutes. The teacher calls for responses and records all responses on the board.

2.2. Categorize the needs identified in terms of fundamental "survival needs" (food, shelter, clothing, health care) and "human needs" (such as relationships, security, respect).

2.3. Compare the survival needs with their previous list of needs. The teacher should elicit that the survival needs are those basic things that we need just to survive. This list should be labeled "Basic Needs."

2.4. Elicit a second list of what we need to be human, to feel like a person, to experience worth and dignity. Label the list "Human Needs."

2.5. Finally make a third list of "wants," items we believe will enhance the quality of our lives or increase our capacities to perform work and leisure activities. Do these wants affect needs in any way? How are the effects felt and by whom?

2.6. Class generates definitions of "Basic Needs," "Human Needs," and "Wants."

2.7. Discuss and compare responses to "What do we need to survive?" "What do we need to be human?" "Why is the distinction important?" Are basic or survival needs the same for people everywhere? How are human needs similar and different? Here reference to cultural differences could be noted.

2.8. Review: The teacher may ask, "What's the difference between a want and a need?" or "What are basic needs? What are the consequences of being deprived of basic needs?" Questioning along the line of, "Is everyone assured of having enough food? Should they be assured of this basic need?" will segue into the next portion of the unit.

2.9. Introduce the concept of rights as conditions or entitlements people should be able to realize in their own societies. If the students have not previously studied the origins and purposes of the Universal Declaration and the covenants, provide them with a brief overview.

LESSON THEME. Food as a Human Right

Learning Objectives. Students will:
- determine how the International Bill of Rights addresses the issue of hunger;
- use the International Bill of Human Rights to support an ethical argument for the right to food;
- take action in support of the right to food.

Materials
- Universal Declaration of Human Rights (see Appendix and Sample 16, Handout #2), International Covenant on Economic, Social, and Cultural Rights (available from the United Nations), Convention on the Rights of the Child (see Appendix). Simplified versions of these covenants and conventions are recommended for use in the senior high school grades; see Chapter 7 for sources.
- Retrieval chart entitled "Legal Standards Upholding the Right to Food," with a column for each of the international human rights instruments used in this unit. The teacher may provide these or have the students make them.

Learning Sequence

Step 1. Overview of the international standards

1.1. Provide each student with a retrieval chart for review and summary of the Universal Declaration of Human Rights, the Convention on Economic, Social, and Cultural Rights, and the Convention on the Rights of the Child; and simplified versions of these international instruments. See Samples 14 and 19 for suggestions for designing a retrieval chart.

1.2. Provide students with background on these documents, noting especially that the Conventions on Civil and Political Rights and on Economic, Social, and Cultural Rights are part of the body of international law, international legal standards designed to implement the purposes of the Universal Declaration of Human Rights. The Convention of the Rights of the Child has the same relationship to the Declaration on the Rights of the Child. Teachers who want to provide a chronology of the international standards will find one in Sample 20, Handout #2.

1.3. Divide the class into three groups. As a homework assignment each group is to study one convention and record on their retrieval charts by number and short quotations the articles and paragraphs that could be cited to support the argument that the right to food is stipulated or implied in the international standards. In preparation, it is important to point out the difference between a right's being stipulated or implied.

Step 2. Reviewing the International Bill of Rights and the Convention on the Rights of the Child

2.1. Ask the students to share the results of their homework and cite the specific articles of the Universal Declaration of Human Rights and the three conventions that may be related to the issue of food. In conducting this lesson, ask that they be sure their retrieval charts show these articles.

2.2. Review the articles in each document that might be cited to support the right to food as a human right. Students should discuss the articles by explaining how they might be interpreted to support this proposed right. Check retrieval charts to be sure all relevant articles are noted.

2.3. What arguments might they construct to make a case that access to sufficient amounts of nutritious food is a human right? Students might present these arguments in class as though before a governmental body that has the power to allocate public resources to provide food. What counter-arguments might they expect? What do they themselves believe? Do all agree? What differences of opinions are espoused by various class members? What reasons can they give for holding their respective opinions? Remember that if the right is to be upheld, a majority must agree, but some may continue to dissent. So long as they are based on clearly stated reasons, all opinions will be considered.

LESSON THEME. Taking Action to Support the Right to Food

Learning Objectives. Students will:
- review some obstacles to access to adequate food;
- apply international standards to these obstacles;
- undertake steps to encourage action to overcome the obstacles;
- assess their learnings in this exercise.

Learning Sequence

Step 1. Assessing Obstacles to the Right to Food

1.1. Organize the class into cooperative learning groups of three or four students. Each group is to identify or select from a list provided by the teacher a specific problem related to access to food, for which they must determine a range of possible consequences. They are to review their retrieval charts on the International Bill of Rights, then assess whether these consequences may constitute or contribute to a violation of any of the articles that can be interpreted to support claims to a right to food. When they find the potential consequences to be in violation of any of the articles identified, they are to compose a letter of appeal to an appropriate body or agency in which they cite the relevant international standards. Possible examples:
- Discontinuation of a local public school breakfast or hot lunch program. Appeal addressed to the school board.
- Limitation on food stamps that would deprive some people of adequate food. Appeals addressed to the relevant government agencies (researching public food assistance programs would be a constructive way in which to identify these agencies); to large food and grocery chain stores requesting they establish a policy for local distribution of remaindered food stock.
- The high cost and poor quality of food in low-income neighborhoods. Appeals to the appropriate representative to a local governmental body, citizens' organizations, and local markets, urging them to join together to change this situation.
- The closing of a nearby soup kitchen. Appeal to the kitchen organizers offering to provide assistance in fundraising and operating the kitchen.
- Famine conditions in an area of drought or war. Appeals to the Congress and the United Nations Food and Agriculture Organization, to the news media urging more coverage, to relevant relief agencies offering help in mailing and other fundraising and information campaigns.

Student letters should include statements describing the probable consequences of the situation, and make reference to the international standards of human rights to support their proposals and uphold the ethical argument they seek to make. They should also try to include some action they themselves might take.

1.2. An actual community problem of lack of access to adequate food among some individuals or groups may be used in place of any of these hypothetical examples. If such a problem is identified, students should be encouraged to reflect upon how the problem affects those who are thereby deprived, the community in general, and themselves.

Group work should be emphasized in this lesson so that the students work together toward the planning of solutions to the problem and actions they themselves might take to contribute toward a solution.

Step 2. Group Reports and Process Assessment

2.1. Each group should select a spokesperson to describe the problem with which they worked and read the draft of one of the group's letters, proposed solutions, and planned actions.

2.2. Each group should discuss their group's process and assess their own work:
- Describe how your group worked together.
- How did you plan the work and use the skills and talents of each group member?
- How would you do this differently if you were to do it again?
- What was your best idea or biggest problem in doing this assignment?

2.3. An alternative method of review and assessment might be to have all students write a process piece during the last five to seven minutes of the class that would describe their individual experiences with the assignment.

Tenth Grade. Actions for the Fulfillment of Human Rights

If history is to be taught so as to prepare students to be agents of historical change, then an historic approach to human rights should provide students with more than a chronology of events, declarations, and conventions. It should also offer accounts of the people and movements that brought about or responded to the events and those who developed and took action to establish the international human rights standards. Tenth grade students are but three years from voting age and at a stage of development at which social responsibility can and should be acted upon. Some may choose to volunteer with one of the human rights organizations listed in Chapter 7. Others may take part in an actual human rights campaign or event. All should be made aware that the history of human rights results from such actions as theirs.

The concept of human rights as an area of human endeavor characterized by courage, struggle, and exciting challenges can be demonstrated by cases and stories of individuals, organizations, and agencies that have made the history of human rights. These stories also illustrate a range of actions taken to overcome human rights violations and to try to bring about a society committed to the values of human dignity and integrity. The following unit offers such illustrations. It is adapted with permission from Jack B. Fraenkel, Margaret Carter, and Betty Reardon, *The Struggle for Human Rights* (New York: Random House, 1976), pp. 37–49.

Learning Objectives. Students will:
- review and discuss actions individuals can take on behalf of human rights;
- review and discuss examples of the efforts of citizens' organizations to reduce human rights abuses;
- review and discuss measures governments can enact to protect human rights;
- review and discuss possibilities for intergovernmental procedures to hold abusers of human rights accountable for the violations they commit.

Materials
- Handout #1, What Individuals Can Do: Rosa Parks
- Handout #2, What Private Groups Can Do
- Handout #3, What Government Agencies Can Do
- Handout #4, What International Organizations Can Do

LESSON THEME. Individual Action for Human Rights: The Rosa Parks Case

Step 1. Ask if some of the students have seen the film, *The Long Walk Home.* Explain that the historical case they are going to read is the actual background of that film. It should be emphasized that the film is a fictionalized version of the experiences of a black family and a white family during the Montgomery Bus Boycott of 1955–1956. Distribute Handout #1, "What Individuals Can Do." Allow class time to read it.

Step 2. To start discussion of the Montgomery Bus Boycott, have the students form small groups of four to six members to discuss the following questions:
- What do you think Rosa Parks might say if someone asked her to explain why she refused to move from her seat?
- What human rights were violated in this instance?
- What methods did Rosa Parks and others use to protect the rights of blacks in Montgomery?
- Do you consider these methods appropriate and effective? Why or why not?
- What other actions might individuals take on behalf of human rights?
- What actions could you yourself take?

Step 3. Have groups report their conclusions to the entire class.

Step 4. Optional. Show excerpts from *Eyes on the Prize* or otherwise review the U.S. Civil Rights Movement, including the writings of Martin Luther King and Malcolm X. Discuss the current state of racial justice in the United States.

LESSON THEME. What Organizations Can Do for Human Rights

Step 1. Distribute Handout #2, "What Private Groups Can Do," and assign it as homework.

Step 2. Organize small discussion groups to address the following questions:
- What effect do you believe the students' letters had on the East German government?
- What values did these students demonstrate?
- How would you explain the success of Amnesty's tactics?

Step 3. Have the groups list actions private agencies can take on behalf of human rights, then share the lists. From these actions have the class select a list of the three they think most effective. Then determine how the class members might contribute to such actions.

LESSON THEME. What Government Agencies Can Do for Human Rights

Step 1. Distribute Handout #3, "What Government Agencies Can Do." Allow class time to read it, or assign it as homework.

Step 2. Raise the following points for discussion:
- The Human Rights Commission of New York City is a governmental organization

charged with the protection of human rights. Can you think of some guidelines that this organization might use to determine whether a New York citizen's rights have been violated? Does our state, town, or city have its own bill of rights?

- Is there a human rights agency in this state, town, or city? If so, try to obtain information about the agency's activities to discuss in class. How can this class support or contribute to the work of that agency?

LESSON THEME. What International Organizations Can Do for Human Rights

Step 1. Distribute Handout #4, "What International Organizations Can Do," and allow class time to read it or assign it for homework.

Step 2. Raise the following points for class discussion:
- What do you think are the strengths and weaknesses of the European Commission? Of the Court?
- What methods was the Commission using to protect the human rights of Greek citizens? Do you consider these methods effective? Why or why not?
- What methods did the UN Human Rights Commission use to promote human rights in South Africa? Do you think this approach is effective? Why or why not?
- Do you agree with the reasons given by Britain and the United States for their votes against the Convention on Apartheid?

Step 3. Provide as a handout the list of human rights instruments and their ratifications (see Chapter 7) and have the students check which ones have been ratified to date by the United States and Britain. Consult the United Nations Human Rights Liaison Office for an update of the list (see Chapter 7 for address).

Step 4. Review the Human Rights Implementation Procedures Chart (See Chapter 7). Pose these questions:
- How might these procedures be improved?
- What machinery and procedures would you suggest for the enforcement of human rights conventions?

Step 5. Some teachers may want to review the texts of the declarations and conventions on racial discrimination, apartheid, torture, and political and civil rights.

Note. There are excellent films and documentaries on the historical events and human rights issues involved in the cases used in this sample. See Chapter 7 for a list of films.

Sample 22, Handout 1.
What Individuals Can Do: Rosa Parks

In today's complicated world, a single individual may feel powerless to achieve anything important. Yet it is amazing how much one person can do—if she or he is determined enough.

In the 1950s, African Americans who lived in the southern part of the United States lived under "Jim Crow" laws. These laws segregated "black" people from "white" people. Blacks were required by law to eat in separate restaurants, to go to separate schools, to drink from separate drinking fountains. In courtrooms they were required to swear oaths on separate Bibles.

Segregation was even evident on city buses. There were no black drivers. The white men who drove the buses often were polite to black passengers, but sometimes they were not. Many blacks reported paying their fare at the front door of the bus and then being told to reboard the bus at the rear door. It was not unusual for a bus driver to pull away before black passengers had time to reach the rear door.

Even when blacks did board a bus, they could not sit in certain seats labeled "whites only." Blacks could sit only in the rear section marked "colored." If the "whites only" section filled up, the drivers would ask black passengers to stand so that the white passengers could be seated. A black person who refused to stand up was arrested.

These were the conditions in Montgomery, Alabama on December 1, 1955, when Rosa Parks, a seamstress in a large department store in Montgomery, boarded a city bus and refused to give up her seat to a white person.

Parks was then arrested, fingerprinted, and charged with violating the city's segregation law.

When word of her arrest spread through the city, the black community began to act. Led by local college students and several ministers, including Martin Luther King, Jr. and Ralph Abernathy, blacks agreed to stay off the buses on the day of Parks's trial.

Thus began the action that became known as the Montgomery Bus Boycott. Black people stopped riding the city's buses. People organized car pools. Many walked great distances to work.

Because the bus company lost 65 percent of its business, it had to cut back its schedule and lay off drivers. Finally, buses stopped running entirely. The business

Excerpted with permission from Jack B. Fraenkel, Margaret Carter, and Betty Reardon, *The Struggle for Human Rights* (New York: Random House, 1976), pp. 37–38.

of white storekeepers suffered. The city of Montgomery had become a non-violent battleground for human rights.

In November 1956, the Supreme Court of the United States ruled that bus segregation violated the United States Constitution. The Montgomery bus company then agreed not only to end segregation but also to hire black drivers and treat all passengers with equal respect.

Sample 22, Handout 2.
What Private Groups Can Do

Most individuals, of course, do not act alone in the cause of human rights. Many join organizations to increase their effectiveness. There are many private groups devoted to problems of human rights, including organizations such as Amnesty International, Human Rights Watch, the American Civil Liberties Union, the National Council of Churches, and many others.

Sometimes groups of private citizens join together with similar groups in other nations to work on problems of common concern. Examples of such groups are the Boy Scouts, the World Council of Churches, and Amnesty International.

Amnesty International was founded to carry out some of the aims of the Universal Declaration of Human Rights, specifically Articles 5, 9, 18, and 19. The organization has official advisory status with UNESCO, the United Nations Human Rights Commission, the Organization of American States (OAS), and the Organization of African Unity (OAU). This status gives Amnesty the right to have its observers attend debates, and provides a direct channel for making its views known to these intergovernmental organizations.

Amnesty has thousands of members in many countries. They work for the release of "prisoners of conscience" in many parts of the world. Amnesty International defines prisoners of conscience as "individuals imprisoned for their political beliefs, religion, race, or ethnic background who have not used or advocated violence."

Amnesty International's research department tries to make sure that the persons they hope to help are really prisoners of conscience and not ordinary criminals.

Amnesty learns about prisoners of conscience mainly through newspapers, radio, and television. It also gets reports from exiles who have had to leave their own countries for political reasons, and from news reporters and travelers.

Most of the pressure exerted by Amnesty comes through private correspondence. Members of Amnesty constantly write letters and postcards to the officials of the government of a country holding a prisoner of conscience. They ask that the prisoner be set free or at least be given a fair trial or a reduced sentence. They try to continue this correspondence until they get some response.

Since governments may wish to forget their political prisoners, Amnesty constantly reminds them of the plight of these individuals. In addition, the prisoners often learn that they are not forgotten or abandoned by their fellow human beings.

Amnesty groups may publicly dramatize the cases of their "adopted" prisoners

Excerpted with permission from Jack B. Fraenkel, Margaret Carter, and Betty Reardon, *The Struggle for Human Rights* (New York: Random House, 1976), pp. 39–43.

through letters to the editor, fund-raising campaigns, appeals to embassies, cables to heads of state, or posters in airports. Sometimes Amnesty sends observers to investigate specific problems. In certain cases it may then submit reports to the United Nations or to other international bodies.

This sort of unofficial pressure by concerned persons has resulted in freeing many political prisoners and improving the situations of many more. Amnesty has worked on behalf of many thousand prisoners of conscience. At least half of these have been released from prison.

Sample 22, Handout 3.
What Government Agencies Can Do

A number of nations, states, and cities have established agencies to protect human rights. Here is an example of the actions of a local government agency.

New York, January 23, 1974

Mrs. Eleanor Holmes Norton,[1] chairman of the city's Human Rights Commission, disclosed yesterday that her agency had denied the Trans World Airlines request to reopen a 1969 case in which a former Jewish employee was awarded $11,899 after the agency found the airline had tolerated religious discrimination.

For 27-year-old Malcolm Rattner, the former employee and a Vietnam veteran, the "decision meant a lot to me."

Mr. Rattner, who now drives a taxi, said: "It means that no one can discriminate because of race, creed, or color, and that New York can be proud of its Human Rights Commission."

Mr. Rattner was dismissed as a TWA ramp handler on September 27, 1969, after 37 days of employment.

In speaking of her agency's action, Mrs. Norton said: "It is easy to believe anti-Semitism has been eliminated in America. This case demonstrates the need for continued vigilance."

The Human Rights Commission decision found that Mr. Rattner had suffered "humiliation, outrage, and mental anguish because of the discrimination." It also ruled that the airline had refused to give Mr. Rattner time off to observe Yom Kippur [the most sacred day in the Jewish calendar] and had failed to give him advance notice of his dismissal. The decision also detailed other anti-Semitic incidents directed against Mr. Rattner. (adapted from a report in the *New York Times*, January 23, 1974)

Excerpted with permission from Jack B. Fraenkel, Margaret Carter, and Betty Reardon, *The Struggle for Human Rights* (New York: Random House, 1976), pp. 43–47.
1. Students of the 1990s may be familiar with Norton, who became a radio commentator, a professor of law and a Congressional representative from Washington, DC.

Sample 22, Handout 4.
What International Organizations Can Do

International organizations are made up of representatives from many nations. One example is the *Organization of American States*, which deals with regional problems of Latin America. Another is the Organization of African Unity (OAU).

A number of nations in Western Europe have formed a regional organization called the Council of Europe. It seeks to protect the human rights of all people in the member nations. It does this through a Commission and a Court of Human Rights, assisted by a Committee of Ministers.

The Commission, composed of representatives of each nation, conducts investigations into alleged violations of human rights. Where actual violations have occurred, the Commission may make the results of its investigations public, as it did in the following instance that occurred in 1969.

London, November 28, 1969

The European Commission for Human Rights has concluded that Greece's military-backed government allowed torture of political prisoners and denied many fundamental human rights.

Its 1200-page report, the result of more than two years of investigation, found that torture and ill-treatment were "an administrative practice" that "was officially tolerated." It charged that Greek authorities had taken no effective steps to stop the practices.

The report represents the efforts of lawyers who took hundreds of hours of testimony and even traveled to Greece for on-the-scene investigations. Some have called their work the weightiest international legal inquiry since the Nuremberg trial of war criminals after World War II.

The report said that competent Greek authorities, "confronted with numerous and substantial complaints and allegations of torture and ill-treatment," failed to take any effective steps to investigate them or to insure remedies for "any such complaints or allegations found to be true."

Here is an excerpt from the testimony of Mrs. Anastasia Tsirka, taken from the Commission's report. Mrs. Tsirka was arrested by the Greek police at the time in connection with pamphlets considered "suspicious":

I say to them (the police), "I am going to have a baby."

They answer: "Who cares about that? It will be another person like you, it is better not to have it." . . .

[An official] ordered [a policeman] to give me 15 Falanga [blows on the soles of the feet] and he gave me 20, I counted, maybe it was not, 18 maybe 21, but it was more than 15. . . .

Excerpted with permission from Jack B. Fraenkel, Margaret Carter, and Betty Reardon, *The Struggle for Human Rights* (New York: Random House, 1976), pp.

I started to scream very loudly and they put a very dirty rag in my mouth to keep my mouth shut.

In 1974 the military dictatorship in Greece was replaced by a more democratic government.

The European Court of Human Rights hears only those cases which the Commission cannot resolve. Usually if the Commission cannot settle a case, it sends its findings and conclusions to the Committee of Ministers. The Committee then either gives the nation involved a chance to correct the violation before a public report is made or passes the case on to the Court.

The Court hears cases from or concerning nations. Individuals cannot submit an application to the Court (though they can to the Commission). Only those cases in which the nations involved have already agreed to accept the Court's jurisdiction are tried. When the Court does reach a decision, however, its decision is final and binding on the parties concerned. No appeal is permitted.

While organizations such as the Council of Europe concentrate their efforts in a single region, the United Nations and its agencies and commissions work throughout the whole world. The UN Human Rights Commission is one such organization. This Commission meets annually to review the status of human rights throughout the world. It has investigated such problems as apartheid and racism, rights of minorities, exploitation of foreign workers, and punishment of war criminals. Here is one example of the Commission's activities.

Geneva, April 2, 1973

The United Nations Human Rights Commission approved today the draft of a convention that would make apartheid, the racial segregation practiced in South Africa, and similar policies of racial segregation a "crime against humanity."

The Commission voted 21 to 2, with 5 abstentions, to ask its parent body, the Economic and Social Council, to endorse the proposed convention for adoption by the General Assembly.

Nations ratifying the pact would commit themselves to take legislative and other measures needed to "combat all manifestations" of apartheid. Those nations would also be obliged to bring to trial and punish those guilty of acts committed for the purpose of establishing and maintaining domination by one racial group.

The United States and Britain voted against the draft, citing legal and technical reasons, including duplication with other United Nations measures against racism. France, Italy, the Netherlands, Austria, and Norway abstained on similar grounds. [Note: This Convention was adopted and entered into force in 1976.]

Most of the work of the Commission has involved investigating and making records of violations of human rights in many parts of the world. These investigations have helped to focus public opinion throughout the world on gross violations of the Universal Declaration of Human Rights.

Eleventh Grade. Crimes Against Humanity—Genocide

For many years the study of the Holocaust has been included in the curriculum of schools concerned with giving students a full and authentic understanding of the major events of the twentieth century, and encouraging them to live and act so as to avoid the repetition of such crimes. More recently the wider topic of genocide has been studied, focusing on the various cases that occurred before and since the Nazis' mass murder of Jews, Romany, homosexuals, and resisters. Genocide continues to be committed as the most horrendous of state crimes, and the failure to prevent or even to reduce the dimensions of these crimes indicates that the lessons of the Holocaust have not been learned. Human rights education must continue to take full account of the whole range of genocidal acts, both historic and contemporary. The February 1991 issue of the journal of the National Council for the Social Studies, *Social Education*, focusing on genocide, listed among the resources for this unit (see Chapter 7 for address), will be especially useful to secondary school teachers and teacher educators seeking to include genocide in their human rights curricula.

We recommend the following sample unit on genocide for the eleventh grade. This is an age at which issues of individual moral responsibility can be introduced and moral reasoning can be explicitly considered. The Nuremberg Principles are recommended for study as the international standards most relevant to the study of genocide and moral responsibility.

This unit was designed by Laura Schneider during graduate study at Teachers College for use in her senior high school English class. It suggests some of the possibilities art and literature offer to human rights education.

Learning Objectives. Students will:
- identify the political and social factors which comprise the process of genocide;
- question, analyze, and discuss the issues of personal and social responsibility for the Holocaust in the context of the story in *Maus* and the history of the period;
- identify historical patterns which predict the occurrence of genocide;
- use journal writing for reflection on personal moral choices;
- generate strategies for preventing and intervening in genocide;
- identify and critique moral choices made by individual characters in *Maus*;
- evaluate consequences of alternative moral choices;
- devise and justify a definition of genocide;
- discuss and define "moral choice."

Materials
- sufficient copies of *Maus* for class use
- Universal Declaration of Human Rights (see Appendix and Sample 16, Handout #2) and Convention on the Prevention and Punishment of the Crime of Genocide (available from the United Nations, see Chapter 7, or may be copied from *Twenty-Four Human Rights Documents* [New York: Center for the Study of Human Rights, Columbia University]), copies for each student
- special issue on genocide of *Social Education*, copies for each student
- Handout #1, Nuremberg Principles
- Handout #2, Moral Exclusion Practices
- world map
- small pads of adhesive-backed paper

STATEMENT OF PURPOSE

Maus is an unusual memoir about a survivor of the Holocaust. Written and illustrated by Art Spiegelman, it documents in cartoon form his father's story as a Jewish merchant who by good luck and ingenuity escapes death in German prison camps. What unfolds is a human account of genocide which illustrates in personal terms the physical and moral conditions in which the Holocaust took place. As a true story, *Maus* offers readers an engaging literary experience in the context of history.

The purpose of this curriculum unit is twofold. First, it will give students an introduction to the topic of genocide through specific study of the Holocaust. Second, it will create an opportunity for discussion around the issues of individual and social moral choice. With these goals in mind, the class can explore the broader concepts implicit in a study of genocide, such as the concepts of responsibility and the prevention of genocide.

While *Maus* will be the key text for launching the study of genocide, the unit is designed so that other non-fiction media can be studied as well. While *Maus* can be used as a shared class text, the study of the Holocaust will be pursued in the framework of a theme study. Other materials can be used with the class as well, and students will be given the freedom to explore their individual interests on the subject of genocide through their independent reading and writing.

The study of literature can create opportunities for cooperative learning and group discussion. When students are encouraged to explore their own thoughts and feelings in writing and to share them with others in discussion, a community is formed in the classroom. By creating a cooperative environment for learning, the fundamental concepts of peace education can be modelled as an alternative for living and learning.

Class or school situation

This material would ideally be used as an interdisciplinary unit on genocide. If World War II were being taught in the history classroom concurrent with the study of *Maus* in the English classroom, students could develop an in-depth understanding of the historical and personal forces that led to the Holocaust. They could be encouraged to make connections between disciplines that would further their knowledge of what the different disciplines are, and how they can help to build and interpret knowledge. The degree of cooperation between teachers could be determined by those individuals; it is recommended, however, that teachers communicate their plans to each other and coordinate their curricula.

Format

Activities are planned for an average 45-minute class period, assuming the standard public high school schedule and format.

The curriculum will be directed by several guiding questions:

- What is genocide?
- What is "moral choice"?
- What moral choices do the characters in *Maus* make and what are the consequences of these choices?
- Who among the characters in *Maus* is responsible for the destruction of human life caused by the Holocaust?
- What and who are the actual historical counterparts to the events and characters portrayed in *Maus*?

LESSON THEME. Moral Choice

Objective. To explore the question: What is "moral choice"?

Step 1. The class read *Maus*, Chapter 5, "Mouse Holes," together. Each student should have a copy of the text to follow along. This chapter will be the focus of several activities for this objective. Distribute Handout #1: the Nuremberg Principles.

Step 2. The teacher focuses on specific scenes in this chapter that deal with moral choices. There are several relevant scenes and characters, such as the merchant who betrays the hiding family. In class discussion relate the Nuremberg Principles to the actions of the characters described in *Maus*, Chapter 5.

Step 3. Students will discuss questions: Did the characters have a choice? If so, did they make a good choice? What seemed to be the values and factors that influenced the choice? What effect did their decisions have on other characters in the book? If their actions caused harm to someone else, is this morally right?

Step 4. Have students define "moral choice" by writing in their journals; then have students exchange journals and respond to each other's writing. (If students prefer not to exchange journals, the definitions can be written on separate sheets of paper, but also recorded in their journals.)

LESSON THEME. The Consequences of Moral Choice

Objective. To explore the questions: What moral choices do the characters in *Maus* make? What are the consequences of these choices?

Step 1. Students form groups of three to five members. Groups are told that they are going to act as a jury for a particular character in the book. They must come to an agreement whether that character made a good moral choice and they must judge that character's actions. Assign a character to each group.

Step 2. Groups receive record sheets on which they answer specific questions they must think about in making their decisions. (Teachers make and distribute these sheets.) Questions "juries" must explore are

· Did the character have a moral choice?

· What was the consequence of that choice?

· What other choices could have been made, and what might have been the consequences of alternative choices? Was the choice a morally good one? What makes the choice morally good or bad?

At the end of the period, "juries" must then defend their judgments to the rest of the class, clearly explaining their reasons for judging the choice they considered to have been good or bad.

Step 3. Students are asked to represent one of the characters who were "on trial" in the previous exercise. They are to write a defense paper explaining what moral choice they made and why. Students will then present their "cases" to the "juries." Because the "defendants" will be appearing before their respective "juries," students may not choose to represent a character they will be judging.

Step 4. Class reads article: "Those Who Said 'NO': German Soldiers, SS, and Police Who Refused to Execute Civilians During World War II" from *Social Education.*

Class discusses the questions: If there are, in fact, morally good choices that could have been made, why didn't more people make them? What leads people to act in a "morally inclusive" (that is, fair, just, and humane) way toward other people?

Step 5. Class reads section of *Maus* in which the Spiegelmans are protected by a Polish woman and her son.

· What motivated these two characters to help the Spiegelmans?

· How do the characters' actions compare with those of other Polish citizens depicted in the account?

LESSON THEME. Genocide

Objectives. To explore the question: What is genocide? To show the development of the idea of moral exclusion and identify systems by which the Nazi government carried out genocide (activities take place over several days).

Step 1. Distribute Handout #2 on Moral Exclusion Practices for the class to read, along with the following articles from *Social Education* as homework:

· "Genocide Against Jews by the Nazi Regime: A First-Person Account";

· "The Forgotten Holocaust of the Gypsies";

· Sterilization of the Handicapped by the Nazi Regime: A First-Person Account."

Discuss each article to review what happened, when it happened, who the victims were, and any reasons they were chosen as victims. What were the goals and purposes of the genocidal acts and why were they deemed necessary?

Step 2. Class makes a time line for the period leading up to and through World War II. For each year, students list the specific actions taken against the Jews and other target groups and note whether these actions appear on the list of moral exclusion practices. This is an on-going activity that evolves as students read *Maus* and as their reading is supplemented with other non-fiction materials. This time line will demonstrate that genocide is often a process of escalating moral exclusion, not merely a singular event.

Step 3. Assign "Genocide: An Historical Overview" from *Social Education* as homework. Hand out Convention on the Prevention and Punishment of the Crime of Genocide. Class will next attempt to define the word "genocide." The definition should account for the following considerations:
* What actions are included in the definition of genocide?
* Who takes these actions?
* Who are the victims?

LESSON THEME. Moral Responsibility

Objective. To explore the question: Who is responsible for the destruction of human life caused by the Holocaust?

Step 1. Class reads the passage from *Maus* that illustrates the roles of several Nazi soldiers in the genocide. Review Handout #1, the Nuremberg Principles, and ask the students to reflect on how these principles apply to the actions of these soldiers. Could they be applied to other citizens who were aware of or participated in the Holocaust? On what grounds?

Step 2. Class discussion of the actions of those characters. Are they responsible for what they did? What motivation did they have for their behavior? What choices might they have had in regard to their actions? (Note: A viewing of the film *Judgment at Nuremberg* is excellent background for such discussion.)

Step 3. Students write an account from the point of view of one of the Nazi characters. What are their thoughts, values, fears, and reasons for their actions? Conduct an informal role play of interviews with different "characters," asking them to respond to questions about why they took the actions they did.

Step 4. View appropriate extracts from *The Nasty Girl* (a feature film made in Germany), or show it in entirely in two class periods.

Step 5. Discussion: If a whole town has some responsibility for the Holocaust, what should be done to hold the citizens accountable for their actions? What are the implications of denial? Could genocide occur in Germany again? Could it happen here? Where has it occurred elsewhere? When? Against whom and committed by whom? What might be done to prevent genocide?

LESSON THEME. Moral Exclusion

Objective. To reflect on the practices of discrimination that help to create a climate in which genocide might occur.

Step 1. Review Handout #2 on Moral Exclusion Practices. Ask the students to think of two types of examples of each practice: examples they themselves have witnessed or have direct knowledge of; examples from other times and places learned through study, reading, or other media.

Step 2. Class discussion of the question: What is moral exclusion? How does it operate? Where does it occur? What is our own experience of moral exclusion? What current problems and crises result from moral exclusion? What actions can we take to overcome moral exclusion and prevent the social damage it inflicts?

Schneider recommends these readings to teachers:

Chalk, Frank and Kurt Jonassohn, "Genocide: An Historical Overview." *Social Education* 55, 2 (February 1991).

Friedman, Ina. "Sterilization of Handicapped by the Nazi Regime." *Social Education* 55, 2 (February 1991).

Kitterman, David. "Those Who Said 'No!': German Soldiers, SS, and Police Who Refused to Execute Civilians During World War II" *Social Education* 55, 2 (February 1991).

Opotow, Susan. "Moral Exclusion and Injustice: An Introduction" *Journal of Social Issues.* 46 (Spring 1990).

Spiegelman, Arthur. *Maus.* New York: Random House: 1986.

Tyrnauer, Gabrielle. "The Forgotten Holocaust of the Gypsies." *Social Education* 55, 2 (February 1991).

Verhoeven, Michael. *The Nasty Girl.* (Michael Verhoeven, director) 1990. Miramax Films. 94 minutes running time. In German with subtitles.

Weitz, Sonia Schreiber. "Genocide Against Jews by the Nazi Regime: A First Person Account." *Social Education* 55, 2 (February 1991).

Sample 23, Handout 1.
The Nuremberg Principles, 1946

I. Any person who commits an act which is a crime under international law is [personally] responsible . . . and may be punished.

II. Even if domestic law does not impose punishment for crimes under international law, the person who commits such acts is still responsible under international law.

III. Even if a person who commits such acts is a Head of State or a responsible government official, [that person] is still personally responsible.

IV. Even if a person committed the criminal act under orders from his government or superior, [the person] is still responsible, if a moral choice was in fact possible.

V. Any person charged with a crime under international law has the right to a fair trial on the facts and the law.

VI. Crimes punishable under international law are
  a. *Crimes against peace*, which constitute planning, preparing, or starting a war in violation of international agreements, and participating in any of those acts.
  b. *War crimes*, which include, but are not limited to: murder, ill-treatment, deportation to slave labor of civilians in occupied territory; murder or ill-treatment of prisoners of war; killing hostages; wanton destruction of cities, towns, or villages; or devastation not justified by military necessity.
  c. *Crimes against humanity*, designated as: murder, extermination, enslavement, deportation, and other inhuman acts against civilians, or persecution on political, racial or religious grounds when such acts are carried out in connection with any crime against the peace or war crime.

VII. Complicity in any of the crimes enumerated in Principle VI is a crime under international law.

Excerpted with permission from Lawrence Metcalf and Robert Low, eds., *War Criminals, War Victims* (New York: Random House, 1976). The principles underlying the judgments of the Nuremberg War Crimes Tribunal were endorsed by the UN General Assembly in 1948, and defined in their present form in 1950 by a panel of experts in international law convened by the United Nations.

Sample 23, Handout 2.
Processes of Moral Exclusion

Process	Manifestation in moral exclusion
Exclusion-specific processes	
Biased evaluation	Making unflattering comparisons between one's own group and another group; believing in the superiority of one's own group
Derogation	Disparaging and denigration of others by regarding them as lower life forms or inferior beings—e.g., barbarians, vermin
Dehumanization	Repudiating others' humanity, dignity, ability to feel, and entitlement to compassion
Fear of contamination	Perceiving contact with others as posing a threat to one's own well-being
Expanding the target	Redefining "legitimate victims" as a larger category
Accelerating the pace of harm doing	Engaging in increasingly destructive and abhorrent acts to reduce remorse and inhibitions against inflicting harm
Open approval of destructive behavior	Accepting a moral code that condones harm doing
Reducing moral standards	Perceiving one's harmful behavior as proper; replacing moral standards that restrain harm with less stringent standards that condone or praise harm doing
Blaming the victim	Displacing the blame for reprehensible actions on those who are harmed
Self-righteous comparisons	Lauding or justifying harmful acts by contrasting them with morally condemnable atrocities committed by the adversary
Desecration	Harming others to demonstrate contempt for them, particularly symbolic or gratuitous harm
Ordinary processes	
Groupthink	Striving for group unanimity by maintaining isolation from dissenting opinion that would challenge the assumptions, distortions, or decisions of the group
Transcendent ideologies	Experiencing oneself or one's group as exalted, extraordinary, and possessed of a higher wisdom, which permits even harmful behavior as necessary to bring a better world into being
Deindividuation	Feeling anonymous in a group setting, thus weakening one's capacity to behave in accordance with personal standards
Moral engulfment	Replacing one's own ethical standards with those of the group
Psychological distance	Ceasing to feel the presence of others; perceiving others as objects or as nonexistent
Condescension	Regarding others as inferior; patronizing others, and perceiving them with disdain—e.g., they are childlike, irrational, simple

Technical orientation	Focusing on efficient means while ignoring outcomes; routinizing harm doing by transforming it into mechanical steps
Double standards	Having different sets of moral rules and obligations for different categories of people
Unflattering comparisons	Using unflattering contrasts to bolster one's superiority over others
Euphemisms	Masking, sanitizing, and conferring respectability on reprehensible behavior by using palliative terms that misrepresent cruelty and harm
Displacing responsibility	Behaving in ways one would normally repudiate because a higher authority explicitly or implicitly assumes responsibility for the consequences
Diffusing responsibility	Fragmenting the implementation of harmful tasks through collective action
Concealing the effects of harmful behavior	Disregarding, ignoring, disbelieving, distorting, or minimizing injurious outcomes to others
Glorifying violence	Viewing violence as a sublime activity and a legitimate form of human expression
Normalizing violence	Accepting violent behavior as ordinary because of repeated exposure to it and societal acceptance of it
Temporal containment of harm doing	Perceiving one's injurious behavior as an isolated event—"just this time"

Excerpted with permission from Susan Opotow, "Moral Exclusion," *Journal of Social Issues* 46, 1 (1990): 10–11.

Eleventh Grade. Regional Human Rights Regimes

The concept of constitutionalism and covenanting for the achievement and protection of human rights, an essential component of education for democracy and civic responsibility, should be a central focus of human rights education at the secondary level. By the eleventh grade students should be familiar with the Universal Declaration of Human Rights and some of the covenants and conventions that address specific sets of rights. They should also understand the distinctions of declarations, conventions, and treaties. In dealing with constitutionalism and covenanting, (that is the ideas that governments should be based on principles of law and that the society is best served by agreement to uphold the principles) the curriculum should present information about the international instruments that provide global standards and those that are regional, such as the African, European and Latin American instruments and systems. Against this background procedures for the enforcement of the covenants can be introduced.

Having pointed out to students that human rights standards derive from the belief that certain forms of human suffering and deprivation run counter to a society's notion of its values and purposes, teachers can also indicate that historic, cultural, and political differences in societies have also produced differences in priorities in regard to human rights. The following lesson does just that with respect to the African Charter on Human and Peoples' Rights. Taken from a revised edition of David Shiman's *Teaching Human Rights* (Denver, CO: Center for Teaching International Relations, University of Denver), the unit was designed for use in grades 9–12. It is included here at the 11th grade level, because the content requires the maturity of senior high school age level. It is especially appropriate for a curriculum that deals with civic education, government and constitutions and provides an opportunity for discussing the collective or group rights called "third generation rights."

Learning Objectives. Students will:
- identify similarities and differences in the perspectives on human rights found in two human rights documents;
- review the reasons African nations included the rights to self-determination and development in their charter.

Materials
- Universal Declaration of Human Rights (see Appendix and Sample 16, Handout #2)
- Handout #1. African Charter on Human and Peoples' Rights

Learning Sequence

Step 1. Begin this activity by pointing out that there are regional documents that re-affirm and expand on the principles found in the Universal Declaration of Human Rights. These include the European Convention on Human Rights adopted by the Council of Europe in 1950, the American Convention on Human Rights adopted by the Organization of American States in 1969, and the African Charter on Human and Peoples' Rights approved by the Organization of African Unity in 1981.

These documents are similar but not identical. Each reflects the history, cultural traditions, ideologies, political, and economic structures of the nations that wrote it. Sometimes these rights are prioritized differently by different nations. We need to understand why all nations don't look at these rights in the same way. To do so, we need to understand how these countries view their historical experiences.

Step 2. Distribute the Universal Declaration of Human Rights, and Handout #1, African Charter on Human and Peoples' Rights. *Note.* This activity is based on the assumptions that students have been introduced to the Universal Declaration and have done some study of African development issues.

Step 3. Have students read the preamble to each document. Ask them the following questions:
- In what ways are the preambles similar?
- What concerns are addressed in the African Charter's preamble, but not in the Universal Declaration's. (e.g., right to development; elimination of colonialism, neocolonialism, apartheid, and zionism; dismantling foreign military bases and racial discrimination)?
- What is the Universal Declaration referring to when it speaks of "barbarous acts which have outraged the conscience of mankind?"
- What foreign powers do you think the African Charter is referring to in the preamble? *Note:* Focus discussion on the clause beginning with "Conscious . . . ."
- Why do you think the African Charter includes peoples' as well as human rights?

Step 4. Divide the class into groups of four to five students. Ask each group to compare the two documents. Using the African Charter as their reference point, have students check off each right that is also found in the Universal Declaration.

Step 5. Have students identify those rights found only in the African Charter. Use these as the basis for the subsequent discussion or students' research projects.

Step 6. Try to build the remainder of the activity around the following rights included in the African Charter.
- right to existence and self-determination (Article 20);

- right to dispose of own wealth and resources (Article 21);
- right to development (Article 22).

Use the following questions to help guide the discussion, or to organize student research efforts:

- Why would Articles 20–22 be found in the African Charter? How do they reflect Africans' view of their past history, particularly colonialism? How do they reflect an African concern with neocolonialism?
- Whom might Africans describe as oppressed peoples on their continent? Consider both past and present instances.
- How do these articles relate to African calls for a New International Economic Order?
- Do you agree with the following assertion by the United States Department of State:

"Experience demonstrates that it is individual freedom that sets the stage for economic and social development; it is repression that stifles it. Those who try to justify subordinating political and civil rights on the ground that they are concentrating on their economic aspirations invariably deliver on neither." (U.S. Department of State, *Country Reports on Human Rights Practices for 1985*, Washington, DC: U.S. Government Printing Office, 1986)

- Compare the above quotation with that found in the African Charter's preamble which begins "Convinced . . . ."

Extension

Similar units can be developed for study of the European and Inter-American human rights instruments and for "The Duties of the Peoples and States of the ASEAN [Association of South East Asian Nations] Nations" devised by a group of nongovernmental organizations (NGOs).

Sample 24, Handout 1.
African Charter on Human and Peoples' Rights

PREAMBLE

The African States members of the Organization of African Unity, parties to the present Convention entitled African Charter on Human and Peoples' Rights;

Recalling Decision 115 (XVI) of the Assembly of Heads of State and Government at its Sixteenth Ordinary Session held in Monrovia, Liberia, from 17 to 20 July 1979 on the preparation of "a preliminary draft on an African Charter on Human and Peoples' Rights providing inter alia for the establishment of bodies to promote and protect human and peoples' rights";

Considering the Charter of the Organization of African Unity, which stipulates that "freedom, equality, justice and dignity are essential objectives for the achievement of the legitimate aspirations of the African peoples";

Reaffirming the pledge they solemnly made in Article 2 of the said Charter to eradicate all forms of colonialism from Africa, to co-ordinate and intensify their co-operation and efforts to achieve a better life for the peoples of Africa and to promote international co-operation having due regard to the Charter of the United Nations and the Universal Declaration of Human Rights;

Taking into consideration the virtues of their historical tradition and the values of African civilization which should inspire and characterize their reflection on the concept of human and peoples' rights;

Recognizing on the one hand that fundamental human rights stem from the attributes of human beings which justify their international protection, and on the other hand that the reality and respect of peoples' rights should necessarily guarantee human rights;

Considering that the enjoyment of rights and freedoms also implies the performance of duties on the part of everyone;

Convinced that it is henceforth essential to pay particular attention to the right to development and that civil and political rights cannot be dissociated from economic, social and cultural rights in their conception as well as universality and that the satisfaction of economic, social and cultural rights is a guarantee for the enjoyment of civil and political rights;

Conscious of their duty to achieve the total liberation of Africa, the peoples of

Adopted by the Organization of African Unity, Nairobi, Kenya, 1981.

which are still struggling for their dignity and genuine independence, and undertaking to eliminate colonialism, neo-colonialism, apartheid, zionism and to dismantle aggressive foreign military bases and all forms of discrimination, particularly those based on race, ethnic group, color, sex, language, religion or political opinions;

Reaffirming their adherence to the principles of human and peoples' rights and freedoms contained in the declarations, conventions and other instruments adopted by the Organization of African Unity, the Movement of Non-Aligned Countries and the United Nations;

Firmly convinced of their duty to promote and protect human and peoples' rights and freedoms, taking into account the importance traditionally attached to these rights and freedoms in Africa.

HAVE AGREED AS FOLLOWS:

HUMAN AND PEOPLES' RIGHTS

ARTICLE 1

The Member States of the Organization of African Unity parties to the present Charter shall recognize the rights, duties and freedoms enshrined in this Charter and shall undertake to adopt legislative or other measures to give effect to them.

ARTICLE 2

Every individual shall be entitled to the enjoyment of the rights and freedoms recognized and guaranteed in the present Charter without distinction of any kind such as race, ethnic group, color, sex, language, religion, political or other opinion, national and social origin, fortune, birth or other status.

ARTICLE 3

1. Every individual shall be equal before the law.
2. Every individual shall be entitled to equal protection of the law.

ARTICLE 4

Human beings are inviolable. Every human being shall be entitled to respect for his [sic] life and the integrity of his [sic] person. No one may be arbitrarily deprived of this right.

ARTICLE 5

Every individual shall have the right to the respect of the dignity inherent in a human being and to the recognition of his legal status. All forms of exploitation and degradation of man particularly slavery, slave trade, torture, cruel, inhuman or degrading punishment and treatment shall be prohibited.

ARTICLE 6

Every individual shall have the right to liberty and to the security of his person. No one may be deprived of his freedom except for reasons and conditions previously laid down by law. In particular, no one may be arbitrarily arrested or detained.

ARTICLE 7

1. Every individual shall have the right to have his cause heard. This comprises:

a. the right to an appeal to competent national organs against acts violating his fundamental rights as recognized and guaranteed by conventions, laws, regulations and customs in force.

b. the right to be presumed innocent until proved guilty by a competent court or tribunal;

c. the right to defence, including the right to be defended by counsel of his choice;

d. the right to be tried within a reasonable time by an impartial court or tribunal.

2. No one may be condemned for an act or omission which did not constitute a legally punishable offence at the time it was committed. No penalty may be inflicted for an offence for which no provision was made at the time it was committed. Punishment is personal and can be imposed only on the offender.

ARTICLE 8

Freedom of conscience, the profession and free practice of religion shall be guaranteed. No one may, subject to law and order, be submitted to measures restricting the exercise of these freedoms.

ARTICLE 9

1. Every individual shall have the right to receive information.

2. Every individual shall have the right to express and disseminate his opinions within the law.

ARTICLE 10

1. Every individual shall have the right to free association provided that he abides by the law.

2. Subject to the obligation of solidarity provided for in Article 29 no one may be compelled to join an association.

ARTICLE 11

Every individual shall have the right to assemble freely with others. The exercise of this right shall be subject only to necessary restrictions provided for by law in particular those enacted in the interest of national security, the safety, health, ethics and rights and freedoms of others.

ARTICLE 12

1. Every individual shall have the right to freedom of movement and residence within the borders of a State provided he abides by the law.

2. Every individual shall have the right to leave any country including his own, and to return to his country. This right may only be subject to restrictions provided for by law for the protection of national security, law and order, public health or morality.

3. Every individual shall have the right, when persecuted, to seek and obtain asylum in other countries in accordance with the laws of those countries and international conventions.

4. A non-national legally admitted in a territory of a State Party to the present Charter, may only be expelled from it by virtue of a decision taken in accordance with the law.

5. The mass expulsion of non-nationals shall be prohibited. Mass expulsion shall be that which is aimed at nation, racial, ethnic or religious groups.

ARTICLE 13

1. Every citizen shall have the right to participate freely in the government of his country, either directly or through freely chosen representatives in accordance with provisions of the law.

2. Every citizen shall have the right of equal access to public service of his country.

3. Every individual shall have the right of access to public property and services in strict equality of all persons before the law.

ARTICLE 14

The right to property shall be guaranteed. It may only be encroached upon in the interest of public need or in the general interest of the community and in accordance with the provisions of appropriate laws.

ARTICLE 15

Every individual shall have the right to work under equitable and satisfactory conditions, and shall receive equal pay for equal work.

ARTICLE 16

1. Every individual shall have the right to enjoy the best attainable state of physical and mental health.

2. States parties to the present Charter shall take the necessary measures to protect the health of their people and to ensure that they receive medical attention when they are sick.

ARTICLE 17

1. Every individual shall have the right to education.

2. Every individual may freely take part in the cultural life of his community.

3. The promotion and protection of morals and traditional values recognized by the community shall be the duty of the State.

ARTICLE 18

1. The family shall be the natural unit and basis of society. It shall be protected by the State which shall take care of its physical and moral health.

2. The State shall have the duty to assist the family which is the custodian of morals and traditional values recognized by the community.

3. The State shall ensure the elimination of every discrimination against women and also ensure the protection of the rights of the woman and the child as stipulated in international declarations and conventions.

4. The aged and the disabled shall also have the right to special measures of protection in keeping with their physical or moral needs.

ARTICLE 19

All peoples shall be equal: they shall enjoy the same respect and shall have the same rights. Nothing shall justify the domination of a people by another.

ARTICLE 20

1. All peoples shall have the right to existence. They shall have the unquestionable and inalienable right to self-determination. They shall freely determine their political status and shall pursue their economic and social development according to the policy they have freely chosen.

2. Colonized or oppressed peoples shall have the right to free themselves from the bonds of domination by resorting to any means recognized by the international community.

3. All peoples shall have the right to the assistance of the States parties to the present Charter in their liberation struggle against foreign domination, be it political, economic, or cultural.

ARTICLE 21

1. All peoples shall freely dispose of their wealth and natural resources. This right shall be exercised in the exclusive interest of the people. In no case shall a people be deprived of it.

2. In case of spoliation the dispossessed people shall have the right to the lawful recovery of its property as well as to an adequate compensation.

3. The free disposal of wealth and natural resources shall be exercised without prejudice to the obligation of promoting international economic cooperation based on mutual respect, equitable exchange and the principles of international law.

4. States parties to the present Charter shall individually and collectively exercise the right to free disposal of their wealth and natural resources with a view to strengthening African unity and solidarity.

5. States parties to the present Charter shall undertake to eliminate all forms of foreign economic exploitation, particularly that practiced by international monopolies, so as to enable their peoples to fully benefit from the advantages derived from their national resources.

ARTICLE 22

1. All peoples shall have the right to their economic, social and cultural development with due regard to their freedom and identity and in the equal enjoyment of the common heritage of mankind.

2. The state shall have the duty individually or collectively to ensure the exercise of the right to development.

ARTICLE 23

1. All peoples shall have the right to national and international peace and security. The principles of solidarity and friendly relations implicitly affirmed by the Charter of the United Nations and reaffirmed by that of the Organization of African Unity shall govern relations between States.

2. For the purpose of strengthening peace, solidarity and friendly relations, States parties to the present charter shall ensure that:

a. Any individual enjoying the right of asylum under Article 12 of the present Charter shall not engage in subversive activities against his country of origin or any other State party to the present Charter;

b. Their territories shall not be used as bases for subversive or terrorist activities against the people of any other State party to the present Charter.

ARTICLE 24

All peoples shall have the right to a general satisfactory environment favorable to their development.

ARTICLE 25

States parties to the present Charter shall have the duty to promote and ensure through teaching, education and publication, respect of the rights and freedoms contained in the present Charter and to see to it that these freedoms and rights as well as corresponding obligations and duties are understood.

ARTICLE 26

States parties to the present Charter shall have the duty to guarantee the independence of the Courts and shall have all the establishment and improvement of appropriate national institutions entrusted with the promotion and protection of the rights and freedoms guaranteed by the present Charter.

DUTIES

ARTICLE 27

1. Every individual shall have duties towards his family and society, the State and other legally recognized communities and the international community.

2. The rights and freedoms of each individual shall be exercised with due regard to the rights of others, collective security, morality and common interest.

ARTICLE 28

Every individual shall have the duty to respect and consider his fellow beings without discrimination, and to maintain relations aimed at promoting, safeguarding and reinforcing mutual respect and tolerance.

ARTICLE 29

The individual shall also have the duty:

1. To preserve the harmonious development of the family and to work for the cohesion and respect of the family; to respect his parents at all times, to maintain them in case of need;

2. To serve his national community by placing his physical and intellectual abilities at its services;

3. Not to compromise the security of the State whose national or resident he is;

4. To preserve and strengthen social and national solidarity, particularly when the latter is threatened;

5. To preserve and strengthen the national independence and the territorial integrity of his country and to contribute to its defence in accordance with the law;

6. To work to the best of his abilities and competence, and to pay taxes imposed by law in the interest of the society;

7. To preserve and strengthen positive African cultural values in his relations with other members of the society, in the spirit of tolerance, dialogue and consultation and, in general, to contribute to the promotion of the moral well being of society;

8. To contribute to the best of his abilities, at all times and at all levels, to the promotion and achievement of African unity.

(The remainder of this document deals primarily with the establishment of a Commission on Human and Peoples' Rights and the manner in which it will operate.)

Twelfth Grade. Comparing National and International Standards

Before completing the last year of high school, students should become familiar with their country's major national standards on human rights. (In the case of the United States, the Bill of Rights and the other constitutional amendments intended to assure civil rights and social justice in the American society. For these purposes the materials produced by the Constitutional Rights Foundation are useful. See Chapter 7). They should also be acquainted with the major international human rights documents and instruments, at a minimum the Universal Declaration of Human Rights. Students should understand constitutionalism as the belief that the most effective way to assure rights is through enforceable law. They should also appreciate the degree to which social values and cultural attitudes affect the development of such standards and the potential for the universal enjoyment of human rights.

High school seniors should have gained an understanding of responsible citizenship that includes obligations to and assurances from local, national, and world society. They should be able to recognize, analyze, and take positions on conflicts and controversies over human rights issues, and understand that such controversies often arise over one right in contention with another or over the interpretation of rights. (See David Shiman's curriculum *Teaching About Human Rights*, published by the Center for Teaching International Relations, for further units on rights in contention.)

Every American secondary school student at some time studies the United States Constitution and the Bill of Rights. It is appropriate in such an analysis to examine the current reality in relation to the concepts of "the founding fathers." Juxtaposing the Universal Declaration of Human Rights against the Bill of Rights provides a valuable opportunity for secondary school students to explore the values and rights enshrined in these documents in light of the realities of contemporary society.

A unit designed by Deborah Johnston for use in a New York suburban high school deals with all these elements. The portion we have chosen as a sample of a twelfth grade lesson calls for a comparison of the United States Bill of Rights with the Universal Declaration of Human Rights.

The unit, with some adaptation, was used in a classroom of high school seniors in the state-required course, "Participation in Government," a half-year course on public policy issues.

Learning Objectives. Students will:
• define and apply the concept of human rights;

- display in written and oral work their understanding of the similarities and differences between the United States Bill of Rights and the Universal Declaration of Human Rights;
- consider the tensions between individual rights and the social good;
- recognize cultural bias as an issue in the formulation and application of human rights standards.

Materials
- Universal Declaration of Human Rights (see Appendix and Sample 16, Handout #2)
- U.S. Bill of Rights
- Transparencies, overhead projector, and markers

LESSON THEME. Students' Concepts of Human Rights

Objective. Students should be able to identify what the term human rights refers to; the international document defining these rights; underlying values; and to reflect on issues related to the universality of human rights.

Step 1. Following or incorporated within a study of the United States Constitution and the U.S. Bill of Rights, raise these questions to open the inquiry:
- What is your concept of human rights?
- What are some of the rights humans are entitled to? (Make a web diagram on transparency to illustrate the varying perceptions of what students think of as human rights).
- Have these rights always existed?
- What conditions led to their creation?

Step 2. Distribute the Universal Declaration of Human Rights. In small group sessions have the students compare the Declaration with the Bill of Rights. (Other national constitutions might also be used as further comparison. In countries other than the United States their own constitutions should be used.) Focus group discussions on these four questions:
- *Similarities:* Does the Bill of Rights embody any of the same ideas as the Universal Declaration? Are they grounded in the same underlying philosophy?
- *Differences:* What rights are in the Declaration that are not guaranteed in the U.S. Constitution?
- Based on what you know about the U.S. legal system and Constitution, does this country's legal and political system respect most of the rights contained in the Declaration?
- What's the catch? What do people have to do in return for these rights?

Step 3. Assign as homework the initial entries in a journal of reflections on human rights. The first reflections should be on "What I see as the major problems in protecting human rights."

Step 4. Call for volunteers to present their ideas from the homework assignment. During the reading of several journal entries as a representative sampling, initiate discussion on the issues being raised by the students. Issues that may be voiced include the opinion that the Universal Declaration is ineffective because there is no agent to enforce it or court system to interpret it. Make students aware of the UN Charter and regional human rights enforcement provisions (see Sample 24). Such assertions might be explored by raising the question of whether the U.S. Supreme Court is an adequate forum for the discussion of individual liberties and whether or not international law can be applied in the domestic court system.

What values are inherent in the Universal Declaration? Define values. Have the class generate examples of values they hold. List on the board the values which provide the backbone of human rights as seen in the Declaration and the Bill of Rights. What do these values say about our culture? About the culture of the times in which the documents were drafted? Are these particularly and exclusively Western values?

Step 5. Discussion of Eurocentric/ethnocentric concepts. Are these rights so basic that anyone in the world can accept them, or are they contrary to certain cultures or political systems? Provide examples of religious and social customs around the world that may be contrary to strict interpretation of the document (i.e., religious requirements for holding political authority, behavioral and social restrictions on women, rejection of the concept of children's rights, etc.) What issues are raised by extending or applying these concepts of rights to other cultures? It would be appropriate here to mention the Convention on the Elimination of All Forms of Discrimination Against Women and the Convention on the Rights of the Child (see Chapter 7 for abbreviated versions) and the controversies that have surrounded their ratification and implementation in some countries.

LESSON THEME. How Do These Rights Affect You, the Members of the Class?

Objective. Students will review human rights conditions in their own country and consider the human rights issues in their own lives.

Step 1. In a summary discussion, consider the following questions:
- Are any of the rights in the UDHR not recognized in our country?
- Does the United States fully observe the rights embodied in the Bill of Rights?
- Is your life affected in any way by human rights issues?
- Are there injustices in your life or community not recognized in international standards? Should they be so recognized? If so, why?

Step 2. Elicit responses from students on these two questions and for homework, ask them to generate a list of ways they see human rights being upheld or violated in their daily lives. For the next assignment, list ways to protect or implement their own rights.

Step 3. In the final class session call for the lists of violations and implementations. Pose the following questions:
- What are the causes of the violations?
- What are the reasons for the implementations?
- What can you do to overcome the violations and strengthen the implementations?

Twelfth Grade. Moral Development— From Awareness to Commitment, the Making of Human Rights Heroes

Because the framework and approach put forward here is values based and normative in its pedagogical purposes seeking to develop commitment to standards of ethical behavior, the following unit is offered as one example of how more mature students might be helped to reflect on the process of moral development as it relates to issues of personal and social responsibility.

As with other developmental processes, the attitudinal and behavioral evolution from the practice of moral exclusion by perpetrators and/or observers of human rights violations to the embrace of moral inclusion and solidarity with the victimized (sometimes to the point of assuming the risks and consequences of victimhood) appears to follow identifiable stages. These stages, outlined below, indicate changes in stance toward the violations, and in attitudes toward the victims. They are essentially learning stages in which knowledge, primarily although not exclusively acquired through direct experience of a human rights violation, or interactions with the perpetrators or victims, leads to a process of moral reflection and choice-making that moves the learner to higher levels of understanding of the individual, social and ethical implications of the violations. This process often convinces the learner that action must be taken to end the violation and the conditions causing it. It can lead to commitment to take such action and sometimes to accepting personal risks, injury, or sacrifice to overcome the violation, even martyrdom on behalf of the victims. The new knowledge and deeper understanding usually involve changes in values and world views that can be described in the ultimate form as accepting and internalizing the universality and inviolability of human dignity, and the inclusion of all humanity in the learner's moral community.

The literature on political violence and genocide identifies three major sets of actors in cases of severe and large scale human rights violations: perpetrators, victims, and bystanders. While persons in all three categories can and do undergo cognitive and affective changes, the phases of the development of moral inclusion outlined here are most often experienced by bystanders and those close to the originating perpetrators or acting under their direction. Literature and films frequently use this theme of moral "conversion," and thus provide many excellent cases for study. Suggested here are several popular feature films that can be used in senior high schools. One, *Romero*, is selected as a particular example to demonstrate and facilitate discussion of one such case.

In introducing the process of moral development depicted in any such films, novels, biographies, or histories, the teacher should stress that there is nothing immutable or inevitable about such processes. Sometimes they may evolve in a different sequence or pattern, and it is not unusual for people to return to former attitudes, old values, and old opinions. Nor is it impossible for people to move from a more to a less morally inclusive attitude. People seldom, however, move from one phase to another without a particular experience to facilitate the change. What is significant is that people can change and that change derives mostly from experience, learning, and reflection.

Note. It is important for the teacher to be very familiar with whatever film is selected as the example. At least two preparatory viewings are advised.

Learning Objectives. Students will:
- observe a process of attitudinal and value change;
- identify phases in the development of a morally inclusive attitude;
- assess the probable factors that led particular individuals to change their views and positions or to take significant action on behalf of human rights.

Materials.
- Some readings on the case, event, or conditions upon which the selected film is based
- The article "Moral Exclusion" by Susan Opotow from *Journal of Social Issues* 46, 1 (Spring 1990)
- Handout #1, Practices of Moral Exclusion (note: Handout #1 for this sample is Sample 23, Handout #2)
- Handout #2, Phases in the Development of Moral Inclusion
- Handout #3, Outline for Discussion of *Romero*
- Video of feature film: example, *Romero* (see Chapter 7 for others)

Various relevant films are available for rental and purchase on video. Other possibilities: *The Dry White Season* or *The Official Story*. Novels and television series may also be used for demonstrating and discussing the development of morally inclusive attitudes.

Learning Sequence

Step 1. Present the concept of moral exclusion and provide examples. Assign background reading including Susan Opotow's article, "Moral Exclusion."

Step 2. Introduce the film, describing it as a case in which a person moves from moral exclusion to moral inclusion through a series of "threshold experiences," events that move them to a different view or new understanding of a situation, a person, or a set of social conditions.

Step 3. Ask the students to view the film (or read the novel, etc.) with an eye to identifying these threshold experiences. Ask them to try to record the process and phases they observe the protagonist experience.

Step 4. Show the film. If you do not have a block of time or a series of classes permitting the showing of the entire film, select and show the crucial scenes depicting the "threshold experiences," being careful not to "dismember" the film. If possible make one edited tape for classroom use showing these crucial scenes. It is also advisable to have students view the entire film outside of class, if at all possible.

Step 5. Organize discussion groups of five to seven students, asking them to outline the process and name the phases of change evident in the key character or characters. Then have the groups report to the class. Emphasize especially the challenges to authority, unjust laws and structures, or inhumane conditions that the central characters risked.

Step 6. Distribute Handout #1 on Practices of Moral Exclusion and ask the groups to identify specific practices depicted in the film.

Step 7. Distribute the description of phases outlined in Handout #2 on the Development of Moral Inclusion and ask the students to compare it to their own outline of the phases. Identify the "threshold" events and the challenges experienced by the main characters that lead them to another phase.

Step 8. Ask the students to write a reflective essay on the significance of individual learning and personal development to the process of moral inclusion and the growth of the human rights movement.

Step 9. Ask the students to cite other such cases and what might have led to the changes. Make a list of outstanding "actors" for human rights, people whose values and views changed and the contributions they have made to social justice and human dignity.

Step 10. Make a list of films that depict the development of morally inclusive attitudes. Have students briefly report on their memories of how the central characters change. On the basis of this discussion organize a human rights film festival and try to schedule it for the entire school, or for the community.

Sample 26, Handout 2.
Phases in the Development of Moral Inclusion

Consideration of human rights issues usually focuses on rights violation, both the perpetrators and the victims. However, intervention to halt, remedy, and prevent violations is mainly the sphere of the bystander, or those not directly involved. Most citizens and students fall into this category. Thus the attitudes, concerns, and actions of bystanders are crucial to the achievement and maintenance of human rights.

The universal recognition of the full range of human rights for all peoples of the world depends in large part on widening our moral community and extending its boundaries to include all human beings. The development of morally inclusive perspectives is a learning process. Moral inclusion is a capacity which can be developed through both experiential and academic learning. This unit is an academic learning process based on the experiential learning of actual or fictional persons depicted in film. The films offer an opportunity to observe particular phases in the process of learning to be morally inclusive. In these films we see bystanders move from lack of awareness to commitment to intervene to remedy human rights violations. Sometimes the phases of the learning process can be identified in some specific experiences of these bystanders. These experiences can be classified as roles in relation to the human rights issues and violations concerned. A number of such roles or learning phases are described below.

Spectator

The first phase a bystander usually experiences is moving from ignorance to some knowledge of the violations. We can refer to this as the *Spectator* phase. The bystander is simply an onlooker who sees a violation, but does not attribute a moral aspect to it or have any personal concern or lively interest in it.

Observer

When, however, the interest of the spectator is aroused for any of many possible reasons, then the bystander starts to pay attention, to seek information intentionally, to try to observe more than the surface events, and to look for causes, patterns, and consequences of the violations. Such bystanders have become intentional *observers*.

Developed by Betty Reardon for a course on "Human and Social Dimensions of Peace: Human Rights and Responsibilities," offered at Teachers College, Columbia University.

Witness

If the learning process continues, such observers often develop a concern about the violation that leads them to want to make others aware. In this phase of speaking about the violation, telling what one knows, the bystander becomes a *witness* who tells what she or he knows of the case to others, sometimes publicly to the media.

Advocate

When the concern of the witness phase deepens, bystanders are sometimes moved to speak out publicly against the violation on behalf of the victims, to join advocacy groups, write letters to the editor, speak to schools, church groups, etc. Such people *advocate* the cause of the victims.

Activist

When advocates take direct action toward remediation of the problem, such as attempting to influence the policies of governments, or intervening in the actual situation (such as going to the scene of a violation to try to restrain the perpetrators or assist the victims), they have moved to the acceptance of personal responsibility and risk. It should be noted that without the willingness of some advocates to take some risks, a situation of violation is seldom likely to change. *Activists* are essential to major progress in the field of human rights.

Solidarity/Victim/Martyr

Activism is most often pursued within one's own group or country, but some activists actually join in *solidarity* with the struggle and suffering of victims to work for human rights as a member of the victimized group. Such an activist risks being victimized herself even to the point of losing her life and thus becoming a *martyr* in the struggle for human rights. Do you know of such martyrs who are now considered heroes of human rights?

Sample 26, Handout 3.
Outline for a Discussion of *Romero*

• What are the major human rights violations depicted?

• Who are those shown as victims, violators, and bystanders?

• What are the values and moral rationales expressed by each of the following characters:
> the priest who is murdered;
> the priest who is tortured;
> the priest who becomes a guerrilla;
> the father-in-law of the Minister of Agriculture;
> the colonel, lieutenant, and President-Elect;
> the wife of the Minister of Agriculture;
> the young girl working in the community;
> the guerrilla in the van.

• What concepts of rights and "humanity" does each hold? What are the elements of "moral exclusion" and "moral inclusion" in their positions?

• Trace the phases of learning and growth experienced by Romero in his encounters with those listed above as he moves through the "bystander" roles of:
> Spectator (sees the violation);
> Observer (pays attention to it);
> Witness (speaks about it);
> Advocate (speaks for the victims);
> Activist (acts on behalf of the victims);
> Member (joins the victims);
> Martyr (becomes a victim of the same or related violations, sometimes losing life).

> What of the many other committed activists? Do you know of such people who devote many hours of their lives to the struggle for human rights? Develop a list of such people, and post it as a "Human Rights Honor Role" in your classroom.

• What role does information and learning play in the struggle for human rights? What are some ways in which we can encourage learning about human rights issues?

Developed by Betty Reardon for a course on "Human and Social Dimensions of Peace: Human Rights and Responsibilities," offered at Teachers College, Columbia University.

Twelfth Grade. Global Issues—Human Rights and Responsibilities

This senior high school study of major human rights violations covers the development of concepts and standards of human rights as outlined in major international instruments of human rights, examines crucial human rights topics and inquires into possible approaches to the protection and fulfillment of human rights on a global scale. It also can serve as general global issues course exploring world problems from a human rights perspective.

Feature films are used to illustrate the problems, and students are asked to work together on reports on potential remedies to be presented in class. This course comprises eleven units, each of which should take about three class sessions including an introductory discussion of the issues and the relevant international standards and human rights conventions, a viewing of selected portions of the film (students should be encouraged to view films in their entirety outside class), and a post-film viewing discussion focusing as much as possible on remedies and strategies for overcoming these human rights violations. Most films included in this course outline are available at video rental stores. All conventions and declarations and some relevant Human Rights Fact Sheets are available from the United Nations Center for Human Rights (see Chapter 7).

Learning Objectives. Students will:
- review the major human rights violations which underlie some of the most severe global problems;
- become familiar with the most important international standards, declarations, covenants, and conventions the United Nations has produced to protect human rights;
- learn of the historical and conceptual development of human rights as a major trend in modern history;
- consider strategies and policies for the remediation of human rights abuses.

Framework of inquiry to be applied to each unit. The first five questions are to provide a basis for reviewing the fundamental circumstances of the human rights problems. The last three questions are to be used as a guide to the preparation of student reports on proposed remedies.
- What conditions led to the human rights abuse in this case?
- Who were the perpetrators and what were their apparent motives?

- Who were the victims, and which human rights standards were violated?
- What actions, if any, were taken by bystanders?
- What *could* have been done to prevent or stop the violation?
- What *was* or should have been done to remedy the violation?
- Were any of the international instruments on human rights applied? Could any have been applied?

Materials
- Text, *Breakthrough* 10, 2–3 (Winter/Spring 1989), special issue on human rights (available from Global Education Associates; see Chapter 7 for address)
- Materials packet prepared by teacher and students. Provide students with the guiding questions and ask them to collect news stories, magazine articles, and so forth related to the questions. Ask them also to look for poems, novels, and other films. The videos listed with the units are generally available at rental outlets
- Human rights documents as noted in each unit, available from the United Nations (see Chapter 7). The conventions used in this syllabus also appear in *Twenty-Four Human Rights Documents* (New York: Center for the Study of Human Rights, Columbia University)

Learning Sequence

Unit 1. Introduction to the international standards and the historical development of concepts of human rights.
- Reading: Richard Claude and Burns Weston, "Human Rights: A Multidimensional Struggle That Takes Human Suffering Seriously," *Breakthrough.*
- Videos: *Right Relations* (Lucas Productions); *The Universal Declaration of Human Rights* (Amnesty International).

Unit 2. Crimes against peace: war, genocide, and individual responsibility. Nuremberg: the trial, the principles, perspectives on accountability.
- Readings: "Nuremberg Principles" (see Sample 23); Convention on the Prevention and Punishment of the Crime of Genocide.
- Video: *Judgment at Nuremberg.*

Unit 3. Refugees, the consequences of war, and ethnic repression.
- Readings: Adolfo Pérez-Esquivel, "The Human Right to Justice and Peace," *Breakthrough*; Convention Relating to the Status of Refugees.
- Video: *El Norte.*

Unit 4. Political crimes: civil and political rights, ideological conflict, ideological repression.
- Reading: International Convenant on Civil and Political Rights.
- Video: *Romero.*

Unit 5. Political crimes: disappearance and torture.
- Readings: Convention Against Torture and Other Cruel, Inhuman, or Degrading Treatment or Punishment.
- Video: *The Official Story.*

Unit 6. Racism: the crime of apartheid.
- Reading: International Convention on the Suppression and Punishment of the Crime of Apartheid.
- Video: *A Dry White Season.*

Unit 7. Poverty and colonialism: economic and social rights.
- Readings: Oscar Schachter, "True Rights," *Breakthrough*; International Covenant on Economic, Social, and Cultural Rights.
- Video: *Sugar Cane Alley.*

Unit 8. Exploitation of the vulnerable: the rights of children.
- Reading: Convention on the Rights of the Child, (see Appendix)
- Video: *Salaam Bombay.*

Unit 9. Sexism: the rights of women.
- Readings: Elise Boulding, "A Twentieth-Century Movement for Social Transformation," *Breakthrough*; Convention on the Elimination of All Forms of Discrimination Against Women.
- Video: *Raji and Kamala.*

Unit 10. Crimes against the earth: environmental rights.
- Readings: C. G. Weeramantry, "Science, Law, and the Citizen," *Breakthrough*; Rosalie Bertell, "Health as a Human Right," *Breakthrough.*
- Video: *The Emerald Forest.*

Unit 11. Envisioning a culture of human rights on Planet Earth: "scenario" on a human rights regime. The assignment is to spend time in groups developing an "image" of a future global order guided by concepts and standards of human rights, and to write the story of how it was achieved for presentation and discussion in class.

Chapter 7
Resources for Human Rights Education

Teachers and teacher educators seeking to undertake human rights education will find a variety of useful sources on which to base appropriate learning experiences for their students. A growing number of curricular materials and other teaching aids, many pamphlets and publications distributed by human rights organizations, and the popular media provide rich sources of information and descriptions of events that are very useful as bases for lesson planning and class discussions. Newspapers are probably the best source of succinct coverage of the major current human rights issues and events. We recommend maintaining a human rights bulletin board for posting newspaper clippings and materials from human rights organizations.

We offer here listings of some of the most useful resources: the names and addresses of education organizations concerned with human rights; human rights advocacy organizations; curricular materials; feature films and extracts from some of the major human rights documents featured in the sample curricula in this volume. Please note that the list is not exhaustive, nor does it include all the resources suggested in the individual samples. The author welcomes suggestions for additions for an updated list.

All these resources can be integrated into the conceptual-developmental framework presented in Chapters 1 and 2.

Educational Resource Organizations

The following educational organizations and agencies produce or distribute curricular resources, ideas for teaching activities, and information of interest to human rights educators in universities as well as elementary and secondary schools. Some publish newsletters for teachers. The purpose of these groups is to educate, not to advocate.

Center for Teaching International Relations
University of Denver
Denver, CO 80208

Center for Peace and Conflict Studies
Wayne State University
2319 Faculty Administration Building
Detroit, MI 48202

Compiled by student researchers in the Teachers College Peace Education Program.

Center for the Study of Human Rights
1108 International Affairs Building
Columbia University
New York, NY 10027

Constitutional Rights Foundation
601 South Kingsley Drive
Los Angeles, CA 90005

Defense for Children International
30 Irving Place
New York, NY 10003
(Note: DCI is also an advocacy agency for children's rights)

Educators Against Racism and Apartheid
164-04 Goethals Avenue
Jamaica, NY 11432

Educators Network
Amnesty International
53 W. Jackson, Room 1162
Chicago, IL 60604-3507

Educators for Social Responsibility—Metro
475 Riverside Drive, Room 450
New York, NY 10115

Educators for Social Responsibility
23 Garden Street
Cambridge, MA 02138

Human Rights Center
University of Ottawa
57 Louis Pasteur
Ottawa, Ontario, Canada, K1N 6N6

Human Rights Internet
400 Washington Avenue
Montgomery, AL 36104

Institute for the Study of Genocide
John Jay College of Criminal Justice
City University of New York
899 Tenth Avenue, Room 623
New York, NY 10019

International Labor Rights Education and Research Fund
Box 68
110 Maryland Avenue NE
Washington, DC 20002

NAACP Legal Defense and Educational Fund
99 Hudson Street, 16th floor
New York, NY 10013-2815

National Institute for Citizen Education in the Law
711 G Street
Washington, DC 20003

Office on Global Education
2125 Charles Street
Baltimore, MD 21218

People's Decade of Human Rights Education
526 W. 111th Street, Suite 3B
New York, NY 10025

Reach Center for Multicultural and Global Education
293 North McLeod Street
Arlington, WA 98223

Shalom Education
1448 E. 53rd Street
Chicago, IL 60615

Teaching Tolerance
400 Washington Ave.
Montgomery, AL 36104

UNESCO-UN Liaison Office
3 United Nations Plaza
New York, NY 10017

UNICEF
3 United Nations Plaza
New York, NY 10017

United States Institute of Peace
1550 M Street NW, Suite 700
Washington, DC 20005-1708

World Affairs Council of Philadelphia
1314 Chestnut Street
Philadelphia, PA 19107

World Goodwill
113 University Place, 11th floor
Box 722, Cooper Station
New York, NY 10276

World Order Model Project
475 Riverside Drive, Room 460
New York, NY 10115

World Without War Council
175 5th Avenue
New York, NY 10010

Advocacy Organizations

Many of these organizations publish newsletters and other informational materials that might be adapted for classroom use. Educators should, however, take into account that the materials are designed for advocacy, not education. The primary functions of these organizations are the relief and prevention of human rights abuses and the implementation of human rights standards.

Africa Watch
485 5th Avenue
New York, NY 10017

Albert Einstein Institute
1430 Massachusetts Avenue
Cambridge, MA 02138

Allard K. Lowenstein International Human Rights Law Project
Yale Law School
401A Yale Station
New Haven, CT 06520

American Association for the Advancement of Science
Clearinghouse on Science and Human Rights
1515 Massachusetts Avenue NW
Washington, DC 20005

American Association for the International Commission of Jurists
777 United Nations Plaza
New York, NY 10017

American Bar Association
1155 E. 60th Street
Chicago, IL 60637

American Civil Liberties Union
132 West 43rd Street
New York, NY 10036

American Committee on Africa
198 Broadway
New York, NY 10038

American Friends Service Committee
1501 Cherry Street
Philadelphia, PA 19102

American Jewish Committee
165 East 56th Street
New York, NY 10020

American Near East Refugee Aid
1522 K Street NW, Suite 202
Washington, DC 20005

Americas Watch
485 5th Avenue
New York, NY 10017

Amnesty International USA
322 Eighth Avenue
New York, NY 10001

Archbishop Oscar Arnulfo Romero Relief Fund/ Humanitarian Law Project
8124 West 3rd Street
Los Angeles, CA 90048

Asia Watch
485 5th Avenue
New York, NY 10017

Aspen Institute for Humanistic Studies: Program on Justice, Society and the Individual
1 Lincoln Plaza
New York, NY 10023

B'nai Brith
823 United Nations Plaza
New York, NY 10017

B'nai B'rith International
1640 Rhode Island Avenue NW
Washington, DC 20036

Bread for the World
802 Rhode Island Avenue NE
Washington, DC 20018

Cambodia Documentation Commission
251 W. 87th Street, Apt. 74
New York, NY 10024

Campaign for Peace and Democracy
Box 1640, Cathedral Station
New York, NY 10025

Campaign for Political Rights
201 Massachusetts Avenue NE
Washington, DC 20002

Canadian Human Rights Foundation
3465 Rue Côte-des-Neiges, Suite 301
Montréal, Québec, Canada H3H 1T7

Center for Concern
3700 13th Street NE
Washington, DC 20017

Center for Immigrants' Rights, Inc.
48 St. Mark's Place
New York, NY 10003

Center for Migration Studies
209 Flagg Place
Staten Island, NY 10304

Center for Victims of Torture
722 Fulton Street SE
Minneapolis, MN 55414

Children of the Dawn
56 Clinton Street
Guelph, Ontario, Canada N1H 5G5

Children's Defense Fund
122 C Street, NW
Washington, DC 20001

Christian Church (Disciples of Christ)
International Human Rights Program
222 S. Downey Avenue, Box 1986
Indianapolis, IN 46206

Coalition for a New Foreign and Military Policy
120 Maryland Avenue NE
Washington, DC 20002

Committee of Concerned Asian Scholars
50700 South Woodlawn Avenue
Chicago, IL 60637

Council for Human Rights in Latin America
3835 SW Kelly Street
Portland, OR 97201

Cultural Survival Inc.
11 Divinity Avenue
Cambridge, MA 02138

Eritrean Relief Committee
475 Riverside Drive, Room 251
New York, NY 10115

Foundation for Human Rights and Democracy in China
733 15th Street NW, Suite 525
Washington, DC 20005

Freedom House
48 East 21st Street, 5th floor
New York, NY 10010

Fund for Free Expression
485 5th Avenue
New York, NY 10017

Helsinki Watch
485 5th Avenue
New York, NY 10017

Human Rights Internet
1338 G Street SE
Washington, DC 20003

Human Rights Internet
Harvard Law School
Pound Hall, Room 401
Cambridge, MA 02138

Human Rights Watch
485 5th Avenue
New York, NY 10017

Indian Law Resource Center
601 E Street SE
Washington, DC 20003

Institute for the Arts of Democracy
36 Eucalyptus Lane, Suite 100
San Rafael, CA 94901

Institute for the Study of Human Issues
3401 Market Street, Room 252
Philadelphia, PA 19104

Inter-American Commission on Human Rights, Organization of American States
1725 I Street NW
Washington, DC 20006

International Catholic Child Bureau
323 E. 47th Street
New York, NY 10017

International Commission of Jurists
American Association for ICJ
777 United Nations Plaza
New York, NY 10017

International Committee of the Red Cross
Liaison Office to the United Nations
815 2nd Avenue, Room 510
New York, NY 10017

International Human Rights Law Group
1346 Connecticut Avenue NW
Washington, DC 20036

International Indian Treaty Council
777 United Nations Plaza
New York, NY 10017

International League for Human Rights
432 Park Avenue South, #103
New York, NY 10016

International Rescue Committee
386 Park Avenue South
New York, NY 10016-8860

International Women's Action Watch
Humphrey Institute of Public Affairs
301 19th Avenue
Minneapolis, MN 55451

Interparliamentary Human Rights Program
International Secretariat, Congressional
Human Rights Foundation
901 31st Street NW
Washington, DC 20007-3838

Latin American Documentation Center
1312 Massachusetts Avenue NW
Washington, DC 20005

Lawyers Committee for Human Rights
330 7th Avenue
New York, NY 10001

Lawyers Committee for International Human Rights
36 W. 44th Street
New York, NY 10036

Lawyers for Children
850 7th Avenue
New York, NY 10019

Meiklejohn Civil Liberties Institute
Box 673
Berkeley, CA 94701-0673

Middle East Research and Information Project
Box 3122
Washington, DC 20010

Middle East Watch
485 5th Avenue
New York, NY 10017

Minority Rights Group
35 Claremont Avenue, #4S
New York, NY 10027

NAACP Special Contribution Fund
4805 Mount Hope Drive
Baltimore, MD 21215

National Abortion Rights Action League
1101 14th Street NW
Washington, DC 20005

National Council of Churches
Human Rights Office
475 Riverside Drive
New York, NY 10115

National Institute Against Prejudice and Violence
31 S. Greene Street
Baltimore, MD 21201

National Organization of Women
1000 16th Street NW, Suite 700
Washington, DC 20036

New England Human Rights Network
c/o American Friends Service Committee
2161 Massachusetts Avenue
Cambridge, MA 02140

Office of Tibet
107 E. 31st Street
New York, NY 10016

Orville H. Schell, Jr. Center for International
Human Rights
401-A Yale Station
127 Wall Street
New Haven, CT 06520

Older Women's League
730 11th Street NW, Suite 300
Washington, DC 20001-4512

Oxfam America
115 Broadway
Boston, MA 02116

PEN American Center
568 Broadway
New York, NY 10010

Refugee Voices
713 Monroe Street NE
Washington, DC 20017

Solidaridad/Solidarity
1114 Noble Street
Houston, TX 77009

Southern Poverty Law Center
400 Washington Avenue
Montgomery, AL 36195

Survival International (U.S.A.) for Street Children
2121 Decatur Place NW
Washington, DC 20008

United Nations Association of the USA
485 5th Avenue
New York, NY 10017

United States Catholic Conference, Office of
International Justice and Peace
1312 Massachusetts Avenue NW
Washington, DC 20005

*U.S. Department of State, Office of Human Rights,
Bureau of Human Rights and Humanitarian
Affairs*
Washington, DC 20520

United States Institute of Human Rights
200 Park Avenue
New York, NY 10017

Wheat for Peace
3835 SW Kelly
Portland, OR 97201

*Women's International League for Peace and
Freedom*
1213 Race Street
Philadelphia, PA 19107-1691

Curriculum Resources—General

While curriculum resources in human rights are far from adequate in quantity and variety, there are a growing number of published materials from which teachers can choose for developing human rights units suited to their respective teaching needs. There are as well several listings and bibliographies that include content descriptions and ordering information for a range of resources that can be adapted to peace and human rights education. These are listed first.

Annotated Lists and Bibliographies

Human Rights: A Selection of Films, Booklets, and Photos. United Nations, 1988. Available from United Nations Department of Public Information, United Nations, New York, NY 10017.

This pamphlet contains descriptions of a wide range of materials suited to senior high school and above.

Human Rights Education Bibliography. Amnesty International, May 1992. AI Index: Pol 32/01/92. Distri: SC/GR/P6. Available from AI International Secretariat, 1 Easton St., London WCIX8DJ, United Kingdom.

This is probably the most comprehensive of all bibliographies of materials for teaching about human rights and peace, both print and visual in several languages. Lists materials available from various European countries, Canada, and the United States.

General Curriculum Resources for All Levels

The resources listed here are not designed for particular developmental levels. They include general suggestions to be adapted for various levels, or sample approaches for a range of levels.

ABC of Teaching Human Rights: Practical Activities for Primary and Secondary Schools. UN Centre for Human Rights, Geneva. Available from UN Sales Section, New York, NY 10017.

This booklet aims at fostering awareness and comprehension of human rights by providing basic information about rights and respect for self and others, within the context of the Universal Declaration of Rights. Activities for children of all age groups are outlined; those for younger children focus on nurturing their sense of self worth and respect for others. These activities were designed to make the idea of human rights more meaningful. The exercises for older children deal with current issues and promote a greater understanding of the issues.

While part of the text contains traditional instructional materials about human rights, the central theme of the book is for children to experience human rights through various activities. There is a particular emphasis on role playing for older children, while activities for the younger ones are more exploratory in nature. This is an excellent guide for practical applications in the classroom.

Approaches to Human Rights Teaching: Material for Schools, by Helena Allahwerdi and Lisa Jaaskelainen. Finnish National Commission for UNESCO, Helsinki, 1989. Available from UN Sales Section, New York, NY 10017.

This is a detailed, well organized book of approaches, activities, and games teaching human rights to children. The book was developed for Finnish schools but the material may be used anywhere. The book covers teaching values and encourages participation and action on the part of students. It presents implementation models for schools along with particular methods of instruction. Activities, games, and literature are outlined according to themes such as non-violence and the environment. There is a special chapter devoted to apartheid.

In the Child's Best Interest: A Primer on the UN Convention on the Rights of the Child, by Kay Castelle. Defense for Children International-USA, New York, 1990. Available from Defense for Children International-USA, 210 Forsyth St., New York, NY 10002. $5.95.

Describes the Convention in simple terminology; explains why there are special rights for children with elaboration and statistics on child rights violations. The articles of the Convention are interpreted and illustrated by drawings done by children all over the world.

In the Spirit of Peace: A Global Introduction to Children's Rights, by Kay Castelle and Dennis Nurske. Defense for Children International-USA, New York, 1990. Available from Defense for Children International-USA, 210 Forsyth St., New York, NY 10002. Grades 5–12, $7.95.

Examines, from a multicultural perspective, 23 children's rights issues as they pertain to children of countries and cultures all over the world. Each right is developed into a lesson designed specifically for the classroom. Readings are paired with discussion questions, background information, and related activities and often illustrated with cartoons, maps, and other images from a variety of cultures. The UN Convention on the Rights of the Child is used as a framework, dividing the rights into survival, protection and development.

Learning the Skills of Peacemaking: An Activity Guide for Elementary Age Children on Communicating, Cooperating and Resolving Conflict, by Naomi Drew. Rolling Hills Estates, CA: Jalmar Press, 1987. $21.95.

An exceptional curriculum filled with concrete activities that allow children to learn self-awareness, sensitivity to others, mediation, compromise, and cooperative problem solving. It consists of fifty six lessons that focus on each individual's personal responsibilities as well as on developing a respect for human differences, tolerance, acceptance, and cooperation.

Reaching Children: In Celebration of the Rights of the Child: An Activity Based Teachers Unit, by Marilyn Stroud. UNICEF. Available from U.S. Committee on UNICEF, 333 E. 38th St., New York, NY 10016. Free on request.

A wonderfully written and illustrated pamphlet presenting ten articles of the Convention, with details of child rights violations in different parts of the world and descriptions of UNICEF activities to deal with the problems. Twenty-six activities are then outlined in conjunction with the various articles.

Teaching Human Dignity: Social Change Lessons for Every Teacher, by Miriam Wolf-Wasserman and Linda Hutchinson. Education Exploration Resource Center, Minneapolis, 1978. Available from Education Exploration Center, Box 7339, Powderhorn Station, Minneapolis, MN, 55407.

Stories, poems, comments, and reflections on issues of social change dealing with racism, ethnic studies, women's studies, minorities, and colonialism. Other elements such as art, music, drama, math, science, and the media are used to illustrate the theme of social change.

Todos los niños tienen derechos, by Kay Castelle. Defense for Children International-USA, New York, 1991. Available from Defense for Children International-USA, 210 Forsyth St., New York, NY 10002. $5.00.

This is a wonderful story of a journey of discovery and self exploration about a young girl from a foreign planet who explores planet earth and its children in a variety of circumstances. With each encounter, she confronts human rights violations and the need for the Convention on the Rights of the Child. The book is beautifully illustrated and includes discussion questions and answers as well as activities, games, and quizzes related to the book and the Convention. The Convention on the Rights of the Child is presented as well in a simple and coherent fashion, synthesized into ten themes. Suitable for upper elementary and lower secondary school classes.

World Concerns and the United Nations: Model Teaching Units for Primary, Secondary, and Teacher Education. UN Fellowship Program for Educators and UNESCO Associated Schools Project, 1983. Available from UN Publishing Office, New York, NY 10017.

Contains materials on a variety of global issues relevant to human rights.

Teacher Background Materials

Few teacher educators and classroom teachers have a background in human rights subject matter or the theoretical basis of human rights education. The following materials can help provide such background.

Periodicals

Periodicals, occasional papers, and special issues of journals on human rights are particularly useful in teacher education because they provide subject matter background along with rationales for and approaches to human rights education.

Breakthrough (Winter/Spring 1989), Special Issue on Human Rights. Available from Global Education Associates, 475 Riverside Dr., New York, NY 10115.

This may be the best short introduction to human rights history, standards, issues, and controversies. Highly recommended as an essential handbook for teachers, useable as a text for senior high school.

Children at Risk (1992). Division for Church in Society, Evangelical Lutheran Church in America, 8765 West Higgins Rd., Chicago, IL 60631-4190.

This publication deals with the plight of children in various parts of the world and the human rights violations that must be acknowledged and addressed by the international community at large. It is furnished with articles, photographs, prayers for peace from the Christian, Islamic, and Jewish traditions, as well as letters from children in various parts of the world.

Human Rights Teaching. Occasional paper issued by UNESCO, 7 Place de Fontenoy, 75700 Paris, France. Deals with particular issues providing useful substance for teaching.

Social Education 55, 2 (February 1991). Special Section on Genocide, edited by Samual Totten, National Council of the Social Studies. Available from the Council.

Provides an historic overview and inquiry into moral and ethical concerns. Excellent case materials and extracts from primary sources and first-hand accounts.

Social Education 56, 4 (April/May 1992). Special Section on The Rights of the Child, edited by Beverly C. Edmonds and William R. Fernekes, National Council of the Social Studies. Available from the Council, $7.50.

A compilation of articles by social studies professionals about teaching children's rights. Topics covered include analysis of the Convention on the Rights of the Child, civic skills, student activism and participation, multiculturalism, children's rights in foreign countries, and child labor. The relationship between teaching about the rights of the child and the social studies discipline is also explored. Resource and organization lists are included as well.

UNESCO Courier: Children in Danger (October 1991). UNESCO, 31 Rue François Bonvin, 75015 Paris, France. $3.90.

This issue explores the plights of children in various countries and focuses on themes of multiculturalism, children of the streets, gangs, stress, poverty, child labor, and the Convention on the Rights of the Child. The articles on the various topics are beautifully illustrated by colorful art work done by children from all over the world. Authors of the articles are also leaders in fields related to children's issues and are from different countries worldwide.

Winning Ideas to Stop Racism. March 1992. Anti-Racism Campaign, Department of Canadian Heritage, Ottawa, Ontario, K1A 1K5.

> Produced by a project for eliminating racism and racial discrimination. The publication is a compilation of prose, poetry, art work, cartoons, visual graphics, and quotations dealing with racism submitted by Canadian children from schools across Canada. The publication is in both English and French and is a wonderful reflection of children's thoughts and feelings about the highly emotional topic of racism. (Sample 17 contains some extracts.)

Other Background Materials

How Children Learn About Human Rights, by Wilhelmina Hill and Helen K. Mackintosh. Federal Security Agency, Office of Education, Bulletin 1951, No. 9, Washington, DC.

> This article is particularly important in light of the fact that it was written in the early 1950s and was published by a government agency. While the article is dated, it draws on the United Nations call for integrating the study of human rights into the schools curriculum. The authors discuss the use of situational learning, problem solving, books, and stories to build attitudes and understanding. They are optimistic in their belief in children's capacities for processing and understanding the concepts of human rights. The book also provides examples of what some schools were doing to integrate this teaching into the curricula.

Human Rights Education in Schools: Concepts, Attitudes and Skills, by Derek Heater. Strasbourg: Council for Cultural Cooperation/School Education Division, Council of Europe, February 1984.

> A history of the evolution of teaching human rights and an elaboration on the central concepts, including justice, equality, discrimination, freedom, and self-determination. It advises teachers on how to introduce human rights and the relevant vocabulary. The writers distinguish between teaching values, intellectual processing, and action skills.

Teachers' Handbook: Teaching the UN Convention on the Rights of the Child. UNICEF-UK, Save the Children and Oxford Development Education Unit, 1990.

> This is a companion guide to a series of three books teaching about the protection, participation, and provision articles in the Convention. It provides background for the teacher about the rights of the child and how various disciplines can include teaching about these rights. It also includes an official text of the Convention with unofficial summaries of the provisions.

Teaching and Learning About Human Rights, by Ian Lister. Strasbourg: Council for Cultural Cooperation/School Education Division, Council of Europe, July 1984.

> This publication focuses on the content, methods, materials, and projects in human rights education. It looks at human rights teaching from an historical perspective, drawing on social studies, history, and other disciplines. Concepts of rights and related duties, obligations, and responsibilities are also examined.

United Nations Materials

In addition to the materials listed above, the following are a sample of background materials available from the Department of Public Information, United Nations, New York, NY 10017.

Human Rights. Human Rights Fact Sheets Nos. 1–16, Centre for Human Rights, United Nations, Geneva.
> This series treats particular issues and problems in human rights. Excellent for teacher background and for short readings for senior high school. The series is ongoing, so more sheets are likely to be published.

Human Rights: Questions and Answers. 1987.
> A discussion about rights and the role of the United Nations and related organizations in their implementation. Particular international issues such as torture, apartheid, and cultural rights are explored and the text of the Universal Declaration of Human Rights is included.

Objective Justice.
> A review dedicated to the promotion of justice through self-determination of peoples, the criminalization of apartheid and racial discrimination, and the advancement of human rights.

Materials on the Convention on the Rights of the Child

Convention on the Rights of the Child. Department of Public Information, United Nations, New York, May 1991.
> This short booklet provides an introduction to and history of the United Nations promotion of specific rights for children through the Convention on the Rights of the Child. It includes a highlighted summary of the Convention and a detailed presentation of articles 1–54. A basic straightforward outline of the Convention, suitable for teachers and older children.

Convention on the Rights of the Child: Information Kit. United Nations Center for Human Rights, New York, NY 10017 and UNICEF, 3 United Nations Plaza, New York, NY 10017. Free on request.
> This packet is prefaced by a letter from the UN Under-Secretary-General for Human Rights and the Director of UNICEF, followed by an in-depth overview and history of the Convention. The ratification and implementation of the Convention are discussed, as are the flexibility of the articles and their universal approach. In particular, those provisions dealing with survival and development, name nationality and identity, exploitation, adoption, gender inequality, and education are explored. The text of the Convention is included along with an unofficial summary of the main provisions.

The Convention on the Rights of the Child: The 1989 Convention and Related Information. United States Committee for UNICEF, 333 E. 38th St., New York, NY 10016. Free on request.

Includes a copy of the text of the Convention and background information of the Convention and its ratification with particular emphasis on letter-writing in the U.S. for the purpose of ratification.

The Rights of the Child. Stamp Booklet and Highlights of the Convention, United Nations Postal Administration, PO Box 5900, New York, NY 10163-9992. Also available at the United Nations Department of Public Information. Free on request.

Traces in very clear and basic terminology the history of the Declaration and Convention of the Rights of the Child, from the founding of the United Nations to the present and makes projections for the future. The four main categories of the Convention are highlighted: Survival, Development, Protection, and Participation. The booklet is illustrated with children's artwork; stamps may be ordered commemorating the Rights of the Child.

Universal Declaration of Human Rights, illustrated by Jean Michel Folon. Amnesty International-Belgium, 1989.

This is a presentation of the Declaration in the six official United Nations languages—Arabic, Chinese, English, French, Russian, and Spanish. The text is illustrated by wonderful artwork by the Belgian painter Folon.

The Universal Declaration of Human Rights: An Adaptation for Children, by Ruth Rocha and Octavio Roth. United Nations Publications, 1989. Available through Amnesty International or UN Sales Section. $10.00.

A beautifully illustrated adaptation of the Universal Declaration with very basic and simple terminology expressing the actual content of the declaration. Suitable to upper elementary and secondary grades.

Curriculum Resources by Grade Level

The following materials have been reviewed by several of the resource researchers who worked on the Columbia project. They have been organized for the convenience of teachers, according to the developmental levels followed in the main text. Many can, of course, be adapted to other grade levels, but we feel them to be most suited to the levels for which they are listed.

The Early Grades, K–3

As of this writing, not a great deal of curricular material is available specifically designed for human rights education at this level. However, much children's literature focuses on the values and concepts central to the goals and purposes of human rights education. One source of information on such books is the Council for Children's Interracial Books (see list of Resource Organizations).

Included here are descriptions of a few selected curricula, some designed for a range wider than K–3.

Education for International Cooperation and Peace at the Primary School Level. UNESCO, 1983. Available from UNESCO, 7 Place de Fontenoy, 75700 Paris, France. Pages 21–37, Human Rights: The Needs and Rights of the Child. Pages 123–35, UNESCO Recommendation for Education for International Understanding, Cooperation and Peace and Education Relating to Human Rights and Fundamental Freedoms. Available from UN Sales Section, New York. $8.00.

This publication focuses on how international understanding can be promoted in both the home and the school. Related and adaptable methods of instruction including projects, discussion questions, exchange programs, and teaching materials of various countries are reviewed, and particular techniques and activities related to teaching human rights and the rights of the child are discussed. There is also a chapter dedicated to socio-affective teaching methods. The book uses the United Nations and related agencies as examples of organizations committed to international understanding and human rights.

Human Rights for Children: A Curriculum for Teaching Human Rights to Children Ages 3–12. Human Rights for Children Committee, Hunter House, Box 2914, Alameda, CA 94502.

This resource funded by Amnesty International is organized around the ten principles of the 1959 Declaration of the Rights of the Child. Suggestions for a variety of activities for teaching the concepts and purposes of each principle are offered for the "young child," "the primary child," and "the upper elementary child." Each subject area includes an annotated list of relevant children's books and a bibliography describing other selected teaching resources.

The Middle Grades, 4–6

Teachers in the middle grade level of elementary school have a wide variety of general global education materials to choose from. Only a few, however, are particularly designed for and adaptable to human rights education. Some of those few are noted here.

Food First Curriculum, by Laurie Rubin. Institute for Food and Development Policy, San Francisco, CA, 1984, $12.

Tailored for 6th grade with modifications for 4th–5th and 7th–8th. Deals with issues of world hunger and food distribution.

Human Rights, by Samuel Totten and Milton Kleg. Enslow. 1989.

This well-documented survey tells the history of human rights from ancient Greece and China to the present. Offering interviews and eyewitness accounts that vividly show what effect the denial of human rights has upon people's everyday lives, the book discusses such topics as racism, genocide, discrimination, torture, hunger, and political prisoners. The book emphasizes that every person has not only the right to live by her or his own beliefs, with respect and dignity, and without fear and repression, but also the responsibility to protect these rights. To this end, the book offers specific suggestions on how readers can actively work to protect human rights.

New Tools for International Understanding: A Peace Education Curriculum for Elementary and Secondary School Students, by Dale Hudson. Available from Global Educators' Marketplace, Box 165, Kapaau, HI 96755.

   Although not a human rights curriculum as such, this is an excellent collection of learning activities based on the core value of the universality of human dignity or "The Oneness of Humankind." It comprises lessons that make a fine introduction to the topics of constructive human relations and positive peace.

The United Nations: A Right to Rights, by Dorothy Hoffman and Mary Eileen Sorenson. Educating for Peace Project, United Nations Association of America and United Nations Association of Minnesota. $6.95.

   General introduction to UN work in the area of human rights; contains specific lessons on how the international standards are developed and applied.

The Whole Child: A Project to Introduce the UN Convention on the Rights of the Child. UNICEF-UK, Save the Children and Oxford Development Education Unit, 1990.

   This is one of three books designed to introduce the Convention on the Rights of the Child. It deals with those articles which cover the child's participation in his or her own development. It is a wonderful compilation of innovative, experiential approaches and child-centered activities about a child's basic cultural identity and involvement in the wider society. The perspective is on the experiences of a British or European child, but many activities are suitable for children anywhere, and most may be easily adapted.

Junior High School, Grades 7–9

At the junior high school level there are now more materials specifically focused on human rights. What follows are some of the most recent of these.

Children Hungering for Justice, by Carla van Buren. Produced by the Office on Global Education, available from the Center for Teaching International Relations, University of Denver, Denver, CO 80208-0268.

   A curriculum on hunger and children's rights for grades 9–12, this three part unit makes the important links among hunger, social justice, and international human rights standards.

Flight to Hope: A Catholic Refugee Awareness Project. Catholic Consortium on Refugee Awareness Education, 1990. $10.00.

   This material includes eight lesson plans that incorporate a holistic approach to teaching about refugees, including clever games and activities that encourage the child to take the perspective of the refugee child and closely examine government attitudes toward the issue. The approach has a religious bent and biblical teachings are offered as supplemental to the curriculum. There is an informative section specifically for teacher training and sensitization to the topic. Adaptable to secular settings.

Human Rights, by Carole A. Balkey and Andrea Gabriel (Amahengelo Oluntu). Community Law Centre, 249 Berea Rd., Durban 4001, South Africa, 1991.

This book represents a curricular and a political breakthrough in South African education. Presented in both English and Zulu, it is the result of cooperation between the Centre and the National Institute for Citizen Education in the Law in Washington, DC. The 30 articles of the Universal Declaration of Human Rights are explicated with text and illustrations accompanied by challenging questions for class discussion. It is suitable for a variety of uses in grades 7–12 in all English-speaking countries.

Human Rights: Today's World, by Charles Freeman. Available from Social Studies School Services, Box 802, Culver City, CA 90233.

Are human rights a purely Western concept? Which rights are more important—the social and economic rights espoused by Communist states or the individual freedoms proclaimed by capitalist governments? Drawing on examples from all over the world, this thought-provoking resource surveys the history of human rights and investigates the status of human rights in the contemporary world. The UN Universal Declaration of Human Rights is reprinted in full at the end of the book. Middle grades and up.

It's Our Right: A Project to Introduce the UN Convention on the Rights of the Child. UNICEF-UK, Save the Children and Oxford Development Education Unit, 1990.

This material, another of the set of three, deals with those articles of the Convention on the Rights of the Child which cover provision for the child's physical and emotional development, including nutritious food, clean water, and health services. It examines these rights and introduces case studies on the lives of children in both the UK and other countries.

Keep Us Safe: A Project to Introduce the UN Convention on the Rights of the Child. UNICEF-UK, Save the Children and Oxford Development Education Unit, 1990.

The third in the series, this publication expands on the protection articles, rights that require adults to care for children by protecting them from psychological, emotional, physical, and sexual maltreatment. The right to rehabilitation is stressed throughout. As in the other two books in the series, related articles are discussed in the various experiential activities, which deal with children all over the world where protective rights are not recognized.

Peacemaker: Module One—A Post Primary Peace Programme. Teacher's Book and Students' Worksheets. Joint Peace Program, Irish Commission for Justice and Peace and Irish Council of Churches, 1991. Available from Peace Education Program, 48 Elmwood Ave., Belfast BT9 6AZ, Ireland.

This compilation is aimed at facilitating growth of peacemaking skills and attitudes in students. Several units focus on the development of self esteem, communication, and acceptance of self and others. There is a Christian perspective to the teaching modules, including a focus on reflection, Bible, and prayer. This may be adapted to other grades and to secular settings as well.

Taking a Stand Against Human Rights Abuses, by Michael Kronenwetter. Watts, 1990.
A variety of teaching activities and approaches to a major obstacle to the enjoyment of economic rights. A timely overview of the current status of human rights in the world, punctuated with dramatic case studies, not only of people whose basic human rights have been denied them, but also of people who work to end these abuses. After an historical overview of human rights, from the writings of John Locke through the UN Universal Declaration of Human Rights, chapters discuss "Why Governments Abuse Human Rights" and "People Taking a Stand." Describing organizations such as Amnesty International which work to make people aware of human rights abuses, the book also suggests how to join a human rights organization and stresses the importance of taking a stand on issues that affect one's life.

Teaching About Food and Hunger, by George Otero and Gary Smith. Center for Teaching International Relations, University of Denver, Denver, CO 80208-0268, 1989.
This resource provides approaches to teaching about the denial of the most fundamental of economic rights.

Teaching About Human Rights. 1991. Education Information Programme, Special Programmes Section, Department of Public Information, United Nations, New York, NY 10017.
A compilation of readings and classroom examples on various aspects of human rights with a special emphasis on the rights of the child. A companion video "About the United Nations: Human Rights" is also available. A major theme of the activities is discrimination and taking action against it. The United Nations and related agencies are also explored, and guidelines are provided as to how to initiate a "Human Rights Society." This material is suitable for upper primary as well as secondary students.

Senior High School, Grades 10–12

There are more materials available for high school than for any other level. A number of the items listed above for junior high school are also used in senior high school. Those listed below are among those we believe to be the best for the upper grades.

Civil Justice, Constitutional Rights Foundation and Scholastic, 1988. Available from Scholastic Inc., New York, NY. $8.25.
An introduction to civil law in the United States. The book addresses the interests and concerns of students and explains the practical steps they should take to protect their rights as citizens, consumers, workers, witnesses, or family members.

Exploding the Hunger Myths, by Sonia Williams. Institute for Food and Development Policy, San Francisco, CA, 1987.

> This curriculum provides materials very useful to exploring the right to food and the social responsibility of citizens to work to fulfill it. It also offers an excellent basis for studying obstacles to human rights such as poverty, scarcity, and aspects of the global resource distribution system.

Human Rights for All, by David McGuoid-Mason, E. O'Brien, and E. Greene, 1991. A publication of Lawyers for Human Rights (South Africa) and the National Institute for Citizen Education in the Law (USA). Available from the Institute, 711 G St., Washington, DC 20003.

> This is probably the best conceptual introduction to human rights for the high school student. It covers fundamental definitions and classifications and provides a comprehensive overview of rights, economic and social as well as political and the rights of those under arrest. It contains lively learning activities and suggestions for action on behalf of human rights. A landmark in human rights curriculum material for South Africa and all other English-speaking countries.

Teaching Human Rights, by David Shiman. Center for Teaching International Relations, University of Denver, Denver, CO 80208-0268, 1993.

> Probably the most comprehensive curricular resource for the secondary level. Organized around issues and topics, it provides ample background content, handouts and all that is needed for over two dozen teaching units, all well constructed, explained clearly, and well documented. This is the second edition of a work first published in 1988.

Torture by Governments. Amnesty International USA, 1985.

> This curriculum presents issues related to civil and political rights violated by torture, using poetry, prose, and artwork of those who have endured it. The curriculum consists of readings and related research, action activities, and discussion questions. The material is very serious, explicit, and highly sensitive. Teachers must judge the appropriateness in terms of their students. This material may be used in a number of different disciplines.

World Hunger and Social Justice, by Gary McCuen. GEM Publications Inc. Hudson, WI, 1986. $12.95.

> A textbook reviewing the crisis in world hunger in terms of economic variables and foreign relations, and focusing on a new world order. Activities and discussion questions are suggested for reasoning and skill development.

Selected Films

We use art and literature to teach and learn about social issues because they express aspects of human experience which cannot be captured by sources produced from research and journalism, and thus are not usually found in texts and news media. Understanding the human dimension of issues such as those related to human rights and peace is essential to the development of solutions to the problems they pose. To explore questions of rights and responsibilities we must confront specific instances arising from actual historical events as experienced and imagined by others. We can learn much by reflecting on the experiences and reflections of others. This experience and reflection has been the inspiration of many feature films.

Films are a particularly useful art form for educators seeking to put flesh on the bones of the abstract value issues and policy decisions that lie at the core of most human rights and peace questions.

Art forms can be most instructive and enriching when viewed from various perspectives. Viewing films outside class is best done in cooperative learning groups; sharing perspectives, reflections, and assessments will enable you to learn more from the films and generate more ideas about how they can be used for teaching purposes.

Because we are specifically concerned with issues and dilemmas of rights and responsibilities, groups are urged to direct discussion particularly to those scenes and aspects of the films which most sharply focus on such issues and dilemmas. As they reflect upon these aspects and scenes, they should note how various attributes of the medium beyond the scenario are used to convey a point of view, raise a question, or emphasize a dilemma.

It is essential that all films be previewed prior to showing. If the film cannot be shown in full in class, select the most significant portions and try to arrange for a full viewing. It is useful to discuss each film after class and again after the entire film has been viewed.

Most of the films listed below are available on video unless otherwise indicated. All films are in English or have English subtitles and all are feature films. Some were made for television.

Some feature films and many documentaries are listed and annotated in Anne Gelman and Milos Stehlik, *Human Rights Film Guide*. Chicago: Facets Multimedia, 1985.

The following are a few of the many films that can be adapted to human rights education. They are listed here because they have proven useful in exploring the human rights topic under which they are listed.

APARTHEID
Cry the Beloved Country
Cry Freedom
Voices of Sarafina
Place of Weeping
A Dry White Season

CHILDREN
Fannie and Alexander
Pixote
Los Olvidades
Salaam Bombay

ECONOMICS AND POVERTY
Grapes of Wrath
Sugar Cane Alley

ENVIRONMENT
The Emerald Forest
The River
The Mosquito Coast
Medicine Man

ETHNOCIDE
The Searchers
The Fringe Dwellers
Where the Green Ants Dream

GENOCIDE
The Mission
At Play in the Fields of the Lord
The Killing Fields
Little Big Man
Dances with Wolves
Hotel Terminus
The Red & the Black

HOLOCAUST
The Diary of Anne Frank
Nuremberg Trials
That None Should Die—Le Chambrun
Au Revoir Les Enfants
The Music Box
The Wansee Conference
Weapons of the Spirit
Judgment at Nuremberg
Shoah

INDIVIDUAL RESPONSIBILITY
Thomas Moore
Joseph Schultz
Judgment at Nuremberg
Hans Yegerstadter
Salvador
Romero

POLITICAL REPRESSION
Yol
Missing
Z
The Trial
Prisoner Without a Name—Cell Without a Number
Danton
State of Siege
One Man's War

Appendix: Selected Human Rights Documents

This appendix includes, first, a list of major United Nations human rights instruments, in order by the date on which each entered into force. Next are excerpts from or adaptations of the three human rights instruments most relevant to a comprehensive approach to human rights education based on the principles of universality and indivisibility: the Universal Declaration of Human Rights, the Convention on the Elimination of All Forms of Discrimination Against Women, and the Convention on the Rights of the Child.

Portions of several other important documents are included with the Handouts to the sample lessons in this volume.

LIST OF MAJOR HUMAN RIGHTS INSTRUMENTS

Universal Declaration of Human Rights (1948)

Convention on the Prevention and Punishment of the Crime of Genocide (January 12, 1951)

International Convention on the Elimination of All Forms of Racial Discrimination (January 4, 1969)

International Covenant on Economic, Social and Cultural Rights (January 3, 1976)

International Covenant on Civil and Political Rights (March 23, 1976)

Optional Protocol to International Covenant on Civil and Political Rights (March 23, 1976)

Convention on the Elimination of All Forms of Discrimination against Women (September 3, 1981)

Convention against Torture and Other Cruel, Inhuman or Degrading Treatment or Punishment (June 26, 1987)

Convention on the Rights of the Child (September 2, 1990)

UNIVERSAL DECLARATION OF HUMAN RIGHTS (1948)

Preamble

Whereas recognition of the inherent dignity and of the equal and inalienable rights of all members of the human family is the foundation of freedom, justice and peace in the world, . . .

Whereas it is essential . . . that human rights should be protected by the rule of law, . . .

Whereas the peoples of the United Nations have in the Charter reaffirmed their faith in fundamental human rights, in the dignity and worth of the human person and in the equal rights of men and women, . . .

Now, therefore,

The General Assembly

Proclaims this Universal Declaration of Human Rights as a common standard of achievement for all peoples and all nations, to the end that every individual and every organ of society, keeping this Declaration constantly in mind, shall strive by teaching and education to promote respect for these rights and freedoms and by progressive measures, national and international, to secure their universal and effective recognition and observance. . . .

Article 1

All human beings are born free and equal in dignity and rights. They are endowed with reason and conscience and should act towards one another in a spirit of brotherhood.

Article 2

Everyone is entitled to all the rights and freedoms set forth in this Declaration, without distinction of any kind, such as race, colour, sex, language, religion, political or other opinion, national or social origin, property, birth or other status. . . .

Article 3

Everyone has the right to life, liberty and security of person.

Article 4

No one shall be held in slavery or servitude. . . .

Article 5

No one shall be subjected to torture or to cruel, inhuman or degrading treatment or punishment.

Excerpted from U.N.G.A. Res. 217A (III), 3 (1) U.N. GAOR Res. 71, U.N. Doc. A/810 (1948).
Note: The masculine pronouns used throughout the Declaration reflect the usage of the time. As the Preamble makes clear, it refers to both men and women.

Article 6

Everyone has the right to recognition everywhere as a person before the law.

Article 7

All are equal before the law and are entitled without any discrimination to equal protection of the law. . . .

Article 8

Everyone has the right to an effective remedy by the competent national tribunals for acts violating the fundamental rights granted him by the constitution or by law.

Article 9

No one shall be subjected to arbitrary arrest, detention or exile.

Article 10

Everyone is entitled in full equality to a fair and public hearing by an independent and impartial tribunal, in the determination of his rights and obligations and of any criminal charge against him.

Article 11

1. Everyone charged with a penal offence has the right to be presumed innocent until proved guilty according to law in a public trial at which he has had all the guarantees necessary for his defence.

2. No one shall be held guilty of any penal offence on account of any act or omission which did not constitute a penal offence, under national or international law, at the time when it was committed. Nor shall a heavier penalty be imposed than the one that was applicable at the time the penal offence was committed.

Article 12

No one shall be subjected to arbitrary interference with his privacy, family, home or correspondence, nor to attacks upon his honour and reputation. Everyone has the right to the protection of the law against such interference or attacks.

Article 13

1. Everyone has the right to freedom of movement and residence within the borders of each State.

2. Everyone has the right to leave any country, including his own, and to return to his country.

Article 14

1.Everyone has the right to seek and to enjoy in other countries asylum from persecution.

2. This right may not be invoked in the case of prosecutions genuinely arising from nonpolitical crimes. . . .

Article 15

1. Everyone has the right to a nationality.

2. No one shall be arbitrarily deprived of his nationality nor denied the right to change his nationality.

Article 16

1. Men and women of full age, without any limitation due to race, nationality or religion, have the right to marry and to found a family. They are entitled to equal rights as to marriage, during marriage and at its dissolution.

2. Marriage shall be entered into only with the free and full consent of the intending spouses.

3. The family is the natural and fundamental group unit of society and is entitled to protection by society and the State.

Article 17

1. Everyone has the right to own property alone as well as in association with others.

2. No one shall be arbitrarily deprived of his property.

Article 18

Everyone has the right to freedom of thought, conscience and religion. . . .

Article 19

Everyone has the right to freedom of opinion and expression; this right includes freedom to hold opinions without interference and to seek, receive and impart information. . . .

Article 20

1. Everyone has the right to freedom of peaceful assembly and association.

2. No one may be compelled to belong to an association.

Article 21

1. Everyone has the right to take part in the government of his country, directly or through freely chosen representatives.

2. Everyone has the right of equal access to public service in his country. . . .

3. The will of the people shall be the basis of the authority of government by universal and equal suffrage. . . .

Article 22

Everyone, as a member of society, has the right to social security and is entitled to . . . the economic, social and cultural rights indispensable for his dignity and the free development of his personality.

Article 23

1. Everyone has the right to work, to free choice of employment, to just and favourable conditions of work and to protection against unemployment.

2. Everyone, without any discrimination, has the right to equal pay for equal work.

3. Everyone who works has the right to just and favourable remuneration ensuring for himself and his family an existence worthy of human dignity, and supplemented, if necessary, by other means of social protection.

4. Everyone has the right to form and to join trade unions for the protection of his interests.

Article 24

Everyone has the right to rest and leisure, including reasonable limitation of working hours and periodic holidays with pay.

Article 25

1. Everyone has the right to a standard of living adequate for the health and well-being of himself and of his family, including food, clothing, housing and medical care and necessary social services, and the right to security in the event of unemployment, sickness, disability, widowhood, old age or other lack of livelihood in circumstances beyond his control.

2. Motherhood and childhood are entitled to special care and assistance. All children, whether born in or out of wedlock, shall enjoy the same social protection.

Article 26

1. Everyone has the right to education. Education shall be free, at least in the elementary and fundamental stages. . . .

2. Education shall be directed to the full development of the human personality and to the strengthening of respect for human rights and fundamental freedoms. . . .

3. Parents have a prior right to choose the kind of education that shall be given to their children.

Article 27

1. Everyone has the right freely to participate in the cultural life of the community. . . .

2. Everyone has the right to the protection of the moral and material interests resulting from any scientific, literary or artistic production of which he is the author.

Article 28

Everyone is entitled to a social and international order in which the rights and freedoms set forth in this Declaration can be fully realized.

Article 29

1. Everyone has duties to the community in which alone the free and full development of his personality is possible.

2. In the exercise of his rights and freedoms, everyone shall be subject only to such limitations as are determined by law solely for the purpose of securing due recognition and respect for the rights and freedoms of others and of meeting the just requirements of morality, public order and the general welfare in a democratic society.

3. These rights and freedoms may in no case be exercised contrary to the purposes and principles of the United Nations.

Article 30

Nothing in this Declaration may be interpreted as implying for any State, group or person any right to engage in any activity or to perform any act aimed at the destruction of any of the rights and freedoms set forth herein.

CONVENTION ON THE ELIMINATION OF ALL FORMS OF DISCRIMINATION AGAINST WOMEN

The Convention on the Elimination of All Forms of Discrimination Against Women is essentially an international bill of rights of women and a framework for women's participation in the development process. The most concise and usable document adopted during the UN Decade for Women, it is the result of several decades of work by the UN Commission on the Status of Women and international women's organizations. The Convention spells out internationally accepted principles and standards for achieving equality between women and men. . . .

The thirty articles of the Convention are condensed below. The full text of the Convention in any of the United Nations languages can be obtained from the United Nations Department of Public information in New York or from the Branch for the Advancement of Women in Vienna. Additional materials on the Convention and on CEDAW, Committee on the Elimination of Discrimination Against Women, can be obtained from IWRAW (see organizations list for address).

Countries that have ratified the Convention "condemn discrimination against women in all its forms" and "agree to pursue by all appropriate means and without delay a policy of eliminating discrimination against women" (Article 2). The first five articles of the Convention outline the general premises of eliminating discrimination and the general obligations undertaken by States parties; the last thirteen articles detail the establishment, functioning, and administration of CEDAW.

Article 1. Definition of discrimination
    —any distinction, exclusion or restriction made on the basis of sex, which has the purpose or effect of denying equal exercise of human rights and fundamental freedoms in all fields of human endeavor.

Article 2. Policy measures to be undertaken to eliminate discrimination
    —embody the principle of equality in national constitutions, codes or other laws, and ensure their practical realization
        —establish institutions to protect against discrimination
        —ensure that public authorities and institutions refrain from discrimination
        —abolish all existing laws, customs and regulations that discriminate against women

Article 3. Guarantees basic human rights and fundamental freedoms on an equal basis with men

Article 4. Temporary special measures to achieve equality
    —temporary special measures may be adopted and must be discontinued when equality is achieved
        —special measures to protect maternity are not considered discriminatory
        —practices based on the inferiority or superiority of either sex shall be eliminated

Adopted 18 Dec. 1979, entered into force 3 Sept. 1981, G.A. Res. 34/180, 34 UN GAOR Supp. (No. 46), UN Doc. A/34/46, at 193 (1979). The excerpted form here is used by permission of the International Women's Rights Action Watch (IWRAW).

—measures should ensure that family education teaches that both men and women share a common role in raising children

Article 5. Sex roles and stereotyping
—social and cultural patterns must be modified to eliminate sex-role stereotypes and notions of the inferiority or superiority of either sex
—family education shall teach that men and women share a common responsibility in the raising of children

Article 6. Prostitution
—measures shall be taken to suppress all forms of traffic in women and exploitation of prostitution

Article 7. Political and public life
—the right to vote in all elections and be eligible for election to all elected bodies
—to participate in formulation of government policy and hold office at all levels of government
—to participate in non-governmental organizations

Article 8. Participation at the international level
—the opportunity to represent their country at the international level and to participate in international organizations

Article 9. Nationality
—equal rights to acquire, change or retain their nationality
—equal rights to the nationality of their children

Article 10. Equal rights in education
—equal access to education and vocational guidance
—the same curricula, examinations, standards for teaching and equipment
—equal opportunity to scholarships and grants
—equal access to continuing education, including literacy programs
—elimination of stereotyping in education and textbooks
—measures for reduction of female dropout rates
—equal participation in sports and physical education
—equal access to health and family planning information

Article 11. Employment
—the same employment rights as men
—free choice of profession, employment and training
—equal remuneration, and benefits, including equal treatment as to work of equal value
—social security
—occupational health and safety protection
—prohibition of dismissal on the basis of pregnancy or marital status
—maternity leave
—provision of social services encouraged, including child care

—special protection against harmful work during pregnancy

Article 12. Health care and family planning
    —equal access to appropriate pregnancy services

Article 13. Economic and social benefits
    —equal access to family benefits; loans and credit
    —equal right to participate in recreational activities, sports, cultural life

Article 14. Rural women
    —recognition of the particular problems of rural women, the special roles they play in economic survival of families and of their unpaid work
    —ensure their equal participation in development
    —right to participate in development planning and implementation
    —access to health care and family planning services
    —right to benefit directly from social security
    —right to training and education
    —right to organize self-help groups and cooperatives
    —right to participate in all community activities
    —right to access to credit, loans, marketing facilities, appropriate technology, and equal treatment in land and agrarian reform and resettlement
    —right to adequate living conditions; housing, sanitation, electricity, water, transport, and communications

Article 15. Equality before the law
    —guarantee of same legal capacity as men; to contract, administer property, appear in court or before tribunals
    —freedom of movement; right to choose residence and domicile
    —contractual and other private restrictions on legal capacity of women shall be declare null and void

Article 16. Marriage and family law
    —equal rights and responsibilities with men in marriage and family relations
    —the right to freely enter into marriage and choose a spouse
    —equality during marriage and at its dissolution
    —the right to choose freely the number and spacing of children; access to information, education, and means to make that choice
    —equal rights to guardianship and adoption of children
    —the same personal rights as husband; right to choose family name, profession, or occupation
    —equal rights and responsibilities regarding ownership, management, and disposition of property
    —a minimum age and registration of marriage

Articles 17–22 (detail the establishment and function of the Committee on the Elimination of Discrimination Against Women (CEDAW)

Articles 23–30 (detail the administration of the Convention)

CONVENTION ON THE RIGHTS OF THE CHILD

Preamble

Appendix

230

The preamble sets the tone in which the 54 articles of the Convention will be interpreted. The major United Nations texts which precede it and which have a direct bearing on children are mentioned, as is the importance of the family for the harmonious development of the child, the importance of special safeguards and care including appropriate legal protection, before as well as after birth, and the importance of the traditions and cultural values of each people for the child's development.

Article 1. Definition of child
Every human being below 18 years unless majority is attained earlier according to the law applicable to the child.

Article 2. Non-discrimination
All rights must be granted to each child without exception. The State must protect the child against all forms of discrimination.

Article 3. Best interests of the child
In all actions concerning children, the best interests of the child shall be a major consideration.

Article 4. Implementation of rights
The obligation of the State to ensure that the rights in the Convention are implemented.

Article 5. Parents, family, community, rights and responsibilites
States are to respect the parents and family in their childrearing function.

Article 6. Life, survival, and development
The right of the child to life and the State's obligation to ensure the child's survival and development.

Article 7. Name and nationality
The right from birth to a name, to acquire a nationality and to know and be cared for by his or her parents.

Article 8. Preservation of identity
The obligation of the State to assist the child in reestablishing identity if this has been illegally withdrawn.

Article 9. Non-separation from parents
The right of the child to retain contact with his parents in cases of separation. If separation is the result of detention, imprisonment, or death, the State shall pro-

Adopted 20 Nov. 1989, entered into force 2 Sept. 1990, G.A. Res. 44/25, 44 UN GAOR Supp. (No. 49), UN Doc. A/44/49, at 166 (1989). The summary here was prepared by UNICEF.

vide information to the child or parents about the whereabouts of the missing family member.

Article 10. Family reunification
Requests to leave or enter a country for family reunification shall be dealt with in a humane manner. A child has the right to maintain regular contact with both parents when these live in different States.

Article 11. Illicit transfer and non-return of children
The State shall combat child kidnapping by a parent or by a third party.

Article 12. Expression of opinion
The right of the child to express his or her opinion and to have this taken into consideration.

Article 13. Freedom of expression and information
The right to seek, receive and impart information in various forms, including art, print, writing.

Article 14. Freedom of thought, conscience and religion
States are to respect the rights and duties of parents to provide direction to the child in the exercise of this right in accordance with the child's evolving capacities.

Article 15. Freedom of association
The child's right to freedom of association and peaceful assembly.

Article 16. Privacy, honor, reputation
No child shall be subjected to interference with privacy, family, home or correspondence.

Article 17. Access to information and media
The child shall have access to information from a diversity of sources; due attention shall be paid to minorities and guidelines to protect children from harmful material shall be encouraged.

Article 18. Parental responsibility
Both parents have common responsibilities for the upbringing of the child and assistance shall be given to them in the performance of the parental responsibilities.

Article 19. Abuse and neglect (while in family or [other] care)
States have the obligation to protect children from all forms of abuse. Social programmes and support services shall be made available.

Article 20. Alternative care for children in the absence of parents
The entitlement of the child to alternative care in accordance with national laws and the obligation on the State to pay due regard to continuity in the child's religious, cultural, linguistic, or ethnic background in the provision of alternative care.

Article 21. Adoption

States are to ensure that only authorized bodies carry out adoption. Inter-country adoption may be considered only if national solutions have been exhausted.

Article 22. Refugee children

Special protection is to be given to refugee children. States shall cooperate with international agencies to this end and also to reunite children separated from their families.

Article 23. Disabled children

The right to benefit from special care and education for a fuller life in society.

Article 24. Health care

Access to preventive and curative health care services as well as the gradual abolishment of traditional practices harmful to the child.

Article 25. Periodic review

The child who is placed for care, protection, or treatment has the right to have the placement reviewed on a regular basis.

Article 26. Social security

The child's right to social security.

Article 27. Standard of living

Parental responsibility to provide adequate living conditions for the child's development even when one of the parents is living in a country other than the child's place of residence.

Article 28. Education

The right to free primary education, the availability of vocational education, and the need for measures to reduce the dropout rates.

Article 29. Aims of education

Education should foster the development of the child's personality and talents, preparation for a responsible adult life, and respect for human rights as well as the cultural and national values of the child's country and that of others.

Article 30. Children of minorities and indigenous children

The right of the child belonging to a minority or indigenous group to enjoy his or her culture, to practice his or her religion and to use his or her own language.

Article 31. Play and recreation

The right of the child to play, to recreational activities, and to participate in cultural and artistic life.

Article 32. Economic exploitation

The right of the child to protection against harmful forms of work and against exploitation.

Article 33. Narcotic and psychotropic substances
Protection of the child from their illicit use and the utilization of the child in their production and distribution.

Article 34. Sexual exploitation
Protection of the child from sexual exploitation including prostitution and the use of children in pornographic materials.

Article 35. Abduction, sale and traffic
State obligation to prevent the abduction, sale of or traffic in children.

Article 36. Other forms of exploitation

Article 37. Torture, capital punishment, deprivation of liberty
Obligations of the State vis-à-vis children in detention.

Article 38. Armed conflicts
Children under 15 years are not to take a direct part in hostilities. No recruitment of children under 15.

Article 39. Recovery and reintegration
State obligations for the reeducation and social reintegration of child victims of exploitation, torture, or armed conflicts.

Article 40. Juvenile justice
Treatment of child accused of infringing the penal law shall promote the child's sense of dignity.

Article 41. Rights of the child in other instruments.

Article 42. Dissemination of the Convention
The State's duty to make the Convention known to adults and children.

Articles 43–54. Implementation
These paragraphs provide for a Committee on the Rights of the Child to oversee implementation of the Convention.

Index

This book was set in Baskerville and Eras typefaces. Baskerville was designed by John Baskerville at his private press in Birmingham, England, in the eighteenth century. The first typeface to depart from oldstyle typeface design, Baskerville has more variation between thick and thin strokes. In an effort to insure that the thick and thin strokes of his typeface reproduced well on paper, John Baskerville developed the first wove paper, the surface of which was much smoother than the laid paper of the time. The development of wove paper was partly responsible for the introduction of typefaces classified as modern, which have even more contrast between thick and thin strokes.

Eras was designed in 1969 by Studio Hollenstein in Paris for the Wagner Typefoundry. A contemporary script-like version of a sans-serif typeface, the letters of Eras have a monotone stroke and are slightly inclined.

Printed on acid-free paper.